TUCO

TUCO

The Parrot, the Others,
and a Scattershot World

A Life with Birds

BRIAN BRETT

GREYSTONE BOOKS

Vancouver/Berkeley

Greystone Books Ltd.
www.greystonebooks.com

Cataloguing data available from Library and Archives Canada
ISBN 978-1-77164-063-3 (cloth)
ISBN 978-1-77164-064-0 (epub)

Editing by Nancy Flight
Proofreading by Stefania Alexandru
Jacket and text design by Nayeli Jimenez
Jacket photograph by Sharon Doobenen
Printed and bound in Canada by Friesens
Distributed in the U.S. by Publishers Group West

We gratefully acknowledge the financial support of the
Canada Council for the Arts, the British Columbia Arts Council, the
Province of British Columbia through the Book Publishing
Tax Credit, and the Government of Canada through the Canada
Book Fund for our publishing activities.

Greystone Books is committed to reducing the consumption
of old-growth forests in the books it publishes. This book is one
step toward that goal.

For Nancy Flight

CONTENTS

FOREWORD

———

I WAS BORN INTO story. I didn't know it at the time, as blissfully unconscious of the world as any newborn could be, and probably more distracted by the bright lights and the slap that started me breathing. It was only years later that my mother suddenly blurted out what the doctor told her shortly after I was born: "You're going to have to do something about that boy." This struck me as a tactless thing to say to the mother of a new child, even if it was mixed in with the usual congratulations and smiles from the nurses. At least he recognized I was a boy.

More than six decades later, I now wonder if I was already listening to stories in my mother's womb. Although I had the misfortune to be born strange with my mysterious micro-genitals, I had the luck of a mother with a mind that watched the world like a hawk and a father who could fill any empty space with his tall tales.

You learn to tell stories by listening to them, and my father was an endless story. A man who could overwhelm the silence of death, whether physical or psychological. He wasn't pleased with silence, except when he was still-hunting in the forest. His world was always alive. Born within the sound of Bow Bells (which made him Cockney), he lost his left leg at the age of seventeen, when he smashed up the stolen car he was driving. He became a one-legged bootlegger and potato peddler who could talk himself into trouble and out of trouble with equal ease. He could inhale silence and spit out all of its stories. He could walk into a room full of Italians and, by the time he left, be regarded as more Italian than the Italians.

Naturally, he was disappointed with his mutant child, born with a rare genetic disorder that caused me to present as intersex, without any apparent testicles at all, but that didn't stop him from including me in the mythology of our lives, and my greatest memories come from spending so much of my childhood on the road with him and his trucks full of potatoes and apples and junk collected for resale—every old truck unique and ready for mysteries. It was a road carnival, and he was the ringmaster.

I grew up dancing at the great feast of the world; then suddenly the hammer of life would smash me, and then the dance would begin again, with me a little groggy, yet still kicking, defiant. I never knew when the pain would strike... or the laughter... or the beauty... It was only many years later that I realized how much this attitude represented the play of entropy in our world, but more about that later. There were imaginary snakes under the bed and frosty morning fields and beautiful friends, real rapists and endless bullying, and all the mysteries possible in the running waters of my childhood imagination fuelled by the great talker that was my father in his glory days, and the yakker I became. My actual syndrome wasn't fully diagnosed until I was twenty, and by then the physical and emotional damage had been done. I had seen beauty, and I had been stepped on by beauty.

Later, I would write poems about the painful ice in my bones, the weeks of headaches caused by my syndrome, and the whip-like scorn of my community. I also had the opportunity to witness or hear the stories of Others—a philosophical term that refers to outsiders, outliers, foreigners—and even sometimes participate with them in those tales while traversing the enormous, lush, thriving swamp that is life on this planet.

I learned that Others were not only me but birds, tribes, the religious and the atheists, every colour of our skins, including the childhood friend who vomited all over the classroom floor—even the teacher laughed at the poor kid and the stink of his troubled guts.

My father took me to the Native reservations and the Doukhobor camps and, being a trusting man, dumped me with the local families he hardly knew while he went about peddling his vegetables, and then, later, collected me, dazzled and in awe of these amazing people. And so I'm grateful to the tribes of the world that raised me, took me under their wing, in my homeland when I was a child and when I found my own road later—a world wealthy with stories—doggerel Yukon poets, Cambodian tuk-tuk drivers, Haida and Salish tale-tellers, Sikh farmers, Mayan women, German potato growers, lovers of every kind. They were all talkers.

When you are born strange, you learn to see the strangeness in the world. For years, I didn't even know I was strange, but gradually I became the one pointed out and scorned, often attacked, though I didn't understand why at the time. The children could smell the Other in me, the way a parasitic cowbird chick will peck to death its fellow nestlings or push them out of nests. Of course, I learned to be one of those who quickly scooped up ill or traumatized nestlings and took them home, only to watch them die because I didn't know how to care properly for them like a real bird mother, not in those days. But I already knew my life would be a life lived with birds.

I learned how to behave like an Other. I dwelt in the cave behind my eyes, watching the miracle of the world unfold—a cold-eyed hawk. This cave state is common, according to the stories of other outcasts and the cave tales of mystics and seers and philosophers like Plato.

Because I was an Other I developed my affinity with birds—they had the same hard, weird eye, only it was more visible. Although it began with that identification with their eyes, our relationships grew in many directions. I think I've always been listening to their voices, especially once I recognized they were also treated as Others.

When I reached my teen years my syndrome accelerated and the chemical inferno of my androgyny swept through me. For most of my life, I only discussed my Kallmann syndrome with a few very close friends. It was my secret shame, and it took me decades to recognize there was no shame in any accident of birth, no shame that I looked more like a girl than a boy, or that my bones were already crumbling from osteoporosis while I was still a teenager.

A little more than a decade ago, in my fifties, I went public with my story. It gushed out in a short memoir; *Uproar's Your Only Music,* a diptych of prose and poetry, the prose designed to echo the story told in the poetry half of the book. I had no idea where the memoir maelstrom would lead me when I wrote it.

Instead of wrapping up those early years of anguish, the book opened the floodgates of memory, unleashing an unlikely non-linear trilogy of independent memoirs—each a different way of looking at the world that birthed and kept alive this odd creature. The second book, *Trauma Farm,* is a memoir of my life lived locally in our community, on a small mixed farm. *Tuco* was born out of recognizing I was still suffering from the blows of my childhood and how inspired I was by birds. It gathers up the loose threads of the two earlier memoirs and travels in a third direction. I guess *Tuco* could be called an *adab,* an Arab form of memoir that's designed to be "pleasing, diverting and titillating" while also educational. A meditation on a life.

Each of the memoirs occasionally portrays a few of the same incidents but from a different point of view. My eyes have always been looking, and one thing I've learned is to see events from different angles, different perspectives. That's the road to empathy and the end of Othering.

For the last twenty-five years, I've been fortunate to have an offbeat guide, the parrot Tuco, also an Other yet basking in the glow of his outlier world, like an anarchistic outlaw biker with wings instead of wheels. I eventually grew from a troubled child into a troubled man with a wicked sense of humour and some understanding of what Othering meant, with help first from my father, and later from Tuco as he stood on my shoulder, overseeing our world and its mechanics.

It's said certain religious scholars looked through Galileo's spyglass and saw no moons of Jupiter. Seeing is as much a product of the mind as of the eyes. They saw only what they'd been told to see, being good Christians. Or they decided the moons must be flaws in the telescope, and one, Francesco Sizzi, proved they couldn't exist by using the science of numerology, based on the number seven. Galileo had thought everything through—the mechanics of gravity, the movements of stars and planets—so he saw the moons that were so evident. That's what a good story does for us. We get to see the moons of Jupiter.

THIS IS THE story of me and the birds I have met, and some I haven't met but encountered in my years of reading about their lives and their ecology. It's been a life with birds, and a long learning. A poor man's *Divine Comedy*, from the inferno of childhood to the paradisio of old age, guided by my twisted version of Beatrice, Tuco. Mostly, it's the story of an African grey parrot I named Tuco. I've been told his name is a Mexican slang word for runt. I named him after the ugly/amusing character in the off-centre Sergio Leone cinematic masterpiece—*The Good, the Bad, and the Ugly*. Tuco has been all three of those and more.

He made me want to know what it's like to be a bird.

Milan Kundera said in *The Curtain* that "man is separated from the past (even from the past only a few seconds old) by two forces that go instantly to work and cooperate: the force of forgetting (which erases) and the force of memory (which transforms)." I think I've spent most of my life dancing on the wires of those two forces.

More importantly, in *Testaments Betrayed,* Kundera proposed this fable, perhaps referring to his own, maybe accidental, possible betrayal of a man in the years of communist dictatorship in Czechoslovakia. We all have our foggy stories:

> Man proceeds in a fog. But when he looks back to judge the people of the past, he sees no fog on their path. From his present, which was their faraway future, their path looks perfectly clear to him, good visibility all the way. Looking back, he sees the path, he sees the people proceeding, he sees their mistakes but not the fog. And yet all of them? Heidegger, Mayakovsky, Aragon, Ezra Pound, Gorky, Gottfried Benn, St-John Perse, Giono—all were walking in fog, and one might wonder who is more blind? Mayakovsky, who as he wrote his poem on Lenin did not know where Leninism would lead? Or we who judge him decades later and do not see the fog that enveloped him? Mayakovsky's blindness is part of the eternal human condition. But for us not to see the fog on Mayakovsky's path is to forget what man is, forget what we ourselves are.

It took me years to recognize I was living in a world that could never be made of its parts, because when I look at those parts they are distorted by my gazing through the fog of my own history. This is called the observer effect, sometimes expressed as a version of the Heisenberg uncertainty principle—however you look at an event alters your knowledge of the event. That's why I have sometimes returned to several moments in each of these memoirs— the cliffs are the same, only different, as they say. That's also why I took up this story of my childhood again where *Uproar* began, only travelling in another direction—my life with birds. It is also why this story makes long journeys into asides that might seem meaningless at first. They are all there for reasons that will become apparent as the memoir concludes. As we will see, every story can change meaning, depending on how we look at it, despite our telling it as true as we can and keeping to the facts. It's a shape shifting world.

Throughout this book, I have tried to first-name everyone who appears: famous, infamous, or unknown to the general public. If I'm going to rebel against Othering, it seems clear that those who drift in and out of this story should at least have a name—which isn't always possible, but I call out their names whenever I can, so I ask for the reader's tolerance when I name those whom the reader will never know and who come onto the stage and then move on, invisibly, into the mist.

How do we tell a story? A story of ourselves or a story of a bird, of many birds, and how these many birds connect our many selves within the changing ecosystems of a life. Sometimes we can only learn a story by telling the story in different ways until we understand it.

This is another story of me—my last, I hope—my troubled and ecstatic years in a life where the curtains are slowly being closed by age and pain—a story told with Tuco watching. I like to think I am writing the joint autobiography of Tuco and myself, which happens to include the birds and worlds that surrounded my life. It's a story that tries to climb a mountain, and thus, it wanders much as it stomps along behind the ascents of Dante in his epic poem, guided by my fiercely alive father, a one-legged illiterate Virgil leading me up through hell, and then the wicked angel Tuco accompanying me in my later years. This path has had dead ends and distractions: the birds, the family, tribes, nations. There are the bullies who Other us—all of us—and the recognition that sometimes we are the bullies. In the end, we are each outsiders and outliers—and this is just one path in the fog of our journeys, and the story of a few who danced on the mountain, wings raised and flashing in the grey mist of history.

But already my desire and my will
were being turned like a wheel, all at one speed,
by the Love which moves the sun and the other stars.

The closing lines of The Divine Comedy
by Dante Alighieri, translated by C. H. Sisson

Chapter 1

GOOD MORNING

THERE'S A VOICE in the darkness. There's always a voice, the haunt, the reminder, the irrevocable voice, and it is calling my name: "Brian." What an odd word. A collection of syllables, common to several northern European cultures, a noise growing louder as the sunlight grows brighter.

"Brian? Brian!"

I'm rising out of a deep place, almost a blue sea, into a warm saffron dawn, but there was this mad cascade of blue feathers raining around me.

"Brian? Where are you?" Oh no, it's him—Tuco—and it's dawn, and I am being dragged out of an outrageous dream.

Somehow I've become an Indio peasant named Brio in a Latin American village, tormented by two young macaws shouting obscenities at my friend Javier and me from the perimeter of the village.

I am holding a double-barrelled shotgun and aiming at an empty sky. Both barrels fire with a bang and blue feathers rain down like blue snow. Feather by feather, squawk by squawk. Feathers and more feathers raining out of the sky and the parrots are still swearing at me.

I

Dozily, I lie in bed watching that saffron sky grow more vivid, more red in the window. Sharon has already left for work. As for Tuco, I briefly want to strangle him, and he probably wants to bite me for my tardiness. In the end, I don't know him. I don't know what he thinks, or even how well he thinks, though I'm convinced he's smarter than I am in ways I'm not intelligent enough to understand. I've spent twenty-five years working in the same room, my office, with this African grey parrot, considering—because of him—birds and dinosaurs, language, and the relationship of my species to the ecology around it. The bird keeps dragging me back there—this weird parrot growing more weird every year. Spawner of distorted dreams of poor peasants in a jungle village, twisted commentator on my behaviour, king of the house, yet confined by me and his own initiative to a few square feet around his cage, except when we are touring the realm of the house for guests or play. Memory bird, he inspires me to journey into my past, as my dream replays itself in my thoughts, going back to the beginning.

"They're as blue as heaven, as beautiful as a woman. They haven't fledged yet. They're still in the nest."

"Are you sure?"

"Every feather is blue-gold, and their eyes are like wet black pearls. One bird will fix your child's teeth, Brio. It will repair your old truck, rebuild the verandah. Two birds? Then we will have earned more than we could earn during six months. The mother feeds them every day—truly the bird that lays the golden eggs. I have a buyer, but what can I do with this withered hand and missing fingers?"

"How much money?"

"Five hundred American dollars for the two. They're rare and expensive. We will bring the big coffee sacks." Javier hunched over and made a gathering motion. "When the tree hits the ground we must be quick, while they're stunned, or they will run away."

"What if they die when I cut the tree down?"

"Then they die. They're only birds."

It's so cozy in my bed that I don't want to go anywhere, and I'm deconstructing the memory of this deranged dream, understanding where a lot of it came out of my own life. Even the insults of the macaws echo the insults of my childhood and my idiosyncratic appearance.

Brio's axe struck the tree. A chorus of shrieks erupted from the nest. The hyacinth mother swooped down, the handle of the axe clipping her leg in mid-air. She limped hastily across the ground, her screeches bone-chilling as she flapped into the air again and circled erratically, looking stricken.

In my bed, remembering this dangerously close to patronizing dream of poor Latino peasants and Indios, it's obvious how much my relationship with Tuco is manipulating me, changing my attitude to the world around us, though I've never imagined myself as a slow-thinking, muscle-bound, impoverished young Indio peasant before this morning. Yet I often suspect this bird knows more about me than I do. I have learned so much from him.

"Get in here!" he shouts. "Good morning. Good morning!" Yes, it is that. Every morning is good when you're Tuco. And he wants out.

Brio attacked the tree with rage, chipping huge chunks out. Then he moved to the side and pounded at the back cut. Two young macaws peered over their nest's edge; then suddenly, simultaneously, whipped around and shat upon Brio.

"Oh Javier, I'm covered in excrement! This is too disgusting!"

There was a cracking noise from the palm. It began to topple. The macaws leaped out of their nest and flew up into another palm as the tree slammed to the ground. Disgusted, Brio stared briefly at them before he took his axe and his windbreaker and trudged away, stepping over the coffee sacks, not even speaking to Javier.

"They hadn't fledged yet, Brio. I swear. This is their first flight."

The two young macaws began to howl like old drunken sailors.

Javier slithered behind, becoming lizard-like, while Brio strode toward the village, thinking of his wife. It was always the hope in her eyes that killed him.

3

"This is too disgusting," cried one of the now-fledged macaws.

"Harder, Brio, drive it harder. Open her up. Oh, you are so strong."

The two men stared at the forest canopy in horror. Then they scuttled forward, followed by the taunts of the macaws.

"Oh Brio, what mighty arms you have."

Dreams are slippery creatures and tend to lose their details, and this one is so complex and filled with brightness and noise, I know I will have to write it down as soon as I've dealt with Tuco. I've always dreamed in colour as well as black and white, including long conversations or diatribes (usually at my expense). I learned the art of dreaming extensively during the years I'd lie in my dark bedroom, my head spangling with migraine headaches.

Then I realize I had been looking down from the nest, that I was all of them, young gangster macaws and Javier and Brio, and Brio's wife resembled Sharon when I first met her thirty-five years ago, as if I were turning the dream world around like a sorcerer's glass ball, making it into my living world. I was even the mother parrot, examining my hurt leg.

The feathers were easy to understand. In Gustave Flaubert's short masterpiece *A Simple Heart*, the senile, kindly old housekeeper—dying—gazes upward and sees a giant parrot fluttering above her, welcoming her to the kingdom of heaven. Somehow, her confused mind has transformed the family parrot into the Holy Spirit as she rises out of her body within a brilliant ascending stream of feathers. I always loved that image of the journey to heaven—a cloud of multicoloured feathers.

Where did this blue hyacinth macaw and her nestlings come from? That's also easy, only parrot smuggling is not such a joke as my dream. In the real world, usually the birds die. Where did Tuco come from? Well, that's a story, all right. Creatures common to our lives—the birds are everywhere, though as a species we generally ignore them aside from our few feckless heroes defending their habitat and those content to tick them off their birdwatcher's life list, mostly because we regard them as Others, when we aren't extinguishing them or treating them badly—or eating them.

ALL OF US are born into different cultures, including cultures within cultures. We break down and assemble numbers in magical ways and call ourselves accountants, tallying the score of businesses and lives. We can play with electricity like fire in a wire; we can comfort anguished, confused, and sometimes violent widowers in a community home; and we can take clocks apart while barely old enough to hold a screwdriver. For a number of my friends, rearing their children is the meaning of their lives.

My first bird captured me. My early relationships with birds were disastrous, yet I kept hungering for their companionship. I am a child of the bird.

At a very young age, I was gifted a canary and kept him in my bedroom. Known for my sudden outbursts of rage and irritating excitement, or my silences, I assume my mother thought I needed a friend. It took decades before I understood how much my syndrome affected my behaviour.

The canary sang his angel songs, and I doted on him. I let him out and was careful not to step on him. He would fly to me when I called and feed in my palm. His name has become foggy with time, but I'm sure it was Yellowbird, because that's what I named my best go-cart. This was more than fifty-five years ago. He would sing to me whenever I arrived home, until one day, returning from school, I entered my room and found him strangled and bled out between the bars of his cage, where he had hung himself trying to join my world while I was gone.

That was a weeper, and a learning experience about our tendency to design objects for animals that suit our taste more than the needs of the animal. It was a lovely canary cage, yet the bars were too far apart for my tiny canary.

My father was a bird lover too, and maybe I inherited the trait from him. I learned a lot at his feet. Since he was my Virgil, my guide through the dark world toward light, he had a journey and he was determined that I accompany him. There was no abandoning hope in his mind, but somehow he made sure there was a lot of birds on our journey. When he was a young man, his parents kept a one-legged rooster in their city yard. His name was Charlie. He was fierce. My grandfather adored him, though the mailman stopped delivering mail out of fear of the rooster. Charlie would stay within the locked yard and had a little chicken door to the basement, where he could sleep in the rafters at night.

Every time Mother visited Father when they were courting, she would have to cross the empty yard like it was a no man's land. Out of nowhere, old Charlie would fly into the air, talons forward on his good leg so that it resembled a multi-pronged spear, and then he'd shred her nylons. Nylons were rare and expensive in those days, and every bad encounter with Charlie meant a bitter loss for her. She hated that bird. He would hop around the yard, pumping his wings and crowing. Another great victory. He was a real Gaddafi of the bird kingdom, crowing his gaudiest. Getting past Charlie always struck me as one of the weirder courtship challenges for a woman I ever heard about. The stories about Charlie taught me how much pride a bird can have, and also how frail life is. One cold winter day, he didn't show up, and when my grandparents went into the basement, they found him frozen solid, still standing, one-legged, on his rafter.

Today, to keep chickens in many cities you need a government inspection and a coop that would be considered a mansion by any homeless person—the growing number of rejects and rebels who gather in increasing numbers on city streets in North America as they are systematically Othered by our government, an organization originally invented to help the weak and protect us from ourselves.

You are supposed to practise biosecurity with your coop—biosecurity, an oxymoron if I ever encountered one. There's never safety for the birds and the beasts, especially if we're around. Still, it's become a mighty strange world when you are told to decontaminate your granddaughter and her clothing after she's collected the miracle that is a chicken egg.

A big honk erupts from my office, followed by the crash of Tuco's toys being whacked around in his cage. He's annoyed now. He wants out, and I usually obey, but this morning I'm defiant, sunk into the luxury of my bed. The wood stove has died, and the electric heat is not turned up, so the house is chilly—morning cool—a briskness that usually gets me up and skipping to the tea kettle and relighting the wood stove on the colder days of winter that Tuco least appreciates.

"It's co-l-l-l-l-l-d-d-d-d-d-d-d," he moans. "Get me outta here." Actually, I don't think he's cold at all in his shroud of grey feathers. He merely understands cold, and enjoys imitating my complaints. There's an evil seed in him that delights in the suffering of others, especially me.

THE EYES OF birds hooked me when I was too young to know much but big enough to have a heart that went out to every living creature, especially those with feathers and a suspicious gaze. That's how I ended up in the rafters of a barn, enthralled, hypnotized, an odd child-creature, paying homage to my first bird-god in its nest.

It had a small face about the size of a saucer, with two black button eyes, and a fluff ball of Ookpik-style feather down surrounding his hissing little demon gaze, scary-howling at me, though the bird was only slightly larger than a kitten.

I was half-hanging from a rafter in the decrepit building near sundown, next to my friend. Maybe we were ten years old, distracted while the mother barn owl silent-fluttered in the rafters, making close passes at us. Then we heard a noise outside, and we bolted down to the ground like rats on a sinking ship and headed out the side door as that voice in my head shouted: "Run!"

The old farmer, who must have been just past forty but seemed ancient to someone so young as me, came crashing in the side door as we went out the opposite door. He had *the gun*—the legendary salt-and-pepper scatter-gun. Stories about that shotgun were passed from child to child, and now it was our turn. We ran like the wind around the barn and toward the field, but the big barn door swung open. He'd easily guessed which direction we were going.

We didn't look back because we knew about the scatter-gun, and we assumed the dreaded farmer might be crazy enough to salt our faces and blind us. In those days, if a farmer was being tormented by young vandals like us—curious kids and idiots, seekers of barn owl chicks—well then, it was our fault.

Salt-and-pepper shot was still common, at least as far as I knew, in the mythic world of childhood. Shooters self-loaded their shells, opening their 12 gauge or .410 gauge bore shotgun cases, dumping out the lead shot, refilling the paper shell with rock salt and cracked pepper, and sealing it with melted wax. These were known as scatter-guns because they were often sawed off, and the shot spread rapidly, so it didn't do much damage. It was also known as scatter shot. These guns hardly needed aiming, yet they delivered a hefty sting at close range, which is where we were when the barn door kicked open.

My friend was the first victim; he was a classic scrawny, freckle-faced redheaded kid of the fifties. I think he was Irish. I heard the big bang behind us, and I saw him lifting, or jumping (or both), off the ground, his mouth gaping.

My bottom was next, and I think the whack came before I heard the bang. All I know is that I seemed to be running on tip-toes for a second, my jeans flattened against my ass as I felt the incredible sting of the first time I was shot. All for a little owl.

I've been shot twice in my life, both times because of birds.

Whoa, that hurt, yet when we finally found ourselves out of range and dropped our pants, there were no holes in our blue jeans. Luckily. That would have got my ears boxed at home—as well—for being naughty enough to incite the wrath of a local farmer, though, in this case, my father also would have been outraged by a stranger's use of a scatter-gun on me, and news of it would have probably led to a physical altercation. Our asses were chicken-poxed with tiny welts, as if the salt had invisibly pierced our pants, though the pain and speckling were relatively short-lived. Since we knew we deserved it, we didn't think much about the behaviour of the cranky farmer. In fact, it was a badge of honour. We'd been shot!

Narrating this incident, I begin to wonder what kind of farmer he was. There was maybe a milk cow and an old mare out in the scrubby thistle field. Some pigs one summer in the shed attached to the barn. A small chicken coop near the house. And cars; there were old cars, new cars, cars in various states of repair and disassembly everywhere. It suddenly dawns on me that perhaps this wasn't a farm; maybe it was a chop shop, replete with stolen cars being unassembled and resold? Or is this just my older imagination running wild? My naïveté in those days and the possible real reason for the scatter-gun—to keep nosy children away—now strike me as hilarious.

However, the baby barn owls, those little hissing demons, were worth a load of salt in the ass. Their faces stayed with me long after the lightning strike of pain that followed that haunting vision in the sun-slivered rafters of the dark barn. This was one of those early days when I first glimpsed the dreaming of life with its painful beauty, its cute saucer-faced fluff-devils, standing their ground against rogue kids armed with impossible curiosity—the day I had my ass spanked in a scattershot world of alchemy and danger.

I never knew where this world of pain and delight was coming from—still don't—nor did I understand why, yet I sensed it coming at me. Something was wrong. Wrong because I was different.

I was fascinated by lizard-like eyes and scatter-guns and breath-less runs across dusky fields, followed by long periods of weeping and manic laughter, occasionally at the same time. Nothing made sense. I was alone inside my head from an early age, a gimped kid like my dreamed double Javier with the crippled hand in the jungle of the blue-bird dream, only it wasn't my hand then, not yet; this was a few years before I shotgunned that while duck hunting. No, it was the glue that made a man. I was a fake little man who wasn't a man. Deeply alone, unaware of the extent of my loneliness, though it became clear in the next few years as I ricocheted back and forth between reaching out like a fledgling bird into the sky or hiding like a coward in the darkness of myself.

And somehow the birds always attracted me, the memories returning over and over, examined at different angles, from first consciousness to twenty-five years in the same room with a crazed parrot, who took it on himself to explain the real world to me, because I always seemed to attract pain. Like my first day of school—a little chick surrounded by bullies—I grabbed a handful of pea gravel and hurled it at the bullies, only to hear the ominous tick of the gravel against the window and see the teacher look up. And thus I found myself lectured and punished for fighting back while my assailants gloated outside the windows. I was a classic, doomed kid; still, that never stopped me from fighting back. Then, later, coming home from school—I don't recall if it was the same day, but I suspect it was because of the way the bullying and the punishment mingle with that huge sky in my memories.

There was a wide horizon as a few of us children crossed the lonely lower field that led to the forest path and my first conscious murmuration. Hundreds, no thousands, many thousands of birds patterning in and out and around each other, flowing harmoniously into the blue-grey sky above the school fields. Maybe because I was so troubled by the school, by the way I'd already become an Other, I focussed on them, silent, delighted, transfixed—possessed by another world. I wanted to merge with that flock, and of course, I knew, even then, I never could.

The birds that perform these aerial ballets have a skill and intelligence almost unfathomable, each sensing the slightest disturbance in the bird ahead, changing, following, and then being followed in a harmony of joy and flight and intuition—the ecstasy of the air and, more importantly, the connection and the celebration in a family of birds.

MY FATHER, INCREASINGLY aware of my feminine weirdness, would try to find manly occupations for me, most of them backfiring. We did succeed at a few enterprises together, keeping pigeons and chickens, and sharing a sudden mutual obsession with go-carting. Near where we lived, a new freeway was being built. The enormously long and closed entrance ramp had a divine slope for go-carting. Too attractive to pass up.

Our prototypes, roughly made with apple crates and lawnmower tires, were a little rickety. The first one exploded into rolling wheels and flying wood parts right under me after I'd gone barely fifty feet. This was a steep ramp for a go-cart. The next one, the Black Rocket, took off, and I roared down the hill while my father thumped his chest and cheered and waved his fists in encouragement, until I hit a stray pebble, which turned the wheel, and the go-cart veered off the freeway ramp onto the grass, where I flew into a complete roll, flattening my nose against the hood, and stopped. Years later, I like to think I crashed into that embankment with extreme prejudice. My nose was slightly bloody, but my skull was miraculously unscathed. I couldn't say the same about the Black Rocket. That was its first and last run. Another go-cart had bit the dust. I looked up the hill as my father, with his wooden leg swinging awkwardly ahead on every step, hopped worriedly toward me, slowing down when he realized I was all right. He wiped my nose with a greasy rag from his pocket, and back to the garage we went.

My crashes didn't bother him. His only comment was "Don't tell Mother."

Our final masterpiece was Yellowbird, yes, named after my dead canary. Talk about a name of doom. This one even had a tubular hood *and* a roll bar. I think Father decided on the roll bar because my nose kept bleeding off and on for a few days after the pieces of the Black Rocket had been snuck into the garage, and Mother eyed us with some suspicion, though no one was volunteering any information.

For us, a successful run was to make it all the way down the long ramp to the near-completed freeway, which wouldn't open for a year. The Yellowbird, finally finished, the paint even dry, my father pushed me off, and I was gone. The Yellowbird was heavier than the Black Rocket, more solid. It took a while to build up speed. When I did accelerate, it scared the piss out of me. I think I was clinging to the steering wheel so hard it was bending. Then came the last curve, and I roared around it on two wheels, briefly glimpsing the top of the hill where my father was stomping around on his wooden leg, fist-punching the air, shouting: "Go! Go! Go!" I think he was determined to kill me or make a "man" out of me. For that moment, I was ecstatically happy. I was his pride. I'd made it to the freeway! So I slammed on the brakes, which did absolutely nothing, and I rocketed forward right across the freeway and into the grassy median with wheels flying into the air. When the go-cart settled in the grass, I was a little winded from bouncing off the bent steering wheel but otherwise fine. So was most of Yellowbird, except that it had somehow lost all four wheels.

Shortly after, my father drove down in the truck, beaming, as we picked up the pieces. Not only had I survived our quest, I had also shown courage. He'd make a man of me yet. And there wasn't much else that could make him happier.

That was the end of my go-cart days. We both knew I'd probably kill myself if we tried anything more difficult. And the broken, wheel-deprived Yellowbird hung like a trophy inside the garage for years, gathering dust.

"Get in here!" Tuco shouts. The sun is shining through his window, and he wants his door open. Then he shrieks, "Baaaaaaad bird," knowing it makes me angry when he nips at his foot to make his scream louder. He never injures himself, but the act is enough to distress me. Thus, he actually is a bad bird, and I haven't even risen from bed yet. "Baaaaad bird." This brings out my stubborn side. I'm not going to be a slave to him every morning. Besides, all this contemplation has only taken up a few minutes.

OUR GO-CART ADVENTURES naturally set me to daydreaming of my Robin Hood stage, when my ever-helpful father, especially when it came to trouble, spent several trips to the woods helping me find good yew shrubs to build a proper English longbow; though it wasn't proper, English, or very long by the time we were finished. It was still a deadly little creation, and I soon learned to handle it with a villainy probably intended to mimic the farmer with his punky salt gun. I could have easily joined Robin Hood's merry band.

The yew is a gorgeous wood, reddish, tight-grained, and supple, a rare tree on my coast and lately used in cancer treatment, which for a while, caused utter devastation in our forests as trees were stripped of their medicinal bark, killing them, until a chemical replacement was thankfully formulated.

There's a reason it was used for longbows. It has a real stretch and a natural tendency to return to form. We found a straight branch and I started whittling. I remember whittling forever, whittling and whittling, followed by sanding... sanding.... After I had the shape that Father approved we steam-bent it into shape. It was kind of laughable when you consider the bows of today—like the compound bow on the wall beside my desk, capable of killing a bear, not that I'd ever be crazy enough to go after a bear with a bow. Still, my little yew bow was a killer. I found some willow shoots, and to make arrows glued split goose feathers onto them. The tips were fire-burnt points, polished with a smooth stone. All delightfully amateurish, Boy Scout style, yet my handmade bow was tight when strung and could fire those arrows sharp and hard and true.

I became a secret stalker, slipping through forests, brush, even a few local gardens and orchards, looking for prey, any kind of prey, no doubt making our neighbours and their cats nervous. I never dragged home any ducks, though this kind of handmade weapon had been our most significant long-distance weapon for thousands of years. And even today in archery clubs, the mechanical boredom of the deadly, modern compound bow has sent archers back to long or recurved bows.

THE SUMMER OF my first bow we camped on a lake in the Interior among the yellow pine mountains of central British Columbia, a legendary "cowboy and Indian country" during the early days of colonialism. However, in the Cariboo, the local Natives were better cowboys than the white cowboys. In fact, they generally were the cowboys. I was in my Davy Crockett and Chingachgook (*The Last of the Mohicans*) stage. I had a "genuine" fake coonskin hat, a pocket-knife, and my bow. I was hunting mountain lions. Fortunately, I never ran into any, though my proficiency increased as I stalked the woods, missing rabbits and grouse and losing arrows.

It was a brilliant blue lake, rich with fat trout, rainbows as well as the larger lake trout. All the lakes of the Interior had exotic names that sounded like witch's spells to my young mind: Lac La Hache, Jewel Lake, Loon Lake, Skaha Lake. This one had calm turquoise waters bordered by pine meadows—open forest that was an invitation, the big yellow pine meadows, the jack or lodgepole pines in the hills—their branches romantic with hanging black tree lichen, or bear hair, a moss commonly used in the traditional diet of the Okanagan people, pit-cooked into dough and then mashed and baked into dried berry-laced cakes that could last for years. I loved the wolf hair, a golden, multi-branched lichen that stuck to the bark of the pines. Sometimes this was shrouded by the spooky, long strands of Methuselah's beard, or Old Man's Beard; a dangly green lichen more common to the coast, though patches appeared in these Interior forests.

I was doing my best Geronimo, sliding noiselessly through the trees, a skill I retain despite being so crippled up. Neither deer nor bears are as wise and sense-sharp as people think, though they're usually far beyond the average city dweller, and these are bush tricks I wouldn't recommend. Still, I so loved stalking a young buck, exhausted and stupid with the rut, following it in the dusk hour until I could stand above it, watching it bed down a few feet away, completely clueless about me, a potential killer. And then once it rested its head on its foreshank, I would slip back into the forest, a proud ghost-watcher leaving him undisturbed. I truly was the last of the Mohicans in my own mind.

This day at the lake was lucky, or I should say, unlucky. I was slipping between the pines, alert, in full stalking mode at the moment I saw the robin, singing away on a branch. I notched the willow arrow and drew the string back, aimed, and fired.

Speared through the breast, the robin fell silently out of the tree and landed at my feet, impaled and very dead. I was horrified. Oh death, you're not real until you are real!

I never told anyone what I had done, but the robin haunted me—still does. I buried it ceremoniously in the yellow grass under the pines and moss and returned to our campfire. I had been made real by the knowledge of the damage I could do with what suddenly had become an abhorrent toy. I had joined the race of casual killers—my species—killing a little bird in song as a childish test of skill. I didn't even eat it.

I've done more than my share of killing over the decades. I always believed that if I am going to eat meat, I have to know the slaughter of it. The carcasses and the skulls seem nearly endless, almost fifty racks of antlers lining my barn. I touch their bare skulls. "I knew you alive, a young buck in its glory, if only for a moment, and what did I learn from your death?" Not much, though the meat was delicious. It's illegal to sell wild meat, and I believe that's an important principle, but I can give it away and always make it a point to tithe some, usually to poor young friends or our farm helpers, and for a while I was known as a source who'd gift high-protein, low-fat, organic wild meat to people struggling with cancer and desperate for real protein.

All the birds I've killed over the decades have flown, one by one, into my mind, like avian spells, thousands of poultry, geese, ducks, pigeons, pheasants, grouse, quail. When I start thinking about the volume that can build up over the decades, I feel like a serial killer, a killer of what I love most, the beauty of the birds. Now, the time has come to expiate my guilt as well as the joy of living among birds.

What I love about many of the great naturalists of the last century, men like Aldo Leopold and Roderick Haig-Brown, is that the few who lived with gun and rod mostly gave them up in their last years, or used them seldom. Haig-Brown, the great fishing writer of the West Coast ended up swimming with the giant tyee salmon while they spawned, using this knowledge to help rebuild the spawning channels. Swimming with the salmon taught him empathy, and by the end of his life he only caught and released salmon for publicity shots for river-saving causes.

Since my life has been lived with birds—dead and alive—they've come to dominate my thoughts and possess me so deeply that my love has increased for them even more in my last years, until I find myself being forced to write our history—the birds and me—this confession and love story. I have always been a sentimental romantic, even while struggling with the rage, the emotional roller coaster generated by my Kallmann syndrome and the traumas of my teenage years as an outsider, when I was not a boy and yet not a girl, an androgyne among the stares and sneers of my community, a target for rapists and bullies. A lot of pain flowed forward from those years, and often I find myself, laughing, declaring that I've now survived five decades of PTSD.

But then memory slides, grows confusing, and I wonder, did I kill the robin the summer before the Cariboo? We fished so many of those lakes. The memory of such a child is dangerous. Perhaps it was the lake where the rattlesnake rattled every time I thumped down the steps of the cabin to race to the water, though the snake never emerged, and I didn't go wandering under the crawl space to learn if it was a real rattlesnake or just a child's fantasy.

I think often of that rattlesnake now. How it was so Other. How it was foreign and dangerous, yet my parents never mentioned it, never seemed to notice it. Was I too alert, or was I so alert I heard what wasn't there? Did I need an Other in the woods, just as I was an Other at home and an Other at my school. When I think about it today, I am grateful for the mystery. I will never know if it was actually there. I'm guessing it was a wild child's fantasy.

I have seen many animals needing an Other. Tuco often invents fake opponents when he is wandering around my office, suddenly flying into wing-flapping attacks at the unseeable, or whipping around when he thinks a non-existent foe is sneaking up on him. Then he will check his feathers, flashing his wings as if searching for an enemy within. An imaginary flea? It's similar to when a cat battles invisible angels in the air.

I also have to laugh when Tuco slides so deeply into sleep that he falls off his perch and lands with a great screeching and thumping and flapping. The first few times he did that at night I thought he was being attacked by a mink that had snuck into the house, and I'd leap out of bed in terror, snatching up any glass or book or sculpture I could use as a weapon. Tuco would strut around the floor of his cage, puffed like a prize fighter, mumbling curses at his fled attacker. Even birds have pride. His ego demanded that he pretend he had been assaulted. Later, over the years, he grew so used to my presence that I could watch him dozing on his perch, head nodding, beak drooping, drifting into a deep sleep, and then suddenly fall off with much flapping and crashing and snatching to arrest his fall. I'd start laughing and he would explode in rage at his embarrassment, and ring all the bells of his little world.

Aside from the robin, I look back with fondness on my childhood explorations of the grass hills and scrub pine forest of the Cariboo and fishing its pristine lakes. Giant enigmatic fish surfacing in the ghost light of night water. The haunting claxons of the ducks on their migrations. The roar of a bear in an alpine meadow. Gazing into campfires knowing that mystery did indeed talk flame and that the language of flame was educating me in the hidden codes of fire, while up in the hills a coyote yapped or a wolf howled. These were the days when the fish were still limitless, the campsites were lonely, and the catch was there for anyone with any skill.

On our journeys to the mysterious Interior of British Columbia we'd take the narrow roads of the Fraser Canyon, and we'd often stop in a rickety little mom-and-pop restaurant beside the road in the canyon. This was a homestyle restaurant—most of which are now extinct—famous for its good burgers and its yappy parrot. We'd often eat there just to meet the parrot. He had a real mouth on him.

I don't know his name, but he was notorious and I'm sure was kept more to attract tourists than out of love, though it's hard to imagine how anyone could not love this bird.

Sometimes he would grow noisy and obnoxious, especially if there were children dining. The owner would ostentatiously take out a cover and drape it over the domed parrot cage. There would be a great deal of muffled screaming and cursing, and then suddenly the parrot's head would pop out from beneath the blanket and he'd call plaintively: "Help! Help!"

This parrot—like most because of their special, agile tongue that can fake not only human language but all kinds of sound effects—understood what could tug at our heart strings. Parrots are emotional, social birds. That's their real intelligence. They know how to mug for their community, whether it's a bird community or a human one.

We were sitting near him one day when he suddenly uttered a screech and the loud sound of a car's tires braking on a road. Then there was an ugly crunching thump, followed by the holler of an injured dog and a yip... yip... yip... yip... in a descending and lengthening series of cries fading down the street. An encapsulation of a car hitting a dog, with all the nuances that most of us wouldn't even be able to recall, let alone repeat perfectly. And why? This bird, more than any other bird of my youth, made me begin to question what language and intelligence are, and I was lost in wonder.

I had met murder in those mountain lakes, and then I met mystery. This incident with the parrot certainly wasn't the first time I realized how little I understood of the world; maybe it was the first time I came to question what we regard as reality. Despite my warm-hearted family and friends, I always carried that distance in me. I was already a loner who liked to dive into company and then retreat to the avalanche of thoughts that had roared through my mind since the beginning of consciousness. With the clueless intelligence of a child, I believed everyone saw the world like I did, but I was the only one who wasn't any good at living in it.

Forty years later, as I was explaining to my mother some details of the tormented childhood I'd navigated through, most of which I'd never before revealed to her, she abruptly blurted out: "But you were the special one." I was shocked that she thought that, especially since being special never had occurred to me during those years. I merely thought I was a hopeless mutant creature. Mother had recognized from the beginning that I was an outsider. Not better or worse, or more loved or less loved, but odd. A lonely outlier—like that feathered, yappy creature in his cage in a remote Fraser Canyon café.

"Brian, get in here!" I smile at the exasperation in Tuco's voice. It's barely past 8 AM and he's now working himself into a frenzy, though another couple of minutes luxuriating in my bed won't ruin his day.

He's ringing his bells like a mad cymbalist. I know he's training me to be punctual with his demands and I have to show independence, or he'll have me at his mercy, but I am awake now and it's a good morning indeed.

Chapter 2

BUYING THE BIRD

VEN THOUGH THE sun is flaring on his cage by the window, illuminating him like a religious painting, I flick on the overhead light and Tuco gives a little jump of excitement. We both know the morning routine. It's been twenty-five years, after all. When I drop his cage door, he always takes a superhero leap through the opening and lands on the last bar of the door, making it bounce even though a chain holds it up. He's both excited and trying to scare me. I usually give him a kiss on the beak and ask, "How the hell are ya?" Then he does a prance, letting me know he's awake and full of piss and vinegar.

These days, I have become jealous of his bird athleticism, and perhaps that's why it's become even more urgent to tell our story. There came the morning I was lying in bed and I realized I would never pass another day in my life without pain. A side effect of Kallmann's is osteoporosis in your teen years, as the lack of hormones sucks the calcium out of the body, making the bones weak and brittle. It affected me most from the lower spine to my feet. The shattered bones of my feet are like corn flakes; the hips and knees and lower back are also wrecked, though these days, it's my collapsed and bent feet and the spreading numbness of neuropathy that hurts most. If I move around for a few minutes, I loosen up enough to walk down the stairs like a man. But unlike Tuco, I'll never be hanging upside down by my feet while arguing with someone.

The nerves at my extremities are also damaged from years of self-abuse with alcohol and chainsaws and mountain-walking in snow. I have powder finger, or white finger, as Reynaud's syndrome is sometimes called. It makes my fingers go white and numb after exposure to cold. The feet are worse, especially my left foot, because of all the nerve damage from those crumbling bones. One doctor wants to fuse the remaining bones together, another suggests amputating the offending foot and insists I'll walk better and with less pain wearing a prosthesis. I'd rather walk with pain for a while yet. Strangely, it's the same leg my father lost in his car crash when he was seventeen. The thought of ending up with a plastic foot on the same leg strikes me as poetic mimicry.

Yet these legs also lasted long enough for me to boot-ski down glaciers and idiotically leap crevasses on those same glaciers; dive among the reefs of Cuba; chase away three cowardly teenage muggers in Casablanca, one with a knife; and deal with another freeway-prowling, knife-flashing wannabe rapist on Highway 5. I still bear the scar from that one on my right palm, and I'm also betting his knife and car keys have remained in the swamp beside the freeway, where I threw them before walking lonely and bleeding down the road.

There's a flash of colour floating down our long gravel driveway. It's the peacock, Yeats, gliding off his big fir at the roadside, where he guards the farm in the night. This large bird's flight, skimming five feet above the road like a torpedo bomber, is always a heart-lifter. I notice Lady Jane, the hen, has already made her descent, and they are soon followed by their son, who is clumsier.

It's more difficult to see the gravelled public back road that leads to the farm now. We spent close to twenty-five years planting trees, and they've filled in well. Tuco's cage is in a perfect position, not only to enjoy bright, indirect sunlight but also to guard the farm, which he's magnificent at, usually the first to give warning of visitors. In the early days, hardly a car went up the road, so it thrilled him if one drove into view. He'd start shouting: "Hi! It's party time! Party time! Yooohhhooo? Come in!" Then, if the car continued up the hill, there'd be silence and maybe a sigh and a long "Awwwwwww" of sorrow. Tuco lives for the party.

I fill his water dish with clean water before I feed him, because once he's had a first snack, he's ready for a bath and maybe a little water fight, which could mean refilling his water dish several times and saturating half the room, including my bookcases and me, with the spray from his aggressively cheeky bathing. Sometimes, on a hot afternoon, I surprise him outside his cage with a water mister. He considers this a challenge to a water fight and opens his wings and dances on his perch, shaking his head with his mouth open to drink and scatter the water from his shower, duck it, or bat it back to me. That also keeps him out of trouble for a good half hour so that I can then refill his water dish while he preens himself, feather by feather, dusting each feather with the secretion that's released by what's known as powder down, a keratin dust that's special to parrot feathers. That's why they're sometimes called powder down birds. Parrots also have an uropygial gland near the base of the tail. It releases an oily secretion, which when rubbed through their feathers makes them waterproof. All this dusting and waxing leaves our room deep in dust, which I'm always failing to clean well enough. Naturally, his bird dust is hard on computers.

When I bring his water dish back, filled with fresh water, he has a little sip and starts hopping on his perch while I dump his old food dish and half refill it with fresh seed, topped with a few vegetables and fruit. If I completely fill the dish, he has a tendency to dive in headfirst in his morning excitement and fling his food everywhere. Seeds dipped in vitamins and minerals are his base feed, though I worry about that. He should eat more fruit and vegetables and nuts. He'd rather have his seeds. I'm careful about the mix I buy, and there's a good local parrot mix. Safflower seed is his favourite, but it's been claimed that too many safflower and sunflower seeds over-excite a parrot because they are too fat-laden. They're the candies of the seed world. I make sure there are only a few in his mix.

Because Tuco is already slightly crazy, like a kid permanently on sugar, I make it a point throughout the day to give him whatever I discover downstairs that's healthy, fetching us broccoli and oranges and grapes to feast on together, and I share my fruit smoothies with him. He loves to eat whatever I'm eating, especially the slices from mandarin oranges. But, like a lot of people these days, he craves pizza, ice cream, chocolate bars, beer foam, and so on. What people don't tell you about parrots is that although they may live to seventy, they are also notorious for dying in their thirties as they develop heart conditions and other ailments, undoubtedly enflamed by poor diet. That's why I'm always trying to lure him into healthy fruits and vegetables. He's a clever beggar, however, and lures too many, including me during my weaker moments, into fulfilling his junk food cravings.

For most people who encounter Tuco, the temptation to play with him is difficult to resist, mainly because he's so game and he's such a trickster. His sense of humour is vast and varied. People are his main entertainment, since he has no other flock to keep him amused. Sometimes I suspect, like Montaigne playing with his famous cat, he takes more joy out of us than we out of him, and he can manipulate guests better than a professional con man. Parrots are wildly gregarious birds.

Tuco has a multitude of favourite games, especially singing and strange-noise contests, most created to lure strangers into his room. Many years ago, after she'd had a few too many glasses of beer, Sharon found herself in a burping duel with Tuco, which they both enjoyed enormously.

Several months later, deep in the night, she needed something in my office. Fearful of waking Tuco (always a fatal mistake), she scuttled into the room and began groping around on my desk in the dark. Tuco sleeps lightly, and he was obviously annoyed at her disturbing his sleep. As she passed his cage in the dark, having found what she was looking for, she'd forgotten Tuco. That was when he let out a loud wet belch behind her ear. Terrified that someone else was in the room, she shrieked, "Gawww!!!"—then fled the room, screaming: "Someone's in there!" Sharon is a classic easy-to-scare victim. Like Tuco, I quickly learned I can make her jump, often hilariously, if I walk up behind her to ask a question while she's vacuuming, and I love it when she shrieks; it's so innocent and real. Alas, after decades together she's learned to keep an eye out for me, but Tuco still startles her.

It took her a moment to realize she'd been surprised by the parrot, who now associated her and excitement with a good, loud, wet burp and ever after has taken to giving her a friendly burp when she walks by, much to her chagrin and embarrassment. Naturally, anybody else silly enough to enter his den in the dark receives a similar treatment.

His finest night moment came with a good friend of ours, Joe, an aging eccentric and marvellous poet. We were having a party on our island farm, which meant many had to stay the night, and we were so crowded that Joe had to sleep on a cot set up in my office. It was a long, rowdy party, and I finally gave up at four in the morning and went to bed. Joe, though in his early seventies then, was wide awake; left alone in the house, he decided to take drastic action and poured himself a large tumbler of Scotch, assuming that would put him to sleep. The lights were out in the office, so he attempted to sneak into his cot past the sleeping Tuco. Bad mistake.

As he passed the cage in the darkness, Tuco let out his best banzai screech, a sound that can practically shatter glass, and even a foot away it can leave your ears ringing for an hour. Joe replied with a leap and a loud "Ahhoooh!" that awoke everyone in the house, splattering his Scotch from one end of the room to the other, dousing the parrot, my computer, and all the papers on my desk. I scrambled out of bed and ran for the office, terrified something had happened to Tuco. I flicked on the light and Tuco started hooting and high-stepping his victory dance. Joe was clinging to my desk for support. I thought he was having a heart attack. I finally got him settled down with some more Scotch and learned the full story. Joe ended up writing a delightful book-length poem, *Parrot Fever*, about his relationship with Tuco.

NOW THAT HE'S been fed and watered, Tuco is climbing over the top of his cage, ringing his outside bells and banging toys and making his general morning ruckus. I shut the door to my office and lock it, a habit I grew into several years ago because of his tendency to fly down and scuttle around on the floor. One day, my mother was visiting, and excited about some incident downstairs, she rushed up to my office and flung open the door, almost flattening Tuco. So I put in a lock. Strangely, the lock comforted me as much as it protected Tuco. Sliding that latch meant I was separated from my physical world and ascending into the world of my confused yet hungry mind. Writing. We were writing together.

I CAN'T SEPARATE myself from the greater world. I've always felt the moral duty to tithe, pay my dues to my community and my culture. This has led me a number of times into quixotic conflicts with friends and enemies, as well as stints in the public arena campaigning for environmental, anti-censorship, and community issues. Out of my tough and molested childhood, I developed a Galahad complex, a tendency to rush in and help friends who don't necessarily want my excitable help. When you're a lonely social creature with a rare genetic condition that affects both your sexuality and your emotional architecture, you can overreact to personal injuries, to you or others, real or imagined. Growing up relentlessly bullied, I even briefly became a bully for a few years in my early twenties, under the first barrage of excessive testosterone injections the doctors inflicted on me. I was determined to right the wrongs done to me and others. It didn't take more than a few months to realize beating up bullies was also bullying. This led me to a lifelong quest for empathy, and the researching of what's called mutual aid—studying and writing about how life interacts with life, each helping each other—human, animal, plant—another reason I ended up spending decades in the same room with a bird, who came to be my spirit guide through the confusion of life.

NEARLY THIRTY-FIVE YEARS ago, I walked past an empty lot in White Rock—a lovely, rickety, seaside community where I lived. The charming old-style house that had been there was gone. All that was left were the cement stairs that led to a cavernous lot.

Incensed by the destruction of my community by clueless developers, I wrote a long harangue for the local newspaper denouncing the developers who were destroying both good houses and good community to erect soulless, boringly designed condos and highrises. It was all part of the malling of America that has occurred for the last sixty years.

Before I knew it, I was commandeered into running for town council, and crazily enough, I won handily.

Although I was only one person on council facing six pro-development opponents (including the mayor), I soon discovered various techniques for dropping monkey wrenches into the gears of the worst schemes. For a start, I read my agenda.

When I first became involved in civic politics, I assumed it was run by crooked and stogie-smoking millionaires who sat around in back rooms dividing up the community. Although I'm sure that happens, I was surprised to discover this wasn't the case here, and probably not the case in most communities. I soon learned the politicians and the developers were so steeped in their social conditioning they couldn't envision another point of view—yet a further example of Othering.

One day, while watching my fellow council members marking their positions on a controversial project, I realized they resembled a flock of chickens, all operating within their pecking order—the mayor presiding above us like a rooster proudly supervising his flock while they decided what he wanted them to decide. It also made me realize that despite my being outnumbered, like a rogue hen, there were a lot of ways I could get around this flock.

I soon cultivated a couple of strategies I stole from Greek myths. One was the story of the race for the hand of Atalanta. Hippomenes was given three golden apples, and as he raced Atalanta, he tossed out the golden apples, one after another. She slowed down to fetch each of them. He won the race. It was always a delight to discover a golden apple in the agenda that I could roll onto the floor of the city hall and soon discover I had the most doctrinaire capitalist supporting an anarchist poet. This would lead, on a few occasions, to the defeat of particularly ugly projects for bizarre reasons.

My other strategy was sneakier. When Jason had to sew the dragon's teeth and create a legion of skeleton warriors destined to attack him, he tossed a stone at one who wasn't looking as it sprouted from the ground. That soldier assumed another warrior had thrown the stone and attacked that soldier instead of Jason. Soon, all the bone warriors were fighting among themselves, and Jason walked away, unscathed. It always impressed me how easy it was to incite the aldermen into conflict over a proposed project. Each had a weak spot, and once I figured out how to tweak that, I could cause mayhem. I was a devil on that town council.

After a few years (and handily winning another election), I realized I had accomplished as much as I could. The second election also took the heart out of me. Although I won by a landslide, a school board candidate, a retired schoolteacher named Clarence White, ran with the creepy slogan "White Is Right." At all-candidates debates he'd brag about how working summers as a drywaller gave him a strong right hand, snorting proudly with the implication. This horrified me, and when I saw he was also winning his seat, I slid into a bottle of brandy.

By the time I walked to city hall for my acceptance speech, I was hammered and enraged. The TV crew saw me coming and, recognizing this was going to be ripe, began filming. Some of my friends still talk about that TV appearance. I couldn't bear watching a replay of it. I was swaying so badly, the cameraman had difficulty keeping me in frame.

I thanked the good people for electing me and then proceeded to tear a strip out of the electorate, telling them they should be ashamed of themselves for electing a politician like Clarence. For unknown reasons, this drunken harangue made me even more popular.

Eventually, I had only one last task in civic politics, a zoning bylaw regulating the size of housing envelopes on the hillside view lots so that the city wouldn't become the ugly, blocky mass of monster houses on tiny lots it now is. Since this was near final approval, I fatally announced I would not run again in the next election. The gears started clicking and skipping and slowing down. The bylaw was obviously being stalled until past the date for filing nomination papers. So I filed to run again, which brought howls of protests and a stream of invective from the pro-development newspaper.

Before I knew it there were articles calling me a crook, comparing me to the disgraced president Richard Nixon and blatantly implying I was the father of illegitimate children. I felt like a nestling surrounded by crows. I was astonished by how a lone voice could create such antipathy in the council chambers (where at least the conflicts were usually civilized), the press, and the business community. Personally, I liked the council members—including one right-wing fanatic whom I respected the most, because even though

I considered his politics loony, he always displayed integrity, and we soon became friendly enemies.

The most damaging attack wasn't the "crook" guff, which was patently wrong, but the article about my having children outside of marriage. Thirty years ago that still stung. Especially when old ladies began phoning Sharon to offer piano lessons for the kids, and babysitting help. Our world has changed much in thirty years. We assumed they felt sorry for Sharon because she was now regarded as a single mother living in sin, even though the children were born during her previous marriage. The reaction was patronizing, and unfair to her, since she's a private person who hated and avoided politics and my public misadventures especially. She was an innocent bystander abused in order to tarnish me. More importantly, it illustrated how strangely the human mind locks onto meaningless issues. I went from the top of the polls to losing by eleven votes.

When I found out that these crappy newspaper articles had actually been placed in the polling booths, I sued for libel—a contradictory act on my part, since I don't believe in censorship. However, the libel altered an election—and that was crooked politics as far as I was concerned. This led to a full week-long Supreme Court libel trial, which I easily won on three counts, though the newspaper even screwed up their apology and had to correct their correction.

The judge cleverly awarded me enough money to defray my legal costs yet discourage me from appealing. She didn't like libel suits and politics mixing, and I agree with her. It could lead to abuse by politicians with thin skins. Plus, she wisely announced that Sharon was even more libelled than I was because she was a non-combatant, which made any appeal of my settlement by the newspaper more dangerous, since it could face a counter-suit from her. I admired the judge's Solomon-like settlement.

Most people aren't aware that court costs are more of a minimum than actual costs. By the time the $30,000-plus award was divided up and the real court costs and expenses were covered and I'd split the remainder with Sharon for her suffering in the conflict, I discovered I had about $1,000 left, and in a moment of madness, now that my political career was over, I decided I would buy a parrot to have someone to argue with.

Alas, this is the way the mind works. That I would so casually take on such an important lifelong obligation never fails to haunt me. Despite my good opinion of myself, I'm usually only just smart enough to know how dumb I am.

BACK IN THOSE naïve days of 1985, I assumed buying a parrot would be simple, though I knew there were rogue parrots out there, mistreated birds who'd lost their way and had become sick and unmanageable—a creature I could never live with.

I came to learn more about the mistreatment of domesticated parrots in later years, though I did some research at the time, under the delusion I was preparing myself for my new companion. Rogue parrots will holler at the top of their lungs from dawn to dusk, attack their owners, eat the furniture if left on the loose, and worst of all, pluck their own feathers until they stand on their lonely perches naked and bleeding from self-inflicted wounds.

There are 372 species of parrot among the three superfamilies—the cockatoos, the true parrots, and the New Zealand parrots. Although they may all be parrots, the different species each have different talents, different diets, and different natures, and have enticed many clueless people into keeping a "pet" parrot. So there's an astonishing range of abused parrots out there.

My first task in choosing a parrot was to decide what kind of parrot I wanted. I began a crash course on the needs, behaviour, and challenges of these species.

We already had a parakeet named Blue, who was deliriously affectionate and lived in the kitchen, where he could supervise us and sometimes call out our names. Our younger son, Roben, had bonded with him, and they spent hours together, Blue riding like a jockey on his shoulder, cheeping instructions.

A friend raised conures, beautiful deep-green, smaller parrots. He'd built an outside cage, with a window he could open to their indoor cage during the summer. I found them irritatingly noisy at times, though they were lovely and affectionate birds.

I took to visiting various parrots and their companions. I soon discovered, as with dog owners and their dogs, and orchid fanatics and their orchids, that people tend, sometimes hilariously, to resemble their companion—whether orchid or dog or parrot.

Of the major parrots there are several extra-fascinating species, and I soon recognized I'd have to choose between a cockatoo, a macaw, an Amazon, and an African grey. The cockatoo is cute and loving, but it has an ear-splitting call and a limited vocabulary. Amazons also tend to be affectionate and don't have a large vocabulary either. Some macaws have a lot to say, and they perform great tricks. However, they can be moody, with a beak that can break a broomstick and a screech that can nearly pop the nails from walls. They're also as smart as orangutans when it comes to escaping. At one parrot sanctuary, I was shown a chain-link wall. A pair of macaws had systematically unscrewed all its heavy bolts until the wall fell down.

I decided on the African grey, which can be affectionate but aloof—many don't enjoy being touched. However, greys are legendary for their enormous vocabulary, their intelligence, and their cheeky, trickster nature.

There were two varieties to choose from, the larger, talkative Congo, and the smaller Timneh, which can be even more talkative. I began following the newspapers and bird magazines, visiting pet stores and rescue centres.

A surprising number of parrot lovers have come to understand the complex needs of these birds, and they aren't shy about making sure their birds find a good home if they have to give them up.

The first man I phoned had a list of twenty questions ready. He started grilling me as if I were a potential son-in-law. He wanted to know how many birds I'd lived with, what kind and what were their fates. This wasn't good. For a start, all birds die eventually.

We soldiered through the questions, and I discovered I wasn't satisfactory, despite my long history with birds and my love for them, or at least, I was lower down the totem pole compared with the more promising applicants who wanted to "friend their bird." He suggested I phone back in a few days in case he didn't approve the couple who'd convinced him they were my betters.

The next owner introduced Sharon and me to her magnificent African grey. As soon as she opened the door to his room, however, he screamed so loud my eardrums vibrated. It was painful. He was all alone in the empty room, chained to a perch, surrounded by a circle of shit and discarded feed, some rotting, on the once-white wall-to-wall carpet. After he screamed at us for several minutes, we exited silently.

"Does he ever stop screaming?" I asked.

She shook her head. It seems he'd started screaming too much and they couldn't bear it. So they closed him up alone in the room, and he's been screaming more ever since. I'd start screaming too, if I spent a couple of years in solitary confinement, truly a "cruel and unusual punishment."

The next woman had an armoured sleeve onto which she coaxed the parrot. He sauntered across the armour and started ripping at it and squawking. "He's progressing very well and becoming much tamer," she assured us. "Sometimes, I can touch him." He made a run along her outstretched arm toward her ear, and she quickly lifted up a metal spatula to stop him from biting her face.

"I think he still needs a little training." I suggested.

She agreed.

At this point, Sharon was becoming terrified. "Are you sure you want a parrot?"

I'm a stubborn man. "Yes."

We decided to call back the owners of the special parrot who needed special friends. There seemed to be a commotion going on in the background. "I can't talk to you right now," he shouted into the phone. "We were showing him to the other prospects and he flew out the window. Can you call back at a better time?"

We called again two days later. The parrot still hadn't been found. The man sounded suicidal—with good reason. Parrots have a notoriously poor sense of direction and have trouble returning home. In our environment, they are soon mobbed and murdered by crows, or picked off by raptors.

Then a good friend, Mary, told us she knew a woman who rescued parrots and lived in a condo in the suburbs. When we arrived, Elaine had several parrots, in varying condition, arrayed about the condo. One was a plucker. She claimed pluckers could be cured and gently blew air at it from her mouth every time it started plucking itself. She had a lot of parrot-whispering ahead, I thought, but she seemed blessed with more patience than I could ever know. She claimed to have already helped several pluckers recover. Once we had done the tour, she introduced us to an African grey named Circles. He looked at us with some curiosity, and when she lowered his door, he strutted out, marched up my arm to my shoulder, and cocked his eye at me as if he were reading my mind.

"Hello," I said.

He studied me with suspicion but was quiet. We discussed him for twenty minutes, while he gazed alertly about the room. According to Elaine, he was only five years old and had been owned by a lovely woman who'd recently met a new man. Unfortunately, Circles had bonded with the woman and squawked loudly at the sight of the man, attempting to bite him at every chance. The poor man announced: "Either the parrot goes, or I go."

Elaine told us, wryly, that judging from the good temperament of the parrot since she inherited it, maybe the woman should have dumped the man. I lowered my arm, and he walked back to his cage door and looked up at me with curiosity.

I like to think we both knew the deal was done.

I bought him for $950, as if he were chattel, a slave-companion. I felt guilty immediately at becoming the "owner" of such a bright creature.

Chapter 3

———————

OUTSIDERS TOGETHER

WHEN SHARON AND I arrived home, our first fear was the cats. The worst among them was the mouse killer, Firecat, a big, orange furry thing who stalked raccoons for amusement, but fortunately, he didn't have much interest in birds. His fluffy fur was so thick it was a kind of armour, and one of his favourite fighting tactics was to lie down casually in front of any invading tomcats. This drove them nuts, and invariably the tom would pounce first. However, since Firecat's fur was impenetrable, the tom would be caught off guard and out of position, just as Firecat whipped around and shredded him. Firecat's one weak spot was his relatively furless ears, and by the time he died in his ancient old age, they were only stumps. We spent a lot of money at the vet's trying to save that beautiful cat's ears.

Firecat showed far too much interest in the parrot. Sharon was terrified. I didn't know what to do, so I set the cage down on the kitchen table. I had my suspicions about what would happen from the way he angled his head, sizing up Firecat. "I guess we're going to have to learn how he deals with cats," I said.

The bird sat nervously on his perch, watching the slow, stalking approach of the cat. This was nerve-wracking.

"Here, kitty kitty kitty," he said, his voice utterly innocent. He followed this up with a pitch-perfect meow. Firecat couldn't believe his luck as he leaped onto the chair and put his front paws on the table. "Meow," repeated the bird. It was becoming obvious how this was going to end. I edged closer, starting to worry for the cat (which is what most parrot owners will warn you about). The look in the parrot's eye signalled he had the rather dumb Firecat sized up. "Here kitty...."

Firecat pulled himself onto the table and approached the cage, nose to the bars. Idiot that I am, I was too slow pulling him away.

The parrot eyed him a moment before it leaped, fabulously fast, uttering an ear-splitting screech, latching onto the bars and attempting to rip the nose off the cat, who had already lunged backward, high in the air, and, I swear, made a sharp right turn mid-air, plunging out the open back door, not to be seen for several hours, and only then slinking nervously into the bedroom.

That's when we decided Circles was far too sucky a name for this treacherous creature, and he was renamed Tuco, after the monstrous yet amusing Latino bandit.

I mounted his cage on a plywood board on top of my filing cabinet in the middle of my office. The board provided an overhang, which reduced the danger from any surprise attackers climbing up from below. However, I soon learned my greater problem would be protecting the other inhabitants of our home from him. I couldn't keep him locked in the cage, so I usually opened it in the morning when I entered the office, and he took to scouting expeditions around the house, startling Sharon and the children and making life miserable for the cats. One of his favourite tactics was to dive-bomb a cat while it was sleeping on a chair, brush-cutting it, and then disappearing before it had a chance to fully wake. The cats soon learned to walk in fear of Tuco, especially after he figured out the art of weaponry and would snatch up small mislaid objects like spoons or pens and fly off to bomb his catnapping victims.

He also learned to mimic my disciplining of the cats. I'd say, "Get outta here" to any cat dumb enough to wander into my office while Tuco was on the loose. Impressed by how well this worked, Tuco was soon screeching, "Get outta here"—imitating my voice, only louder and with a mean Long John Silver accent. This truly confused the cats, and they obeyed him instantly.

Tuco came with a heavy little music box, which the former owner claimed he loved. The music would pacify Tuco if he became wild and obnoxious. The box played "Feelings," a song so treacly I could understand why it drove him into silence. I kept it on the board, beside his cage (in case I felt the need to torture both of us), until the day Tlell, our lovable husky cross, flopped down below the board and soon began snoring. Tuco scuttled out of his cage, deciding this was going to be more fun than the usual afternoon nap. He tugged at the heavy little box, wiggling it around, which made me curious, so I stayed at my desk—until I suddenly realized he'd pulled it over above the dog's head. He whipped around and started pushing it. I leaped to my feet and shouted, "Watch out!" so loudly the dog looked up, startled, just as the box crashed to the floor where her head had been resting a half second earlier. You can never be fast enough with that parrot. He's always one step ahead of me.

Tuco strode, cackling, his shoulders twice as wide as a minute earlier, back to his perch. I retired the busted music box to the garbage can.

It wasn't long before Tuco had become a menace to everyone, especially Sharon, whom he dotes on, and whenever she entered my office, he took to ripping up any paper he could find (usually my manuscripts or mail), as if he were making a nest.

Basically unteachable, he constantly impresses us with what he learns on his own. I tried for ten years to teach him to say "pieces of eight." He thought I was crazy. But he quickly confiscated my gag Long John Silver pirate laugh and made it sound even better. I soon took to parodying his laugh parodying mine. This is not nearly as complex as it sounds. In fact, over twenty-five years, he trained me to mimic him imitating me with a number of phrases. One of his standard lines is "What's that?" with the emphasis on a kind of distorted and melodramatic "that!" a spoof of me after a loud crash downstairs the day a cat knocked a delicate artwork off a coffee table while lunging for a fly. Now I often say it the way he does, even when I'm not with him. And when I hear a weird noise in the house, usually when Sharon is re-engineering the furniture placement, I look at him and say, "What's that?" loudly, to which Sharon invariably replies, "Nothing," even if she's broken a leg off a table. If I ask about the damage later, she always answers, "Oh, that's been like that for a long time." Sharon and Tuco have both got my number.

One of his triumphant moments arrived when a musician friend, Lesley, who was staying with us for a week, tried to teach him to sing the Woody Woodpecker tune. He spent the week staring at her in utter contempt. On the last day of her stay, while Lesley was desperately whistling her heart out, Tuco suddenly said, "Woody Woodpecker." The name was more interesting than the song. She was stunned, because she had never said those words to him, though we later suspected somebody passing in the hall had said, "Oh, you're teaching him to sing 'Woody Woodpecker,'" and he liked that better.

Naturally, a few days after she returned home to Alberta, he began whistling fragments of the Woody Woodpecker tune and continued whistling them for years, except when Lesley was around.

His behaviour soon taught me to respect the remark attributed to Ryszard Kapuscinski:

"Without trying to enter other ways of looking, perceiving, describing, we won't understand anything of the world."

Over the years, Tuco's repertoire became very large. He knows hundreds of words and even rudimentary grammar. Sometimes he'll repeat entire conversations. One of his favourites is lampooning me on the phone. "Hi... hmhmmm... uh ya... no... that's right... Okay... call me... yup... uh huh... Bye...."

Occasionally, he can be mortifying when he suddenly makes a surprise remark: "Not now, Brian. I'm having my period."

TUCO LOOKS UP with those lizard eyes and I have no idea what he's thinking, but I'm assuming it's a bird's version of happiness. He's cadged the remnants of a Fudgsicle from me. We've come to a silent arrangement over the years, one where I'll give him a tiny piece of my treats if he isn't obnoxious while I devour my portion. So I eat it down to a small lump in the middle of the Popsicle stick, and then hand it to him, which he takes gracefully and thanks me with his traditional loud "chuck-chuck-chuck" noise that's as articulate a thanks as this strong-willed bird will give. He knows what "thank you" means. He merely doesn't want to use the term. Sometimes he'll shout it out in the afternoon when he thinks nobody is around. No doubt, he considers gratefulness demeaning. He deserves everything the world gives, as does any creature—so when I tell him to say "thank you," he "chuck-chucks."

The first time I gave him my Fudgsicle remains he gleefully began licking it with his thick grey, slug-like tongue because he loves ice cream way too much—which is why I keep it out of sight. Then it ran down onto his claw. His foot was now sticky. This induced his most baleful gaze, and I could practically see the wheels going around in his small but impressively complex brain. There are relatively few synapses in there, but they're always on and burning white hot. It's not the size of the brain but the activity within it! He flipped the stick around and licked the goo off his leg and claw while continuing to snatch chunks of Fudgsicle. Then the melting goo flowed in the other direction, back onto him again. So he began doing a slow, graceful baton twirl with the stick, preventing it from dripping while he devoured the treat. Once he finished the Fudgsicle, he cracked the stick in half with a triumphant air, tossed it aside, and licked himself clean again. "Chuck-chuck!"

More than his dexterity with his claws and his beak, and his often astonishing intelligence, Tuco's cold eye is magnetic. We often sit staring each other, me trying to figure out what's going on inside his walnut-sized brain. Him? Who knows what he's thinking? But that eye makes me thinks of Robinson Jeffers's stone-chiselled description of the stare of a dying hawk and of William Butler Yeats's epigraph on his gravestone:

Cast a cold eye
On life, on death.
Horseman, pass by!

HE'S A MASTER at faking mechanical sounds. He can do a perfect toilet flushing and, ahem, the occasional loud fart. Sharon tells me she knows where he got that from. I guess it's a guy thing. He can also do a perfect microwave. What's more interesting is that not only are we unable to distinguish his beep from the microwave, but he also has the minute timer down pat. And his ding will start a split second before the actual ding of the microwave. He's become very fond of the microwave, because sometimes it means treats, and he loves his treats. For instance, if I was having some leftover noodle dish or stir-fry, we'd share the vegetables. He loves yarding broccoli and carrot sticks right out of my mouth, and this is how I eventually discovered he's turned on by French kissing.

French kissing a parrot is not smart, because parrots can carry a disease, psittacosis—or parrot fever—that can be passed on to humans. However, since Tuco has been solitary for so long, I'm not worried about him having it. It took me years to understand why he loves rubbing tongues, and we have a lot of fun kissing. If I open my mouth wide enough, he will even stick his head in and check out my dental work. Kinky.

HIS MICROWAVE TRICKS soon taught me another of his skills—his sense of time. He might be unusual here, because I've read in several places that parrots aren't good at music, though I've also seen film of other parrots dancing to tunes like Tuco does, as well as singing. Tuco can carry brief tunes if he likes them, and he is an amazing scat singer. His taste in music is bizarre. On the one hand, he loves tacky pop tunes, like "Sugar, Sugar," sung by the Archies, but he also enjoys Mozart—whereas he considers Beethoven uninteresting, unless it is a rousing movement, such as the inspiring final "Ode to Joy" of the Ninth Symphony, or carries a bold beat, like the opening of the Fifth Symphony. Ta-ta-ta-tum ....

On the other hand, he adores Bob Marley and most reggae tunes, and his all-time favourite is Louis Armstrong's version of "Mack the Knife," which sends him into paroxysms of scat singing, with the addition of whistling and whooping and dancing and bell ringing. Sometimes I play this cut for guests so that Tuco can impress them with his virtuoso backup and best ballet moves, incorporating lots of raised-foot poses, head bobbing and wing stretching in his grey gown of feathers, whistling and cheering and ack-acking and doing marvellous shout-outs at the perfect moment. It's uncanny. Some women, like Sharon, or our friends Lorna and Heidi, can lure him into full John Travolta "Stayin' Alive," *Saturday Night Fever* mode.

MUSIC AND BIRDS. I inherited that strange relationship between the two in my wild years. I was around fifteen lonely walking the log piles on Quadra Island. We were camping at Rebecca Spit. The big, heavy "portable" radio was blasting out early psychedelic rock when an eagle struck me, knocking me off a log and the clunky radio out of my hand. These were the days of "Light My Fire" by the Doors. I landed on my feet, and the indomitable radio kept rocking along while the eagle circled for another attack. I dodged her every time, but it was scary, scrambling under the logs, ducking for shelter at each wing-thundering dive, until suddenly I was face to face with her wounded child, a yearling not in mature colour yet, the feathers still mottled, with no white head and tail. I picked up a stick to hold him back as he struck at me, dragging his shot wing. I pushed him away with the stick and then I felt the beat of his mother's wings directly behind me, and I instinctively swung around, knocking her out of the air while he cowered under the log she had bounced off. I was aghast, horrified that I'd hit her, even in self-defence, but fortunately, she flapped herself into the air again and coasted above me, calling and screaming—like the macaw mother of my dream.

Without thinking, I gathered up the wounded young eagle, the fight gone out of him, and he submitted. As soon as I held him, I felt how scrawny and light he was. Starving. He would die soon. I retreated with him and the still-blaring radio, backward off the beach, the circling mother following until I lost her in the tall, dense cedars and firs, working my way toward our campsite several miles away, lugging the radio in one arm and cradling the eagle in the other.

Exhausted, a couple of hours later, I put the radio down at the campsite's edge and strode proudly up to the campfire, holding my eagle in my hands while he stared defiantly at the awestruck crowd of relatives. I could see the proud smile in my father's eye—his son, the eagle master.

I built a driftwood shelter and kept my father busy catching salmon for the bird. He was a magnificent eagle, and though ferocious with other people, he would let me scoop him up into my arms. There was more to our relationship than my just rescuing and feeding him. He would rest against my shoulder, tenderly, and crook his head toward me, that black, cold eye staring at me, fierce yet emotionless. The eye of the eagle—as with the feather transformation to black and white—only turns gold as the bird matures.

In retrospect, it's amazing how much he let me get away with. He could have ripped off my cheek, disfiguring me in seconds, but although he attacked the bird experts who came to take him to the zoo after we brought the eagle home, he never threatened me. He even attacked the professional bird keeper who lived next door, after the man put on a set of welder's gloves and tried to pick him up.

The eagle's talon went through both sides of the glove and the man's palm, spearing him like bait.

We returned home from Rebecca Spit with him at the end of the summer. The eagle automatically assumed I was the god of the freezer, where he'd perch when he escaped the temporary cage I'd made for him, scaring my mother in the dimly lit indoor garage when she went downstairs to haul out tomorrow's meat. The great temple of the freezer also supplied him with Mother's chickens and Father's hard-fished salmon that he'd spent so many hours catching.

One of the reasons I had to give the bird to the zoo, aside from my parents' advice that his wing needed professional care, was his expensive withdrawals from the family freezer, though that was never stated.

That day, when I enfolded him in my arms for a last time, his steely gaze locked with mine, and it has haunted me ever since. I handed him over to the young Vancouver zookeepers, who told me they'd fix his wing and keep him in one of the bird houses. I was bawling. He was proud and held his head erect. I later learned they took him back to the zoo and immediately put him down, because they'd decided his shot wing would never allow him to fly again. I'm sure they already knew what they were going to do when they picked him up. The liars.

While I nursed my wounded eagle in his driftwood shelter at Rebecca Spit, I invented another sport, probably encouraged by my devilish father. I don't know what inspired us. It might have been initiated by my compulsory duty as official fish cleaner when Father came home with his salmon in those days of plenty, before there - were even licences, let alone limits. However, once our department of fisheries takes over a fishery, it's usually doomed. As with the great cod tragedy of the Atlantic, almost as soon as the government started regulating the Pacific salmon catch, it evaporated. The new regulations almost seemed designed to inspire the corporations to catch more.

I don't know where our brilliantly deranged "eagle-fishing" notion came from, but it came upon Father and me simultaneously, and soon I had his rod and his lightest line and I would knot the line through a salmon's head. Then I would cast the head far out onto the beach and unreel the line until I was back at camp, where I would set the rod down in such a way that the line would unreel if there was a strike, but the rod wouldn't be lost. It wasn't long before I had a bite. An eagle skimmed low along the beach and snatched the head. The fight was on. I spent many days fishing eagles in the sky. It was a real challenge for them, though eventually they always snapped the line and flew away with their prize. This would probably give fisheries officers heart failure today. It still makes me cringe. But then it was a lot of fun, and the eagles always got their fish head.

I even taught Roben how to eagle-fish, though he was more casual than I, notably on the day he left the rod leaning against our camp table with the reel locked. The eagle grabbed the head during dinner and the chase was on, my expensive new rod and reel banging down the rocky beach as the eagle flew off with the salmon head, line, and rod, Roben and I in pursuit, me cursing the fate of my fancy rod. Fortunately, the struggling eagle was attacked by another who wanted the salmon head, and as the aerial dogfight took place above us, we managed to grab the rod and let them break the light line. Then, out of nowhere, a third eagle flew in and caught the prize in mid-air as it came free and flew off with it. We gave up eagle-fishing after this incident.

LOOKING BACK, IT was clear my rescued eagle recognized the thing in me that walked with birds. I have an odd sensitivity to bird emotions that allows me to do things like snatch a panicked flying rooster out of the air and soothe him into silence in my arms in a few seconds—an empathy that probably came out of my outsider years as an androgynous teenager, often treated with affectionate contempt by both my female and male friends and worse by those who weren't friends.

My brief relationship, maybe two months long, with the eagle inspired me to follow even more the literature of those who have bonded with the creature world—whether lizard, bird, insect, fish, or mammal. I swallowed Frank Buck's *Bring 'Em Back Alive*, Gerald Durrell's charming books about his misadventures with the animal kingdom, and *Man-Eaters of Kumaon* by Jim Corbett, who eventually became a world famous conservationist. Discovering that almost every man-eater (more than thirty) he hunted was wounded from gunshots and spears and traps—or disease—he spent the rest of his life attempting to preserve the leopards and tigers of India and other wildlife. Another hunter who hung up his guns for words.

I began reading Jim Kjelgaard's dog stories, and when I learned he committed suicide following years of arthritic pain and depression from a brain tumour, I wondered if that pain might be a reason why he bonded so well with the animal world. Of the early animal writers, the stately Ernest Thompson Seton retains his power. Charles G.D. Roberts is now hokey as well as unnatural. I loved the trickster impudence of the great fake, Grey Owl, and still do. Aldo Leopold remains a god of the wilds. As a child, I was firmly on the side of animal lovers and even the "nature fakers," a term coined to describe so-called naturalists who wrote about anthropomorphized animals, like Jonathan Livingston Seagull, Tweety, and Bambi, and sometimes swept up real naturalists with its wide broom. Not that I didn't love Bambi, but as I grew older, my taste evolved until I could love more the inspired cartoon/film *Bambi Meets Godzilla*, which ends with the cute and scampering Bambi suddenly flattened under a giant lizard's foot. That scattershot world again. My reading of these naturalists helped me to learn that the worst of the nature fakers could be as corrupt as those who profited from destroying the environment.

The nature fakers term has lately evolved into referring to urbanites (or suburbanites) who sentimentally love animals with big brown eyes while not recognizing their true animal qualities. They've drifted into a nature worship that's become cultish and stupid—a reverse and ignorant Othering that can cause enormous damage to the ecosystem. The deer and raccoon feeders don't appear to care about the real ecology around them and the extinctions of orchids, shrubs, bees, and migratory birds caused by encouraging these cute but voracious creatures in an unnatural, unpredated environment. These are the kind of people who create rogue, troubled domestic parrots when the parrot doesn't quite fit their fantasies. You have to spend minutes-hours-days-weeks-months-years tuned to the landscape around you before you can have a glimmer of how complex it is, how little you understand.

AS AN OUTLIER, I spent most of my early years learning the wilderness world, yet the more I learned, the more I recognized how inadequate my learning was, still is, despite a developing awareness of the needs of animals and plants. I soon learned that with plants, especially domestic ones, you can teach yourself to just glance at them while walking by and recognize if they are drying out, need water, fertilizer, more sun, or if the roots are too restricted, though I'm still trying to understand why I killed off a good chunk of my cactus collection last winter when I didn't notice soon enough how they were reacting to a new fertilizer. Another lesson in attention—it needs to be constant.

The problem that keeps me awake at night is my own lack of sensitivity to my community, an uncanny ability to savage friends, lovers, plants, animals, and family in self-defence or the defence of Others, despite knowing better. Although I might have the poet's classic emotional range of manic-depressive, my so-called sensitivity also seeps into an uncommon awareness that might resemble extrasensory perception—a Clever Hans (the horse that could count but wasn't counting, only reading the behaviour of the surrounding people for the right answer) awareness of the way people move and talk. On extreme days, I can behave like a rogue dog in a garbage dump yet simultaneously read the subtle nuances of community and culture. I probably acquired this sensitivity from stepping into "rape cars" during my wandering, hitchhiking years or from dodging pedophiles or strangers who wanted to beat me up merely because of my looks. I didn't need the missing door handle on the passenger door, or rape door as it's usually called, to know what was coming, but I got very good at talking the guy out of it or fighting back like a feral cat. This hypersensitivity can be a depressing paranoia, because it has also made me walk away from safe cars and safe friends. I always considered it a protective form of paranoia in the face of the scattershot world, except the danger isn't always there, which we all need to recognize. Nowadays, this behaviour is regarded as another aspect of PTSD.

Few of us don't have our life-changing moments, incidents we can never escape, accidents or diseases, bells that ring in our consciousness over and over again as we wind our way through our lives. Mine was receiving an odd throw of the genetic dice sixty-five years ago. It took me decades to recognize the concept of closure was more fantasy than reality. Forgetting and forgiving are the real healers of the injured mind.

SINCE IT WOULD take until I was twenty before a specialist even diagnosed my condition, I not only lived an intersex childhood, subject to various clueless medical indecencies, such as spending almost two weeks in the hospital when I was around fifteen, with my thighs sewn to my scrotum because they bizarrely assumed that by dragging down my undescended and unformed testicles, they could ignite my sexuality and cause me to present as a real man with normal sexual organs in the future. Ouch. Like my father, they were determined to make a man out of me without my having much say in the matter, and without their knowing what they were doing. And that's how you give someone permanent PTSD, though I still laugh more than I weep.

During that first week in the hospital I learned how to master the wheelchair and could do wheelie doughnuts down the entire ward. I had a riot in it, though when the wheelchair fell over, the pain in my crotch was as sharp as the pain you get in your head after gulping down too much ice cream. Now I consider those wheelchair acrobatics practice for my final years, which are arriving fast.

I desperately wanted love but didn't understand love or sex, because I was sexless. My skin was so hypersensitive I couldn't wear wool, and I hated being touched. It gave me the creeps. I only loved fur, and I enjoyed running my mother's fur coat across my cheek or my arm, thinking this must be what lovemaking feels like for normal people.

I encountered two comic book characters who wore full leopard-skin bodysuits. Sheena was one of them. Queen of the jungle. In love with both the girls and boys of my neighbourhood but not knowing what love or sex was, I also dreamed I was my dream-lover-hero, a jungle boy, whom I now remember as Korak, son of Tarzan, though I can't find any images on the Internet of Korak ever wearing a full bodysuit. I was both him and the beautiful girls he won, as well as Sheena. Today, I recognize this wasn't sexual desire (though I had sexless romantic dreams about males and females) but a desire to possess beauty and a hunger to "heal" my tender skin during those years of hypersensitivity. Now my face goes red writing these words at the childish kinkiness of these fantasies and knowing that my fur-suited dreams, drifting through the jungle vines and branches, would have been very painful in reality, with the skanky leather of my Korak suit on the inside and the fur outside.

As I grew older, I witnessed love and desire and sensuality all around me, and I was desperate to join in, to be loved, yet all I seemed to attract was pity, pedophiles, and bullies. It was as if everyone, male or female, could also "smell" my lack of hormones, just as I can "smell," like Tuco, the undercurrent of emotions in a room. However, my syndrome also meant I was born with anosmia, the inability to actually smell, despite an enhanced sense of taste, so I'm very sensitive to foods and even the air. I can stick out my tongue like a snake and detect strong odours. This talent isn't always reliable, however, and I've accidentally set more than a few household fires that I didn't catch until almost too late. No, my kind of smell, like Tuco's, is a weird, perhaps hormonal, sensitivity to the emotions of people. An empathy. I'll change where I sit if I sense the power going weird in a room. Sometimes merely shifting places shifts the emotional energy

Birds do this all the time. If you sit with birds, even domestic ones like chickens, you will soon observe how they move around you, as if there's this invisible elastic space between you, a space you can manipulate by moving an arm or leaning a certain way. When Tuco is out with people he has multiple boundaries, and I love watching how he navigates his almost geometric world when he's flying around with several of us in a room or making little charges across the floor to crawl up another chesterfield.

He's always been an Other in human society and has similar fixations to mine, which is one of the reasons why I am the only person who can touch him, though I've been nipped several times when I misjudged his boundaries.

More important than my skin sensitivity were the strange mental side effects of this disease, according to a few texts I stumbled on when I began reading more about my condition; though there was scant literature on the syndrome in 1970, there's a flood these days. The most crucial comment I stumbled upon after my first troubled twenty years claimed the syndrome could lead to premature intellectual leaps, causing the development of intelligence earlier than normal, yet it could simultaneously retard the emotional range of a child when puberty is supposed to begin. I don't know if this is correct in all cases, but it certainly was in mine. I will still often break into weeping, staring out the window of my office, at the ineffable beauty of the world, the same as when I was twelve years old. This is not as uncommon as one might expect. Although he had nothing like Kallmann syndrome, the actor Peter O'Toole once claimed that sometimes he'd weep so hard the tears would squirt out sideways from his eyes.

One of my most horrific moments during my diagnosis came when the doctor had me strapped down and X-rayed without bothering to tell me why. I almost went into a screaming fit as they aimed the machine at the centre of my forehead. Kallmann syndrome can arise out of a damaged, stunted pituitary gland, the controller of all hormones, and in my case it appears to have had an impact on the hypothalamus gland beside it, a gland that affects emotional equilibrium. I started sobbing when the technician strapped me into the machine. "It's in my head! It's in my head!" He never said anything, and now, so much later, I think he was as much a victim as I was. Nobody told him that nobody told me. But there was a kindly nurse there to take me sobbing back to my room, and I'm guessing he called her when he saw my condition.

The specialist constantly pestered me for nude photographs for the medical literature. After all, my syndrome was only first identified in 1944, six years before I was born. That's where I drew the line. I wasn't about to become his prize for a history of deformed patients, though it would have probably been beneficial for future diagnosis, and I'm still conflicted about whether I should have helped out by allowing the medical photographs. Then he changed my life with one sentence.

When I asked him if my syndrome would affect how long I lived, he casually said, "Your kind has no history of living beyond forty." It was so blithely cruel that it left me speechless. That gave me twenty more years at best.

I left that hospital like a rocket just launched—now fuelled on excessive doses of testosterone. They shot me up so hard with the first injection that when I returned to the dark basement room I was renting, I developed a brutally painful erection that had me screaming into my pillow for more than a week. It hurt crazily, and I have a high pain threshold. I even reset my own broken leg once. Now that really hurt. I went back and soon had the injections sorted out to a more comfortable level. This was when I started shooting up in size, from five foot seven and 111 pounds to six foot and 220 pounds.

If there was only going to be twenty years, I was going to live all of them and dance my way through what remained of my life. And I did; I danced hard. Only I never died by forty, much to the amusement of my friends, who tease me often about my longevity, and several have decided cynically that I'm going to outlive them all.

What sticks with me is the casual, thoughtless way this man, a good doctor and undoubtedly a kind human being, could change a life with such an unthinking statement. He thought he was being honest. Instead, he was cruel and probably had no idea that those casual words sent a flaming wound into my heart and forever changed the way I looked at the scattershot world.

Unfortunately, at the hospital I was also tormented by the mostly immigrant janitorial staff, who laughed at my effeminacy and teased me with cruel jokes about pansies and queens. The nurses made up for the men's abuse and mothered me away to safety. The good doctor was a master of tactlessness. He appeared to view me not only as his ticket into the medical history records but also as a live teaching tool, and would casually instruct me to disrobe in front of classes of medical students, who would stare at my micro-genitals and ask me dumb questions about my inability to present as a real male or my misshapen physique caused by the unusual bone growth of a Kallmann child. I had skinny arms that seemed as long as an orangutan's and endless legs, with a tiny torso and a woman's wide hips. Or he would bring them around to my hospital bed in packs of several interns or students, male and female, though there were few women interns in those days, so that they could feel my genitals and examine them blindly under the sheet and ask more embarrassing questions. As demeaning as all this was, I didn't dare complain. I was in shock as the fullness of my condition opened up before me.

None of this was intentionally cruel. He seemed a kindly man. It was only a criminal form of thoughtlessness. Or scientism—the specialist's belief that empirical science is the only authority. The wreckage of my emotional life was not his specialty, so he didn't pay any attention to it.

This is where we need to stray momentarily onto another path up the foggy mountain. Scientism, along with its ugly twin, religious fundamentalism, have had consequences on the story of our species and how we learn to deal with our world.

Scientism and its most vehement proponents insist only science can explain the world. This is, like spiritual fanaticism, a supernaturalist doctrine, and its reliance on reductionist logic—the belief that by examining the parts you can understand the whole of creation—presents a skewed vision of the world. Mary Midgley, philosopher and fierce opponent of scientism, claims it's the same as looking through a number of windows at an aquarium and insisting that one window is the way to look at it all, or that adding up each of the views allows us to see the whole aquarium. This way of looking can never give us the whole aquarium, nor comprehend its constantly changing nature. Science can save lives, yet it's now being used to increase the dangers of climate change as well as diminish them. Science needs moral values to balance its methodology. And moral values are even more difficult to work out than many scientific problems.

Science has strenuously, though unconsciously, supported the Othering of different people, creatures, and landscapes, along with its two-faced stepchild, technology. Obsessive scientism is a cult-like behaviour that at its most fundamentalist dismisses intuition, psychology, anthropology, philosophy, and so on—any discipline that strays from the scientific method. Alas, some of scientism's strongest proponents are superstars in the scientific community who should know better than becoming supporters of this narrow vision.

The optimists continue to believe that cognitive enhancement or cloud bombing or some as yet unimagined technological creation will create a new paradigm to fight climate change and the coming extinction wave. This is why there's such enthusiastic support of the so-called green revolution, which does provide wealth for corporate agribusiness. Aside from a few initial flushes of success, many agronomists consider it more dangerous than helpful, yet such technological striving is always preferred over simpler and healthier solutions, such as the redistribution of wealth and food, and population control. We are a gold rush species. The real green revolution will involve more empathy and less chemistry. But as the philosopher John Gray notes: "If there is anything unique about the human animal, it is that it has the ability to grow knowledge at an accelerating rate while being chronically incapable of learning from experience."

Others, like Einstein, have had a more grounded view of science and the world. "The most beautiful thing we can experience is the mysterious. It is the source of all true art and all science. He to whom this emotion is a stranger, who can no longer pause to wonder and stand rapt in awe, is as good as dead: his eyes are closed." He also knew: "Not everything that can be counted counts, and not everything that counts can be counted."

Although they weren't all alike, a number of doctors in those days also regarded themselves as superior mortals, especially the specialists, and showed little concern for the emotional state of their patients—at least, a number of the specialists I encountered then. It's an entirely different story today.

Almost ten years earlier, a sadistic school principal behaved similarly when he decided to heal my emotionality by strapping the weeping fits out of me in elementary school, culminating in grade six, when he strapped me regularly every time I cried. Thirty-six different times in one year. Like my father, he was determined to make a man out of me, only with a more clinically violent approach.

He was coldly ferocious about his strappings. He owned a professional model strap with a hole punched in it by the thoughtful manufacturer so that it could be hung in a teacher's office as a deterrent. It was a stiff red leather model with raised bumps like sandpaper, which added to the hurt, and he rubbed it with a shiny plastic-like oil at his desk in front of the class, I guess this was intended to show us he meant business. If Mr. Wall really wound up, it would not only hit my palm but wrap around and smack the back of my hand as well, and that hurt extra. We had to stand there, quivering, while he savoured the interval between strokes. In retrospect, it's obvious why I reacted so virulently to that school board candidate Clarence White and his bragging about his strong right hand.

Naturally, I think the only time I never burst into tears was when I was strapped. I might have been a weeper, but I was a stubbornly unique weeper. I didn't even cry the day when, out of mad rebellion, I jerked my hand back just before the strap hit and, caught by surprise, he whacked himself a good one on the thigh and knee, which made him limp around the office for a minute before he returned to do me real harm. If I remember correctly, this time every one of the five strokes on each hand wrapped themselves around both hands.

May you rot in hell, Mr. Wall, terrible creature that you were. But no, I still can't wish that on him, even if there was or is a hell. He taught me the damage men can do in the name of performing good. In the end, I realize he was a virtuous man who thought violence and power cured the strange, the weak, the different—the Other—a surprisingly common viewpoint that continues today.

Every animal wants to control its environment—even insects, with their webs and traps—and the more power it has, the more a creature will manipulate its conditions. I just have to look at Tuco astride his cage, a little King Kong, defiant and all-powerful in his own mind, even if his ego tends to relate to height—it grows with altitude. On the floor, he's a nervous bird, though that won't stop him from chasing me around the room when I'm bare toed and forced to high-step around him like the victim of a tiny toe-biting gunslinger. But generally, the higher his cage, the more cocky he becomes. If he goes on an ego binge for a few days, I hang his cage a foot lower so that I am farther above him, and that shuts up his more obnoxious yammerings.

He's a tough little guy, and if I threaten him with a rolled up newspaper, he'll just chew off the end and spit paper everywhere, creating a real mess. Once, when I grew annoyed as he stood on the open door of his cage, screeching away, I ripped off a piece of paper and made it into a spitball and threw it at him. He batted it away with aplomb. I threw another one. Same thing. He was making sure none went through his door, which resembled a goal. He hates a dirty cage. That's how I discovered Tuco was an ace goalie, and we started playing hockey. He loved it. He's so swift and graceful that it's nearly impossible to flick one past him. And some of his saves are spectacular, the kind that get you on your feet and cheering at a hockey or soccer game.

He's also a sore loser and tends to become angry when I toss something past him. He will throw his toys around, or onto the floor, and grumble and strut like a histrionic baseball batter who's had a fastball whistle past him.

One of the few ways I can intimidate him is with the tanned hide of a mink that a friend prepared for me after I miraculously shot it while it was murdering my chickens in the coop at 4 AM. It went so nuts when I entered the small coop, it raced around the walls about three feet off the ground. I still can't believe I killed it by flashlight with one .22 rifle shot from the hip. An old farmer friend remarked later that if he'd tried that he would have shot every chicken, and the mink would still be stalking island coops.

Anything furry upsets Tuco, and he'll scuttle into his cage and shut up if I wave the mink around. It's cruel swinging that in front of him, and I've only done it in a couple of emergencies and not for a decade now. He probably considers me another version of my cruel schoolteacher Mr. Wall when I haul out that thing.

Fed up with my weeping fits, and realizing that constantly strapping me wasn't working either, the exasperated Mr. Wall brought in a squad of scholastic experts with their folders and charts and tests. This, he casually informed me, was to fulfill the requirements to put me in a home for the mentally retarded. Years later, I've concluded he didn't recognize the cruelty of this revelation. He was just doing his job, like the good doctor.

My high results on the tests, I could tell, shocked Mr. Wall, and he never hit me again. The experts departed with their papers, giving me odd glances as they marched out the door, the same kind of glance I would see in Mr. Wall when he thought I wasn't looking and he was obviously wondering about what to do with me. Now, looking back, I think Mr. Wall spent more time trying to find a way to "improve" me than teaching the rest of the class, but he only had the knowledge and skills of his time, and that wasn't good enough for a mutant creature like me during that era. I had become his "special one" also.

In those days, they couldn't deal with prematurely intelligent manic-depressives, so I was left to rot in the back of classrooms (except for three teachers over the years who opened up different worlds, each in their own way), though I had a level of knowledge high enough for me to graduate from university and the emotional skills of the youngest kid in a kindergarten classroom. An emotionalism that's raged throughout most of my life. Over the years, a few doors kicked in and chair-throwing rages have made me notorious in the literary scene, though they've retreated into the past. I haven't wrecked a room in decades.

ONE DAY, AN incredible teacher with a soft voice, Cecil Reid, a Bella Bella Native who'd earned a master's degree in classics, got annoyed with my continuing disruptions at the back of the room. He plopped a book onto my desk and said something to this effect: "So you think you're tough, eh? You should read this."

And that's how at the age of seventeen I discovered Arthur Rimbaud, the rebel child-poet and permanent outsider. His "Letter of the Seer," written when he was only seventeen and had dropped out of school, became my inspiration. His revolutionary remark in his letter about writing, "I is an other" *(Je est un autre)*—that you had to become what you write—was a revelation in the nineteenth century. To be a true visionary, you had to not just see the Other but be the Other. For him, being a seer demanded an almost hallucinogenic ability to be possessed by empathy.

It's that emotional sensitivity to the Other, my tendency toward empathy and the awareness of my often stupid Othering reactions to the events of life that set me upon the path of this memoir.

The notion of the self and the Other was first discussed by Hegel and since then has gone through many permutations in philosophy and political science. More than a few thinkers, like Rimbaud, have given the idea some real turns. Among the greatest anthropologists of the twentieth century, the ethnographer Bronislaw Malinowski recognized the dangers of looking at strangers from a distance and changed anthropology by demanding the absolute need "to grasp the native's point of view, his relation to life, to realize his vision of his world," in his classic text *Argonauts of the Western Pacific*.

The political thinker Edward Said, who changed the way we think about imperialism—especially toward the East in his searing *Orientalism*—noted that colonialism can only succeed by turning the conquered people into Others. He also illustrated how many Western authors, such as Conrad and Kipling and Yeats, contributed unconsciously to the Othering of the East. Simone de Beauvoir pointed out that Othering is the root behind sexism and the treatment of women as Others in male-dominated cultures, and her lover Jean-Paul Sartre archly had one of his characters in his most noted play, *No Exit*, announce succinctly: "Hell is other people" (*"L'enfer, c'est les autres"*).

MY DECISION TO write this memoir was also partially sparked by reading the brilliant Ryszard Kapuscinski, who also saw our treatment of the Other as the major social problem of our species.

The real magic of Kapuscinski is that he was also working for the Polish secret service while writing some of the best journalism of his era, only from what I have been able to read so far, his spying mostly consisted of catty personal comments about his artistic competitors, comments that he would have known would be loved by his spy bosses but lead to no one being harmed. He appears to have been a clever man, as was Milan Kundera, who allegedly reported the other boyfriend of a friend's lover to the secret police (yes, it was a complex mess), and has consistently insisted it didn't work that way. I believe the murkiness of that affair led to Kundera's allegory of the path and the fog on the mountain I quoted earlier. When I began reflecting on how our mind allows us, despite our best intentions, to misbehave so badly with each other, as Kaspuscinski did on occasion, or people around the world do, keeping thousands of rogue parrots screaming in lonely cages, I realized this is the same condition that has caused so much damage to the earth and to the living things that co-exist with us in what we've labelled the biosphere—that narrow zone so rich with life between the lithosphere, the hydrosphere, and the troposphere (the earth's relatively thin layer of living soil, giant pools of mostly salt water, and the breathable air). Yes, our world has also become an Other.

Yet the gap between Others can be bridged and bridged often. It's happening all around us constantly, as it has happened throughout my life—throughout most of our lives—as everyone from home care specialists to valiant environmentalists rally to save everything—from old people with dementia to panda bears to nightingales to endangered lizards.

I've been fortunate enough to spend so many years with my little guru of Otherness. Soon after he arrived, Tuco got into the habit of sitting behind me on his perch or on my shoulder, while I wrote as he skimmed the growing realm of the Internet. It was evident he found my world fascinating, though limited, and only now, decades since we first met, am I aware of how much he began instructing me in the way of the world from our first meeting.

During all these years, we've been working together on a secret project, and the project is us, though that didn't occur to me for a decade. He's a deceptive non-linear master—my teacher, my sensei, a slapstick guru, and trickster guide to the dubious reality of the so-called the real world. Our connected life has led me to study not only my own pain and frustrations but his as well, and the reaction of various species to the Other. So these words are also a history of our relationship and what he taught me. It's a story we made together.

Chapter 4

THE DINOSAUR BIRD

ACCORDING TO THE poster on the wall, there are 276,000 bottles of dead creatures pickled in alcohol in the Museum für Naturkunde in Berlin. This is a small natural history museum with an enormous collection, specializing in rocks and meteors and the dead creatures of the world.

The jars are contained in a special, glass-walled, temperature-controlled room that's constantly monitored for contamination or evaporation. Hammerhead sharks, snakes, fish, eels, worms, spiders, birds, and mammals creepily peer from the jars perched on seven miles of shelves. It is reputedly the largest collection of pickled creatures in the world. Gazing at these exquisitely beautiful jars and their contents, I realize this array is more about us than it is about studying them. Altogether, including the jars, these halls hold more than 30 million corpses. That's a lot of parrots and pickled fish. And the butterflies—4 million of them. Six million beetles. Then there's the rocks, more than 2,100 meteors. The largest chunk of amber in the world. Crystals bigger than my head. This museum, if nothing else, is a tribute to German efficiency.

It was founded by the explorer Alexander von Humboldt's beloved older brother, Wilhelm, a linguist, using Alexander's naturalist collection and a couple of other collections. Alexander Humboldt's legendary expeditions were not only feats of travel but marvels of scientific study. And much of this museum was built upon his vision of science and his collecting and identifying mania.

Handsome, with an almost unbelievably strong constitution, Alexander von Humboldt was also known for visiting houses of "impure love" and his "shameful passions" for attractive men. He was such a marvellous speaker that when President Thomas Jefferson learned of his arrival in America, he put him up for six weeks in the White House to talk science. Darwin called him the "greatest scientific traveller who ever lived." It's often been said he was the last man whose mind encompassed the sciences of his time. The list of species, animal and botanical; geographic features; communities; colleges and foundations named after Humboldt is interminable. He climbed volcanoes and, with his explorer-companion Aimé Bonpland, was the first European explorer in his era to reach a world record altitude of 19,286 feet on a side trip while crossing the Andes in 1802 (one of four crossings in two years), recording the transit of Mercury and considering the commercial properties of guano in his spare time. The two men discovered the canal-like connection between the Amazon River and the Orinoco and were the first Europeans to encounter a living creature that generated its own electricity, *Electrophorus electricus*, electric eels, which nearly killed both of them.

One of the many stories about Humboldt is that he heard the last few surviving words of the recently extinct Atures people of the Amazon via a lonely parrot he bought in the village this small lost tribe once inhabited before being exterminated by another tribe. Yes, the last speaker of these lost people was a parrot. When Humboldt's parrot died, the spoken language died.

This is an old-fashioned museum, and although some of it is tacky, it's also better than the new attention-deficient museums that spend more on dumb fake phone explanations and computer wizardry than on the natural history itself. Here we meet the stuffed, pathetic corpses of Knut the polar bear and Bobby the gorilla, a dodo, the also extinct quagga, huia, and Tasmanian tiger. There's more than enough sorrow and death and extinction within these walls. We only have to walk through our museums to know our extensive history of Othering.

But there was more to come after the jars and the taxidermy, including the "certified" world's largest fossil of a standing dinosaur skeleton. *Giraffatitan brancai.* And the usual ferocious allosaurus, which can be up to forty-three feet long.

That's when I rounded the corner and saw him, the bird, the bridge, the one, the legendary archaeopteryx.

If we are going to examine our relationship with birds, we have to return to the beginning, and this is it, the most famous fossil in bird history, as well as the most controversial. The dinosaur bird is the cause of the first roaring fossil bird fight. In Germany it is referred to as the *Urvogel,* or the "original bird." Although time has led to the discovery of even older bird fossils, this species was the first encountered by the scientific community. At the Naturkunde they have the best, though not earliest, of the slate fossils of the eleven birds that have now been discovered. It came from the Solnhofen Formation in Bavaria, a limestone quarry that produced the finest slate for lithographers. They've mounted a skeleton based on the fossil, and he's a dead ringer for Tuco, even the stance. A little larger with a rat-like tail once filled out with feathers and a few other small differences, such as number of claws. And oh, he's 150 million years older. I stopped, stunned, in front of him. There's also one other major difference: sharp little teeth. Yet his jaw also resembles a flattened parrot beak—this was a Tuco with teeth.

BEFORE THE DEVELOPMENT of farming, as far as we can tell, almost all tribal cultures regarded the wall between humans and other creatures as porous—or they didn't see a wall at all. We shared the world.

We didn't go to the wilderness. We were the wilderness. *I am Tuco.* This is similar to the philosopher Baruch Spinoza's concept of having a personal relationship with a god that is an infinite inter-dependent living organism in which we are all interconnected. Similarly, some North American indigenous tribes tended to be panentheistic—seeing God alive within everything—as opposed to pantheists, who believe that everything is a god—a larger difference than apparent at first.

As people shifted away from hunting and gathering, and became farmers as well as city folks who managed to live off the produce and the growing apparatus supporting food production, distribution, and protection, our developing technology, everything from the invention of the alphabet to better transport, began chang-ing our attitudes, separating us from the natural world—reducing the genius of the animal kingdom to dumb beasts and convert-ing ecosystems into a commodity. To this day, the high priests of both science and religion exhibit similar cultish behaviour toward animals, even with "friends" like Tuco. The animal world mostly became brute slaves, enemies, or food. The wall, as solid as those in China, Berlin, and Israel, went up, and like those walls it must eventually come down, though nowadays many of our children are afraid to go alone into the magic woods.

WHERE DID TUCO and his ancestors come from? That's a story, a story dancing through our histories and erupting out of many geol-ogies, flashing out of jungles and savannahs, evolving or being bred by us into a multitude of forms and colours and talents.

At first, parrots such as Tuco were probably food and then friends; no doubt he became a god in several eras and landscapes, and today he's become a slot in the commercial pet industry.

Everywhere, the earth surprises us with its treasures revealing themselves, sandstone walkways beside riverbeds suddenly present-ing a hundred feet of dinosaur tracks obviously fleeing—fleeing the way a bird runs. Bones erupt from the dirt. Imagine a huge fossil beak rising out of the ground up to your knee, and that's only half the beak.

By 1850, the concept of evolution was not original. In 1842, the amateurish and wonky yet ingenious *Vestiges of the Natural History of Creation* by Robert Chambers was published and created a sensation, presenting an intelligent design view of evolution— the pseudo-scientific theory that God designed evolution. It was immensely popular and managed to be denounced by scientists, churchmen, and statesmen alike. One theologian, Reverend Adam Sedgwick, went so far as to decide it must have been authored by a woman, because of its "hasty jumping to conclusions." Ah, the Victorian era....

Various people continued ruminating on the concept of evolution, but nobody put it all together until Charles Darwin arrived. His major contribution wasn't the concept of evolution itself, which had been suspected for centuries, but the driving force behind it, natural selection—the mechanism that causes random mutations inevitably leading to evolutionary changes. He also recognized the cultural implications of this brilliant idea, because it meant God was not needed, and this would cause a social uproar that exists even today. So he spent decades painstakingly assembling his research. It was only after Alfred Russel Wallace conceived of the same concept while hallucinating with a fever in the jungles of the Malay Archipelago that Darwin realized he had to advance his book quickly. Wallace sent a brief paper on his theory to Darwin, who reacted with horror at seeing his years of research so hastily and roughly duplicated, but being a moral man he took the high road and "published" Wallace's little paper by having it read aloud along with a short draft of his own ideas and research at a scientific meeting, thereby declaring simultaneous discovery of the theory for both men. The brilliant yet eccentric Wallace was flattered.

The year Darwin had his short paper on evolution and the essay by Wallace read into the record at the Linnean Society meeting nothing happened. Darwin himself couldn't attend. He was too shy to read in public, and besides, he was also at home dealing with a scarlet fever epidemic. Nobody even discussed these world-changing papers. Later that year, Thomas Bell, the president of the society, in his year-end report, ruminating on chairing a dull year, remarked, "The year which has passed has not, indeed, been marked by any of those striking discoveries which at once revolutionize, so to speak, the department of science on which they bear." Was he ever wrong.

One year after the public reading of the evolution papers and the subsequent lack of a reaction, Darwin published his magisterial work *On the Origin of Species*. Although it was a large book, he regarded it as only the first chapter in the epic "big book" he intended to write and never accomplished. If Darwin had died before 1858, he might have merely been regarded by history as the man who wrote a four-volume book about barnacles (with a solid emphasis on their sex lives). He spent eight years studying them, and that study contributed immensely to his thoughts on evolution. If nothing else, Darwin was meticulous. It's been said, with some wryness, that he spent thirty-nine years studying earthworms, which, though not quite true, gives an idea of his stubborn science.

His reputation among scholars in London was solid when *On the Origin of Species* was published. And they knew what was coming. Although the earlier papers he and Wallace had written slipped under the rug, the first edition sold out before it even came off the presses. Darwin was certain the religious community would react vehemently, but he had no idea of the depth of anger and the denials that still foolishly continue 150 years later—after natural selection has long been proven by hundreds of thousands of samples of geological and fossil evidence, embryology, and biogeography, as well as the immense strides in today's molecular biology, genetics, botany, and medicine, based on the overwhelming record of evolutionary and genetic knowledge. It's a problem only for the ignorant, and evolutionary science is now so vast that no individual can even read all of it.

The theory of evolution made humankind rejoin the earth and began the slow healing of the gap that had opened between humanity and the other animals. It also threw us back into the wilderness—we lost our chosen status. This is what might be most repugnant to creationists, who take the beautiful story-myth of the world's creation in seven days as literal truth and add up the begats in the Bible to show that creation was very recent. This notion was fixed in the popular imagination by the venerated Bishop Ussher, who wrote a timeline of the world in the seventeenth century. His complex calculations traced the date of creation to nightfall on October 22, 4004 CE. These calculations were considered serious scholarly work in their era. The facts of evolution and scientific dating techniques prove that our earth is far older: 4.54 billion years old, give or take....

Darwin, prescient of the coming repercussions, cleverly managed to write his 502-page treatise without ever once using the term "evolution," though the word "revolution" is mentioned dozens of times, and he did end his book magisterially with this bombshell: "Whilst this planet has gone cycling on according to the fixed law of gravity, from so simple a beginning endless forms most beautiful and most wonderful have been, and are being, evolved."

The explosion followed. Slowly at first, then in a mounting storm of abuse and controversy.

Thomas Henry Huxley, as rigorous a scientist as Darwin, wasn't fully convinced at first when the theory arrived at his doorstep via a letter from Darwin. Yet he considered it the best theory at the time. He was also noted for remarking about himself: "How extremely stupid not to have thought of that."

When Chambers's *Vestiges of Creation* was released, Huxley criticized its incompetent science, though he also helped Chambers when the man was in need of money, and it was Chambers, whom he met on the street, who urged him to step into the upcoming great evolution debate proposed by Bishop Samuel Wilberforce.

Eventually, Huxley became Darwin's biggest defender and soon found himself dragged into what would become a legendary Oxford encounter with the famous and popular bishop, who was nicknamed "Soapy Sam" due to what Benjamin Disraeli called his "unctuous, oleaginous, saponaceous" manner and speech. Wilberforce was put up to this challenge by Sir Richard Owen, the venerable scientist and founder of the Natural History Museum of London and the man who coined the term "Dinosauria." Unfortunately, though a believer in evolution, he considered Darwin's argument for natural selection full of holes. Being a notorious backstabber in the science world, he decided to inflict Wilberforce on Darwin. This crazy debate is important in that it encapsulates all the attitudes toward evolution and creation ever since.

Soapy Sam was a beloved public speaker and could really boom in the style of his time, whereas Huxley was almost drearily scientific and polite. Darwin's other ally, Joseph Hooker, was sharp and witty on Darwin's behalf. The captain of the *Beagle*, Robert FitzRoy, who had taken Darwin on his great voyage of discovery, spoke for the Church, holding a huge Bible over his head with one hand and declaring that the assembled should believe in God and not Darwin in a style still used by creationists today.

Because the great debate wasn't recorded, there's been much embellishment and many contrary anecdotes afterward. Samuel Wilberforce considered he won it, which few agreed with, and the debate became legendary for his query to Huxley "whether through his grandmother or his grandfather" Huxley descended from a monkey. Huxley later claimed to have muttered: "The Lord hath delivered him into mine hands," and then informed the good bishop he would "rather be born of an ape than be born a man who abused the truth." This remark caused such a ruction among the thousand in attendance (the news of the debate brought an enormous audience looking for entertainment) that a Lady Brewster fainted dead away in shock at Huxley's impertinence.

Amusingly, no one afterward could agree on what exactly was said or whether this exchange even occurred. And this remains the confused state of the so-called evolution controversy today, fuelled by religious fundamentalists and the occasional rogue scientist. These variations tell us much about how strong belief ignores the facts. This refusal to accept facts or the tendency to twist them to fit a belief is called epistemic closure, and it thrives like a virus among us, whether we're young earth believers and intelligent design enthusiasts or closed-minded linguists and fossil researchers.

After the Huxley-Wilberforce exchange in the original debate, Joseph Hooker took up the challenge and scored several rapier-like points at the bishop's expense. In the end, each man walked out believing he'd won the debate, and the historian Michael Ruse claimed "everyone enjoyed himself immensely and all went cheerfully off to dinner together afterwards." Ah, if only such goodwill were the same today.

Shamefully, the evolution controversy has grown vicious over the years, and it's that viciousness that I find more interesting than the debate itself, especially as it relates to bird evolution, which remains a battleground today. Although history has concluded Darwin's theory was the winner, Darwin was lampooned mercilessly in the newspapers of the day and continues to be abused, usually in association with a monkey or ape. The last time I googled "Darwin monkey cartoon" I received more than 23,600,000 hits.

Since Darwin was so shy and well behaved, a legendary outsider yet beloved by many, it was Huxley's lot in life to become his defender. He soon realized, ruefully, that history would regard him as "Darwin's bulldog," and it did, though he went on to other scientific feats and discoveries of his own. In fact, his most controversial moment occurred when the first feathered dinosaur fossil was discovered, my beloved archaeopteryx. He declared it was a transitional creature between the dinosaur and the bird; thus, he was the first, or at least the most famous, to link birds with dinosaurs.

That battle continues to this day, in both the religious and scientific communities, often with less equanimity than exhibited by those participating in the historic evolution debate.

Tuco's opinion of the dinosaur/bird hypothesis is clear. For a start, he's fascinated by dinosaur films, yet he doesn't have a lot of truck with mammals, and if they appear in a film he will create such a ruckus, with screaming and growling and pantomime fights, that we have to remove him from the television room, which I hate doing because he loves watching movies, though he used to annoy us endlessly with his shameless begging for popcorn until I nailed a plastic popcorn dish to his movie room perch, and now Sharon always dumps some popcorn into his dish on her way to the sofa. But not even his beloved popcorn dish will pacify him when a realistic, furry predator appears. He will also growl at photographs of lions or leopards.

One day we were watching a fun but corny Hollywood-style film about a bush-smart Australian named Crocodile Dundee. Mid-film there's a quarrel between the hero and his love interest, and she goes off in a huff to refill her water canteen, which is hanging from a leather cord around her neck. As she's leaning over a quiet stream, a huge saltwater crocodile lunges out of the water. It was scary enough to make Sharon scream. The crocodile misses the woman but grabs her canteen, and for a brief moment there's a tug of war until the cord breaks and the woman falls backward while the crocodile recedes underwater with its trophy. Tuco thought this was the funniest scene he'd witnessed in years, and he let out a loud "Whoopee" as the crocodile lunged and then started cheering for it. He even went "Awww" when he realized the crocodile wasn't going to get the woman. The "awww" made Sharon and me look at each other and then Tuco. He definitely knows which side of the dinosaur bone pile he's on.

Watching television with Tuco is always an education in bird perception. Aside from his dislike of furred creatures (not counting dogs, or at least Olive, our sweet Labrador/Rottweiler cross), he loves naked women and sex scenes, which he accompanies with lots of laughter and wolf whistles and step dancing. He is also fascinated by combat and fighting, but more on that later.

IN 1861, ONLY two years after the publication of *On the Origin of Species*, the ancient fossil of a feather impression was discovered in a quarry in the Solnhofen limestone deposit of Bavaria, and it raised a few eyebrows before it was quickly followed by a fully skeletonized fossil of a dinosaur that resembled a bird. This raised a lot more eyebrows.

The first archaeopteryx resembled roadkill, a flattened mess, missing its head, embedded in a chunk of slate, but the obvious feathers, on what appeared to be a dinosaur, set tongues wagging. Not only did it have many dinosaur characteristics, it also had several features common to birds. Wings, a partially reversed toe, those now-notorious flight feathers, and most importantly, a wishbone—a key ingredient in bird classification. It also was an odd bird. With its feathered legs, it appeared to have four wings, and it probably did more skipping and jumping than long flights.

At the time of the archaeopteryx discovery, the scientist most responsible for bringing this first bird-like fossil to the general attention of the scientific community, Friedrich Ernst Witte, noted in a letter the bird/dinosaur "has characters of both and is strictly none of them."

It was then that Huxley got himself into his second storm, when, after much anatomical study, he famously uttered his theory that birds were descended from dinosaurs and the archaeopteryx was a transitional bird. The insults began flying, but he held his ground, weathering the attacks of his ferocious opponent, the esteemed but now even crankier Richard Owen.

Huxley even shocked Darwin when he declared chickens were basically "an extremely modified and aberrant Reptilian type"— or as Wayne Grady remarked in *The Bone Museum:* "snakes with feet"—a line that gave me some thought after watching one of my chickens running around the back field with a live, writhing snake dangling from its beak.

When I watch Tuco scratching behind his invisible ear, there's a reptilian creepiness in his gestures that reminds me of small lizards, though few, I'm sure, have the dexterity of Tuco, with his two-claws-forward and two-claws-back zygodactyl feet, which nearly give him the dexterity of the human hand and are common to most climbing birds.

The bird/dinosaur archaeopteryx is believed to have arisen since the great Cretaceous-Paleogene extinction 165 million years ago. Science has advanced so far technically that electron microscopes are now being built that can magnify up to 10,000,000x. And these have been put to good use on fossils. At 30,000x, recent microscopy has detected pigment packets in the feathers called melanosomes. These preserved pigment cells dictate the colour of dinosaur feathers, such as the blue-black of the archaeopteryx, which would have resembled the colour of the modern raven. Since the original discovery, at least ten more specimens of this creature have been discovered.

The fossil at Berlin is displayed like a religious object behind a black cloth screen on the wall. You go inside the small room and muted lighting rises, the fossil in its case glowing like a sacred page of history. If you push a button, the fossil will slowly move until it is on its back. And if you are a scientist, the cover will slide off so more exact measurements can be taken under supervision. And that's your daddy, Tuco.

This feathered dinosaur was not a one-of-a-kind species. More recently, many thousands of bird/dinosaur fossils have been uncovered around the world, including, older birds, the aurornis and the anchiornis, and a feathered giant, *Yutyrannus huali*, a thirty-foot-long, three-thousand-pound relative of the *Tyrannosaurus rex*. We used to think of dinosaurs as big lumbering, dumb beasts. Over the years, we have learned they could be as fast as birds, including a number of the larger dinosaurs.

Parrots also have the ability to react quickly. When I'm fooling around with Tuco and accidentally become too scary, he will bite me, sometimes on the lip and sometimes twice before I realize he got me the first time. These bites are invariably my fault, yet I remain surprised at his speed. I have fast reflexes, but I'm no competition for Tuco.

However, if he bites me, he always feels bad and lowers his head shyly, shuffling on his perch, announcing he's a "bad bird." Like every outlier he wants love and approval.

A local businessman on Salt Spring Island once had an African grey with its wings clipped to the bone (a cruel practice), which meant it could never again grow flight feathers and fly, so he would let the bird play in the backyard with his little dog. The bird and dog were inseparable and enjoyed many adventures in the backyard.

One day, the man's wife heard a burst of terrible screaming.

A small hawk, noticing the parrot walking on the ground, had dived, intent on its prey, but since the African grey is so remarkably fast and smart, it had whipped around and grabbed the hawk by the talons, snatching it out of the air, and started beating it against the ground as if it were an old rag doll, aided by the yapping dog, eager to join the fray. At this point, the surprised hawk was trying to scramble away, but it was being whipped around so badly that it couldn't. So it turned and tried to bite the parrot. Eventually it might have gotten a good bite in, but the dog and the hoopla were against it. The woman came rushing out, seized both birds and was bitten by each before she separated them. The hawk wing-shambled away into a stumbling flight, while the dog and parrot strutted about the yard. Victorious.

Sadly, this parrot encountered some bad luck on another day. The dog was let outside and the parrot rushed up to it, all excited to play, startling the little toy dog, which grabbed it and shook it playfully, killing the parrot, despite their loving friendship.

Although a parrot might consider itself a tyrannosaurus, it's merely a little bird in the end. Epistemic closure, that triumph of belief over reality, can kill both birds and us or, more likely, tends to make us look like fools. What deniers of natural selection don't understand is that the evolution battle is already over. Natural selection is reality. And as for the bird/dinosaur controversy, the scientific community is now almost universally on Huxley's side. Religious fundamentalists continue their opposition, more in the manner of FitzRoy waving the Bible around, while the creationists, both scientists and pseudo-scientists, tend to use any minor scientific disagreement to justify their denial of all the science. For complex reasons, a lot of the continuing conflict has focussed on denying the dinosaur/bird connection, perhaps because the prehistory of birds like Tuco remained shadowy until the surge of discoveries over the last three decades. Plus, the recognition that parrots are probably direct descendants of the tyrannosaurus family is just too farfetched for some to swallow, despite the facts. The concept of birds descending from theropods also makes nonsense out of the young earth premise. What we're actually witnessing are desperate attempts to continue Othering the natural mechanics of the world, a common flaw of fundamentalists with an us-or-them vision of life.

The real street fighting in the scientific realm is now over the details, like whether the first birds evolved from climbing dinosaurs and began to fly "tree down" or whether they were crawlers and runners who flew "ground up." As with most of these debates, it is probably a combination of both, yet it remains the subject of much overheated discourse among paleontologists and biologists.

Science has always had its raucous and bitter internal disputes. The hostility of these disputes is what interests me—the blind Othering—the way we treat colleagues with heretic views. Religions and sciences both have their inquisitions and heresies. Religious fights can be more fatal physically. Scientific battles may be career destroying, but they seldom lead to crucifixion or burning at the stake. Knife fighting in the sciences tends toward banishment from the textbooks, public abuse at conference debates, or failure to receive tenure. These disputes can also make for salacious reading. Merely another symptom of the way we treat the natural world, this nasty pack conduct has been evident since the beginning of history.

Pugnacious reactions to the Other are not only a human fault. They're an evolutionary behaviour, evident from earwigs to eagles. One doesn't have to do much thinking to realize how "a stranger coming to town" can be considered a threat.

Several years ago, a friend went on holiday, and before we knew it we'd temporarily inherited a pair of cockatiels. Whereas Tuco's campaigns of household terror have made him cat-proof, I worried the cats might harass the cockatiels, so I took them into my office. Unfortunately, they weren't parrot-proof, and Tuco was soon threatening to rend the cockatiels limb from limb. I was forced to move the cockatiels into a safe place in another room, where they could happily cheep away. I've heard of a number of incidents in which parrots have bitten off the toes of birds clinging to the sides of their cages.

When the cockatiels were finally returned, Tuco cheeped like a cockatiel for weeks, driving me mad with his compulsive cheeping. He'd learned to inhabit the Otherness of the cockatiels. He did the same on another occasion, when our younger son was house-sitting while we were away. The hot water heater in the attic developed a slow leak, dripping down to the floor below. Roben, "cleverly" dealt with the problem by putting a bucket under the leak, leaving it for us to deal with when we returned. Tuco took his "Drip... drip... drip...." revenge for weeks after the heater was replaced. I'm convinced this was his idea of punishment for leaving him with the leaky heater.

Again, he'd become acclimatized, and this we see with both humans and their animal relatives. Once they realize something new isn't a threat, they learn to live with it, even enjoy it. That's how Tuco learned to celebrate the gamut of my home renovation noises, from hammer to saw to drill. He could do them all, sometimes in a burst of simultaneity. That reaction is also how I survived my brutal and bullied young years. When you can learn to celebrate the worst that's thrown at you, you can celebrate life itself.

Othering is a natural reaction to "the strange bird," and you meet it often in the bird kingdom. One of the reasons parrot fanciers are so frightened of parrots escaping into a North American environment is that the local birds will kill them, because they're not local and haven't evolved strategies for survival in North America. They are strangers, and they act strange. There are a number of feral flocks of parrots in North America and Europe, but their existence is precarious, and perhaps ecologically that's a good thing. Invasive species can be dangerous. Othering is a complex issue.

When I look back to my childhood, I realize I was a parrot among crows. The weird kid. The different one—a foreign sensibility in the school hallway. We all know how children can flock and bully, and that's why my earliest school memory constantly returns— the mobbing by that pack of kids. Once again, I am scooping up a handful of gravel to defend myself, followed by the forever tinkle of the gravel against the windows of the classroom and the teacher looking up at me—then the punishment for trying to protect myself. My first lesson in fighting aggression—not fighting is sometimes smarter and often more brave. I never fully learned that lesson, and I've never fully controlled the steroid rages that can occasionally flow like lava through my blood, usually ignited by my "Kid Galahad" complex when I see someone being bullied or buried in lies and I flash back to my own bullied years.

I also had to balance turning the other cheek with my father's opinion about men and cowardice. Several years after that first bitter day of school, I was coming home from the local junior high and a pack of kids jumped me. I dropped my books and ran crying into our nearby house and flung myself weeping onto my bed. Unfortunately, my father was home and had witnessed the whole event from the front room window. He was outraged to see me fleeing a fight, even if it was an unfair fight. Determined, as always, to make a man out of me, he gave me hell and ordered me back out onto the street, alone. So back I went, steeling myself to face impossible odds. Luckily, the older boys had left, and I grabbed my schoolbooks and returned home. Father was proud of my new-found courage (though it was only a greater terror of him), so I learned there were also moments when you had to fight. I thought it cruel of him at the time, still do, but it worked in its way. A crucial teaching event. Ever since then, it's become an almost instinctive behaviour to react aggressively when threatened, which worked in those bullied years. Now it's not good and too inborn and near-impossible to prevent, and I've unintentionally frightened more than a few innocent people who I felt were threatening me or someone else. When the testosterone injections began at twenty, they only increased the ferociousness of my reactions. *Get up. Be a man! Go back and get your books!*

My fear of my father had good reason. Since I was such a rebel kid, there were more than a few times I was backhanded across a room. Also, since he had a wooden leg and I had lightning reflexes, he'd have to throw objects like toolboxes or chairs or gum boots to slow me down so that he could catch up to me. When this was mentioned sideways in a collection of my poems twenty years ago, it caused a family uproar. Finally, my father asked me, "What's this all about? I never hit you!"

"Of course you did."

I could tell he was starting to rile. And that he was deeply hurt. "I never once used my fists on you!"

"I didn't say you did."

I could see the flash of realization in his eyes, and he relaxed. "Oh, that's different then. That was just discipline. What's the problem?" The accusation that he would use his fists on his son was deeply injurious to his moral sense—that was abuse.

"I don't have one. I did then." This was a partial lie at the time, yet I was beginning to understand the powerful moral code of this uneducated man. It's taken me a few more years to actually look back at some of the incidents with a sense of humour and forgiveness. He did the best he could for me with the skills he had.

"Pass the TV remote," he said, calmly ending that potentially explosive conversation.

A few years after the schoolbook-dropping incident, a couple of boys were beating me up beside the school grounds, and a switch went off in my mind as they were kicking me on the ground. I rose.

One punched me, and I went down. Then I got up again. They beat me brutally, but I kept rising to be hit again. After a while, they realized I would not accept defeat, and oddly, that scared them. I had suddenly become more powerful, though it hurt. *Hurt. Hurt. Get up. Go back and get your books!* There were other incidents like this, but I always rose again to the fight. As the carpenter/writer Ross Laird learned: "Wisdom comes from wounds. The deepest wisdom I have comes from the wound."

My acceptance of the beatings by other kids eventually protected me somewhat. There was no point beating someone who welcomed the assault, and strangely, I soon ended up hanging out with the tough crowd of hoods. My outsider weirdness and the way I took ownership of it, along with my uninhibited risk taking, had elevated me into sidekick to the big leagues of the high school hierarchy. *Yellowbird. Yellowbird. Fly, my little Yellowbird, down the hill.* I had inhaled my pain. It's not a route I'd recommend to any child, yet thinking back on these incidents made me consider why human aggression occurs and how it can be deflected or pacified, and equally, how it can be incited. I remember that wry yet horrific scene in the television show *Lillehammer* where the gangster— learning the school bullies have been "talked to" over and over again yet keep on bullying his stepson—tells the victimized child to fill a sock with gravel and use it on the face of the biggest bully the next time they tried anything. A parenting solution that would make any sane person shrivel up with horror today. Yet, in those years of pain, when I was assaulted I also became, on occasion, that little kid with the sock. I always went after the biggest guy when they started on me. Looking back, I realize that I used almost every strategy in the book from fleeing... to pacifism... to being battle-ready... to stalking my bully. We do what we can. I had learned not to give up. *Get up. Go back and get your books.*

Strange angers infest us, and they appear in the strangest places, where we least expect them, and it's easy now to understand how much my childhood led me to question behaviour and any kind of fundamentalism. I've always been fascinated by Gödel's proof, an intellectually foxy theorem—a clever trick of math that, more or less, can't be disproved due to the wicked set-up of its self-fulfilling argument. The publishing of this proof enraged many mathematicians over the years and inspired some impressive rants by scientists who felt they were being insulted by a prank equation. It gradually came to be regarded with respectful bemusement and lately has joined the pantheon of essential mathematical theories, even if it is meaningless. Brilliance often beats meaning. Science is full of such deathtraps, but more important for this history, why would our "dispassionate" mathematicians engage in the virulent arguments and vicious sniping that first greeted Gödel's theorem? A stranger appeared in town and was thought to mock the dignified science when he merely demonstrated math at its most impressive level, and only for the love of the game of math.

Othering was, and still is, being used on everything from math jokes to someone as small and fragile as I was—and to justify ethnic cleansing or the massive pollution that's changing the planet. If Barack Obama has been right about anything, it's that we are all suffering from an "... empathy deficit. We are in great need of people being able to stand in somebody else's shoes and see the world through their eyes." He also once wisely said: "... we have the opportunity to make a habit of empathy, to recognize ourselves in each other...." Gloria Steinem is another who clearly understood the need for empathy, and called it "the most revolutionary emotion."

Science can also be a foggy world, a semi-hidden path in the mists of time. That's why extinction events in the distant past often use estimates, which tend to be virulently attacked. There are no real charts on extinction. What does exist is constantly changing. But it's generally thought that historically one species of bird went extinct every eighty-three years over the centuries. In modern times, since the death of the last dodo around 1681, at least ninety-two species of birds have gone down the funnel of time. It's now being estimated, alarmingly, that a species of bird will soon be going extinct every six months.

The fifth extinction killed the dinosaurs. When I was young, we used to laugh about the dinosaurs—how their stupidity led to extinction. We now know that's not true. There's good reason to suspect the Anthropocene, a new term for the era of human dominance of the planet (since the 1800s), will not last much beyond this century, if even that. Our refusal to acknowledge such a possibility illustrates our classic refusal to acknowledge reality. The dinosaurs were killed off by accidents of time and space, but they still made it through approximately 170 million years. It's we who are the idiots. How dumb we are, despite our idiot claims to intelligence, never fails to impress me. Our era of world power could expire within a few hundred years because of our own deeds.

WHILE THERE REMAIN numberless evolutionary side issues in the scientific community, the evolution of the bird remains hot news. Although the debates have been relatively tame in the last decade, they used to be as brutal as my bullied years. The latest debate has been the nearly played out discussion of whether ancient birds were "top down" or "ground up" fliers. The majority opinion believes they evolved out of the Coelurosauria branch of the theropods into feathered, insulated branch crawlers and, like squirrels, soon glided from tree to tree. This ability to fly allowed birds and a few gliding mammals and amphibians to penetrate what Loren Eiseley evocatively called "the living screen" between the earth and water and the sky.

However, a group of the earliest bird fossils had feathers on all four limbs. There is good argument they were fast ground runners who learned to catch air and lift off as they fled predators—diving off rocks or up into trees. The modern roadrunner, a variety of cuckoo, can troll along at twenty miles per hour. One roadrunner (it's been bragged) was chased by a car for ten miles at thirty-one miles per hour. At least the poor bird survived. Too bad the driver survived, too—another unconscious bully.

A roadrunner doesn't usually leap or fly over obstructions. Instead, it can reverse direction using its vertical tail as a rudder, allowing it to make sharp turns, confounding its predators and idiots with cars. The fastest land bird is the ostrich, which can reach speeds up to forty miles per hour on its powerful legs. Still, the latest research contends that all the modern land running birds descended from flying birds. It's hard to imagine an ancient winged variant of the fabulous extinct, ostrich-like, wingless, twelve-foot-tall moa suddenly fluttering down from the trees, but the world has always been weird.

In 1999, in an open letter to *National Geographic,* the esteemed scientist Storrs Olson, curator of birds at the Smithsonian Institution, while correctly haranguing the magazine for its presumptuous naming of a new scientific discovery of a dinosaur, as an aside, denounced the notion that birds descended from carnivorous theropods and that these dinosaurs had feathers. The letter was so intemperate that it was seized on by Christian creationist institutes, which continue to cite him, no doubt much to his regret, to prove that evolution is a hoax, even though he's a champion of evolutionary theory.

This dogfight arose out of a mangled *National Geographic* article about a fossil bird/dinosaur found in China, which dragged some of the most respected paleontologists through the mud before the smoke cleared. It even sideswiped the illustrious Philip Currie, a founding director of the Royal Tyrrell Museum and one of the major proponents of the theropods-to-birds theory.

Alan Feduccia, a noted paleontologist, following on the trail of Olson, recently took to picking the feathers off dinosaurs again, or at least the theropods. Since he believes that theropods and birds had a common ancestor and were not of the same clade (a branch in the wondrous tree of life), the birds couldn't have descended from theropods. This idea somehow played once again into the hands of those who will use any controversy to argue against the juggernaut of evolutionary theory. When I began writing this book, the bird/theropod thesis was still controversial. Today, Wikipedia begins its article on birds by stating they are descendants of theropods.

When I asked a prominent paleontologist why there aren't more denials of the Olson letter or Feduccia, the reply was sad. There wasn't any point. The science had moved so far ahead, it wasn't worth going back to find someone lost on the trail. Or as the paleontologist Christopher Brochu noted about the venomous exchange of letters over the "storm in a feather" initiated by the *National Geographic* article: "So don't be disheartened. All you're witnessing is the paleontological community exposing itself as a group of bipedal primates before the world. I doubt you'll find a less human group in any other profession."

Further study, to add insult to injury, proved the controversial *National Geographic* bird/dinosaur fossil was a fake, created out of at least three tiny dinosaur fossils, no doubt ingeniously glued together by some poor Chinese farmer who thought he could make a little money on the side. He probably has no clue that he initiated such a dustup in the scientific community and fed the enthusiasms of more than a few anti-evolution fundamentalists. The biggest joke is that all the dinosaurs assembled into this brilliant fake were probably feathered. It's obvious feathered theropods existed, and moreover, there were many of them.

It was soon discovered the fossil was also removed from China without permission. This is an archaeological taboo, which only fuelled the controversy and led to this dogfight further catching the attention of the anti-evolutionists. This famously faked fossil has since been used to "prove" the thousands of feathered dinosaur fossils being found in China today are all fakes, whether they're found by cash-starved farmers (who would have good financial reason to fake a bird fossil) or full-scale archaeological expeditions sanctioned by multiple world scientific bodies with impeccable credentials and detailed records of provenance.

Most of the anti-evolution studies of the dinosaur/bird hypothesis published these days in the popular press ignore the avalanche of evidence and focus on some tiny detail in heated debates among scientists; then extrapolate the minor controversy to disprove everything. These papers soon fade away, until the next one surfaces, usually vouched for by a creation scientist. Whenever a forgery or discrepancy in the fossil record appears it is regarded as total proof of the failure of the last 150 years of research and an enormous authentic fossil record too large to count.

This kind of behaviour most famously arose in the so-called Climategate scandal. The theft of a vast assembly of emails and the quoting out of context of a few too-enthusiastic scientists were used to discredit the works of six thousand scientific studies that were part of the Intergovernmental Panel On Climate Change report. Later, it was claimed a single goofy study of glaciers and a speculative hockey stick graph supposedly illustrated that twenty thousand of the world's top scientists are cheats and/or idiots. The vice-chair of the IPCC noted these were the same kind of distortions and dishonest reporting systemically used in the tobacco controversy last century.

In the end, Climategate and the *National Geographic* fake fossil scandal are part of what's become referred to as the "God of the gaps" school of creation. It's like noticing an unfinished segment of sidewalk and then claiming that proves the entire sidewalk doesn't exist. However, climate change is no longer a debate; it's a reality.

Some "gappers" are convinced they are victims of "evolutionary spin doctoring" used to convince people of "a billion-year-old earth" instead of the real "biblically proven" six-thousand-year-old earth. The shocking number of four in ten Americans, according to a 2010 Gallup poll, still believed the earth is less than ten thousand years old. Only 16 percent believed in an evolution without God. Then again, ignorance does lead to fabulously strange polling—thirteen percent of Americans also believe that Joan of Arc was Noah's wife.

I love the massive and ever-growing body of evidence proving that birds are related to theropods, and it makes me smile, knowing that *Tyrannosaurus rex*—beloved of children who adore scary monsters and star of hundreds of bad movies and good documentaries—along with many of his smaller relatives, shared similar characteristics to the parrot eyeing me balefully in my office. Natural selection, though a wonderful tool of the ecosystem, created many an erratic descendant, and I'm one of those erratics, too.

Darwin never promoted the concept that evolution was progressive. Today, there's enough evidence to prove, despite its most enthusiastic proponents, that the evolutionary ladder isn't a ladder at all but moves in varied directions, mostly toward extinction. Instead of a tree of life, it often seems to me an amoeba of life discovering extinction.

Darwin's concept of natural selection was twisted into "survival of the fittest" by the economist Herbert Spencer. But that's just a tag adopted by the wealthy masters of the gilded age who commandeered Spencer's phrase to cook up a "red in tooth and claw" vision of survival to justify unfettered capitalism that allowed the very rich to grow richer while mistreating the ill, the poor, the uneducated, and the unprivileged, a phenomenon that the present day monopoly capitalism is repeating in this new corporate gilded age. For a start, inherited wealth has nothing to do with fitness.

"Survival of the fittest" should be more properly read as Stephen Jay Gould has stated: "better adapted for immediate, local environment." It has nothing to do with bonkers stock markets or inherited bank accounts.

Like the lungfish, once so exquisitely adapted to a swampy jungle world, now going extinct—our path is predictable unless we reconsider what survival of the fittest actually means. Natural selection is the piece that fits the right spot in a beautiful jigsaw puzzle, not the superior piece on the puzzle board—because there is no superior piece in a scattershot world.

It should also be noted that the lungfish is a victim of what Ronald Wright defined as a progress trap. It took a turn into an evolutionary dead end. Human behaviour often leads to progress traps—the discovery of what appears to be a better technology or route that causes worse damage down the road—such as the invention of the atomic bomb, which ended the war against Japan and will now probably threaten humanity forever. Theoretically good ideas like longline fishing methods can lead to the extinction of albatross species as part of their bycatch.

Rather than being progressive, natural selection is a drift toward more diversity, like the paths of a man on a mountain in the mist, which is why there's such a dazzling yet fragile assembly of life around the planet. It's a messy process. Consider the millions upon millions of extinctions before the human race even appeared. If a niche disappears, so goes the creature. That's another reason why the concept of intelligent design is so strange. Evolution ain't intelligent, and it's not actually designed. It's a force. Evolution is mechanical, and perhaps it's our helplessness before it that makes so many run to their religions.

Although the lies and manipulations surrounding the evolution debate are perilous creations, and emblematic of our dangerous way of interacting with the world, we have to remember that animals also lie. Watch a killdeer drag its "broken wing" across a field, or a peahen's elaborate deception to hide her nest from the cock who will smash the eggs or kill the chicks if he finds them. I once had a dog, Tlell, with a fixation on Christmas nuts (walnuts, hazelnuts, almonds), which I also enjoyed. In my poor student days, I used an apple box artfully draped with a batiked cloth for a coffee table in my living room. Tlell, when I wasn't looking, would suck up a walnut out of the nut bowl on the table and then slide her head into the box beneath so that the batik would conceal her head. Then I'd hear the loud crunch of the nut breaking and the nutmeat being eaten. I could never get angry at this because it made me laugh so much, though eventually I had to move the nut bowl to a higher table. Some would call these deceits a survival tactic; others would call them willfully conceived lies, and both would be right.

Science calls its culprits a number of names—frauds, hoaxers, and masters of the infamous fudge factors (facts that are fudged—bent or invented to prove the thesis). This delicious term probably derives from a corruption of the old English word "fadge," which means "make suit, fit." But it's also said to originate with an infamous Captain Fudge, a ship captain so notorious for delivering a "good cargo of lies" to both his crew and the ship owners that sailors came to shout out "Fudge!" whenever they suspected bullshit. Science long ago learned how to manipulate statistics, but a new political technique surfaced with a vengeance in the 1980s, when publicists realized statistics and facts could be willfully massaged and even misused on a grand scale, allowing corporations like the tobacco companies to baffle the general public, before the overwhelming medical evidence finally caught up with them.

ALTHOUGH I'M A writer and can only live as a writer, treating my years of pain with the medication of words unfolding and leading me to mysterious places, I'm becoming more and more suspicious that my two occupations, writing and farming, are the main culprits in separating us from the natural world. Farming created cities and civilization, and writing was necessary for the record keeping that enabled this civilization. It took me many decades to recognize that writing is the devil-twin of the spoken word. Written texts, strangely, can also distance us while allowing us to communicate across long distances, whereas communication around the fire over a haunch of elk almost always brings us together. Books, unlike the spoken word, were the original human hard drive, the tool that allowed us to store and build upon the knowledge that allowed us to spread like a slime mould across the Petri dish of the planet, or like locusts upon a prairie until our wall of destruction starves us out and we are shut down as the world regrows over millions of years. We truly are phoenixes. Only we will have already scavenged so much of the biosphere that we will never be able to rebuild in the same way. Like the story of all life, we can be beautiful and monstrous simultaneously. Born mutant, I understand why this thought is painful to live with. What we are witnessing in our time is a massive failure to adapt to changing conditions, and we know what that means in the evolutionary world.

Perhaps we will be fortunate enough to return to that condition when there were no walls between us and the real world. Kapuscinski's *Travels with Herodotus* talks about an era when history was oral and changeable, so it was treated with respect—we always had to think about what we heard. In that era, the gods still walked among us and we had to show deference to everyone, because it could be a god and not an old beggar at our doorstep.

Every extinction creates its oddities. The great spreading of the archosaur clade of Dinosauria, beginning as far back as the Permian period, 250 million years ago, led to many varieties of crocodiles, almost all extinct now, and the explosion of bird populations during the glory days of the Triassic period, beginning 200 million years ago. These two clades of archosaur, the crocodile and the bird, somehow survived the great extinction of 60 million years ago. Oddly, birds, like us and crocodiles, have four-chambered hearts. And that's merely one of the many reasons why I enjoy looking up from my desk and giving a smile to Tuco, my friendly survivor of the dinosaur tribe.

The dinosaurs did not disappear with the asteroid. They're still here, in every hedgerow and summer shrub. Padding flat-footed across the glaciers of Antarctica and gliding, giant-winged, for days over the oceans.

Several years ago in Cuba, Sharon and I were staying in a cabin in the natural canals of Montemar, a great swampy nature reserve at Zapata Peninsula, where we'd hired a guide to take us by rowboat to see the birds at the grey hour. This landscape was so swampy we could only stay in a stilt house and had to whistle for a boat to take us anywhere. House and guide were both available for an embarrassingly low cost. The stilt house seemed primitive yet gorgeous until Sharon left the bathroom light on for a few hours during our first night and the white tile wall in the bathroom turned black with bugs. We flicked the light off and dived for cover under the mosquito net around the bed.

Our Cuban guide couldn't speak any English, but he knew every bird. It always impresses me how people can communicate without language. Emotional empathy works every time. We were sitting silently in his rowboat among the clouds of mosquitoes, when suddenly, a hundred feet away, there was an enormous splash and the head of a large crocodile erupted with a heron-like bird in its jaws. Before the bird could even squawk, they were both gone under the surface. We had just witnessed an abrupt and fatal encounter between the two survivors of the dinosaur regime. Our guide just gave us a big toothy, rather evil smile: *"Cocodrilo!"*

Dinosaur nests have now been found worldwide. Some dinosaurs apparently hatched and raised their dragon spawn like birds—many even in colonies of nests. The majority of discoveries have been in Montana at Egg Mountain, the Gobi Desert, and recently, in South Africa, where a ten-foot-long sauropod was nesting as early as the Triassic period, 190 million years ago. One of the nests in the Gobi revealed a fossil mother oviraptor spreading her limbs protectively over her eggs—it's now certain that oviraptors had tail feathers and possibly were completely feathered. These specimens all presumably died in a dust storm, flood, or landslide. This discovery was described along with its location in a fine book, *Dinosaurs of the Flaming Cliffs*. Unfortunately, this made that location too easy to find—those important fossils were soon stolen and smuggled out of Mongolia. Discovered at the last minute by a researcher, some of the major fossils were seized in the U.S. and returned to Mongolia, where they are now on display in the new public museum in Ulan Bator.

Recently, the *Anchiornis huxleyi* has become the latest poster child of feathered dinosaurs. It's an even earlier creature than the archaeopteryx, which might be why it was named after Huxley, who took so much abuse for his dinosaur/bird theory. Like most dinosaur-era birds, its feet were feathered, just as several exotic heritage hens in my chicken coop have feathered legs. The technology has grown so accurate they know its body was grey and black feathered and its crown was rufous.

These new discoveries have been spiced up with more studies of the velociraptor, a carnivorous dinosaur made famous by *Jurassic Park*. Slightly smaller than in the film, weighing about thirty pounds, it had primitive feathers, as can be seen by the presence of quill knobs that hold feathers. It might not have been able to fly, but it could use those feathers for display, to keep a nest warm, and even to aid navigation during a fast escape or chase through the brush. Feathers have multiple uses: flight, insulation, deception, or visual displays for sex and communication.

If we saw a velociraptor today, we might even assume it was a goofy-looking bird, not a carnivorous dinosaur.

I once saw an exhibit of our changing vision of dinosaurs over the last 150 years at the Royal Ontario Museum in Toronto. They began as grey lizards, crawling mostly on their bellies, converting soon into erect green-grey carnivores. Their posture lifted, heads rising higher, their skin colour becoming multicoloured, and then finally, they were covered in bright feathers and, except for the forelegs, could have been giant parrots with teeth. All these new discoveries remind me of Kapuscinski's *Travels with Herodotus*, where he said: "The past does not exist. There are only infinite renderings of it."

Sometimes at night, in bed, I like to imagine the drooling jaws of a brightly feathered yutyrannus. Thirty feet long, weighing three thousand pounds, with eight-inch long feathers, towering over some unfortunate trembling young hadrosaur and whispering: "Dinner time."

Chapter 5

———

WHAT'S THE BIRD?

So what's the bird? Who's this creature inspecting me while standing on my shoulder, his head cocked. Why does he gaze at me so intensely? What's his agenda? What's his mind? And how did he come to make such a deep impression on my life? Why did contemplating him lead me to my past and our Othering.

Birds are a unique aspect of creation, with certain features that distinguish them from all other creatures. That's why they're regarded taxonomically as a class: Aves. And that's one of the few features of the species that is simple. Birds have a special fused collarbone we call the wishbone; this structure allows for the musculature that powers their wings, even if they've abandoned flight, and both flying and flightless birds also have flight feathers. They have air sacs to supplement their lungs. Some also have gizzards. Their bones are mostly hollow, strong, and light. They lay eggs. They have vertebrae, naturally. Their blood is warm, hot even, 104 degrees Fahrenheit, higher than ours, and it can climb 4 degrees higher still. Their little four-chambered heart keeps their blood pumping fast, up to four hundred beats a minute. Hold one in your hands and you will be shocked by their little beating hearts. They have two legs and four toes, though some breeds of chicken tend to have a fifth toe. The toes point forward except for one back toe. Parrots, however, like woodpeckers and ospreys and others, are zygodactyl, with two toes pointing forward and two pointing backward. This somewhat resembles the opposable thumb in primates, at least in usability.

For a couple of years I clipped Tuco's wings slightly. Some parrot owners intentionally clip the young bird's wings back to the bone so that the flight feathers won't ever regrow. This barbaric treatment is dying, along with declawing cats and dogs and other extreme tortures people once performed on their domestic animals. I just scissored the tips (which have no nerves) of Tuco's feathers to keep him from any long-distance performances and accidentally escaping the house, though he would make some spectacularly awkward landings immediately after a trim. Clipping his wingtips caused a lot of complaining and biting on his part, even when I swaddled him with a towel to protect both of us. He hated this treatment, and I hated myself. After a couple of years of torturing him, I decided I'd been misled and stopped trimming his wingtips. He wasn't going anywhere. And if he did, that would be his decision. I know that's a cop-out. The clipping was a terrible experience for both of us, and by then, I no longer feared he'd fly off—foolishly, as it turned out.

About ten years ago, on a summer day, he was wandering around, threatening the cats—the usual—and I didn't know Sharon had left the door open on the main floor. My office is off a top-floor sun-room, and outside is a balcony between bedrooms, opening on the twenty-foot-high front room of our log home. Tuco was strutting along the rail, searching for victims (cats) in the living room below. A gust of wind slammed one of the bedroom doors, startling Tuco, and he soared off the rail to the lower floor, cruising around the adobe wall separating the kitchen and living room, circled the dining room, picked up speed in the galley kitchen, and winged right out the door of the front sun-room, with me following in terror.

The last I saw he was gliding over the low willows, across the ponds and field, and into the cedar forest.

The panic was hammering my heart. Since parrots are notoriously directionless wanderers, I was in danger of losing him. Also, the crows would mob him out here in a landscape where not even another house is visible, and as tough as the little guy is, he didn't have a chance with the local flock of thug crows who'd delight in feeding on his guts. Years ago, I watched a crow eviscerate a fully grown starling on a roof. The victim was pinned on its back, squawking, slashing with its beak even as its intestines were being pulled out.

I grabbed a towel and took the back road through the forest, where I called out, "Tuco!" and heard a squawk. He was clinging to the lower branches of a giant cedar at the forest's edge, panting and out of breath. I tried pulling on the branch, and he started crawling upward. He'd soon be out of reach. Since parrots gain a lot of courage from height, he wanted to move up, where he might prove impossible to lure to ground before dark. So I took a chance and threw the towel over him, and then pulled him back down.

I suspect he was relieved, because he let me take him without a fight and wrap him in the towel so that he couldn't claw or bite me. Rather than covering him, I left his head free, allowing him to see the farm and perhaps be distracted from his terror. Oh, his little beating heart. Walking up the road, I noted he was still panting, no doubt exhausted by his exertions and surprised by the vast, marvellous kingdom he'd suddenly discovered. He did a double take when he saw the peacocks mingling with the chickens. Big birds, and way bigger birds! Many big birds.

Although domesticated parrots tend to fly weakly, the wild birds whoop around with acrobatic charm, along with the feral parrots that have invaded a few major cities in Europe and America despite their tendency to be easy victims for the local predators. The red-masked conures, a flock of parrots gone feral in San Francisco, have become famous and are the subject of a charming documentary, *The Wild Parrots of Telegraph Hill.*

On the other side of the planet, among the delights of the Pincian Hill of Rome, known by the ancient Romans as the Hill of Gardens, is the Villa Borghese, home of the exquisite marble sculptures of Bernini, surrounded by flocks of rose-ringed parakeets, chattering and flying from tree to tree. A real community of vocal hijinking comedians with an intense social life, the feral parrots are a constant joy, rushing about in the trees above, though I suspect they're upsetting the local ecology. I stood under them, safely out of crapping range, for close to an hour as they dominated the forest and ignored tourists. They were on urgent business—parrot politics that only they understood. It involved lots of noise and flying about and hanging sideways from tree trunks. These birds are similar to the Alexandrine parrots that Alexander so doted on during his conquests. The rose-ringed parakeet is now becoming endangered in its homeland due to parrot smuggling, yet feral populations are flourishing in Europe.

Every bird has its own kingdom.

Parrots prefer local living and are not known to migrate any distance. However, populations can spread. Most are defined by their regions, such as the cockatoos of the Australasian region, ranging from the Philippines to Australia. The budgerigars are localized in the drier parts of Australia. The Amazons came out of Latin America, from South America, through the Caribbean to Mexico, along with the macaws. Some Asian parrots have an enormous range. The Congo African grey, however, is generally localized in the Congo, whereas the smaller Timneh, Tuco's clan, is even more localized in western Africa in a small region centred around Liberia, the Ivory Coast, Guinea, Sierra Leone, and Mali.

Although parrots prefer local living, other birds can navigate shockingly dangerous and inhospitable territory. Tiny hummingbirds fly non-stop across the 500-mile Gulf of Mexico. Giant albatrosses spend most of their lives aloft. One banded albatross was recorded to have flown 3,700 miles in twelve days. Arctic terns fly round trip from the Arctic to the Antarctic, 20,000 to 25,000 miles each year. Bar-headed geese have been heard by the famed explorer/biologist Lawrence Swan as they flew directly overhead of Mount Makalu in the Himalayas: 27,824 feet. Others have claimed they heard them flying over Mount Everest at 29,028 feet, high enough to catch the jet stream, a river of wind that can reach 200 miles per hour. Everest is so high and airless that kerosene can't burn on its summit. Nor can helicopters reach its peak. Only geese and us.

As high as the bar-headed geese can fly, even they have nothing on an intrepid but luckless Rüpell's griffon vulture above the Ivory Coast. This massive vulture with a 10-foot wingspan was inhaled into a jet engine at 36,100 feet. The jet landed safely. The bird did not. Birds don't stand much of a chance when they confront our machines head on, such as on our prairie highways, where raptors will whip down to snatch up the latest roadkill only to find themselves suffering the same fate. It's a food chain of death.

The bar-headed geese can attain their altitude from sea level in little over eight hours, flying more than one thousand miles in a day. That's a tough goose.

More interesting is their insistence on migrating this impossible route twice a year even though there's a low pass only several miles away, causing Professor Swan to speculate that they are "behavioural fossils" and, though it's difficult to believe, have been flying the same route since before the slow collision of tectonic plates of the Cenozoic age turned the green valleys and alpine lakes of Tibet into the highest mountain range in the world. Swan conjectured this would make their species "older than the hills below them," migrating patiently until the mountains are worn down into valleys again. The great mystery of migration is regularly on display outside our window, with Tuco and me watching the strangers appear below at the feeders, goldfinches, warblers, sometimes wax-wings, though their population is diminishing.

New Yorkers and Torontonians might migrate to their cottages, and flocks of Canadians spend their winters in Florida, yet seasonal human migrations have always been fairly minor. A few followed game when tribal cultures still thrived. The Inuit tracking caribou, the plains people marching alongside the earth-shaking buffalo migrations. The Sami Laplanders continue following the migrations of the reindeer. The kingdom of flight, however, is the real master of migratory movement. Whereas the epic migrations of the passenger pigeon are now extinct, many others have taken up their niche. More than 5 billion birds move from Eurasia to Africa in the bright autumns, and 5 billion birds also traverse the Americas. Their navigation techniques could still teach our species a few lessons. These skills are varied. Many birds have an internal calendar, and some are believed to use the sun for local orientation, though they don't have an internal clock, like bees, which helps them use the sun for navigation. At night, birds use Polaris and the surrounding constellations for stellar compassing and to provide backup for their magnetic tracking skills. My homing pigeons mostly used geomagnetism, which explains why I lost so many in the narrow, ore-rich chute of the Fraser Canyon. If I had my father release them during his journeys in the less narrow pass from the Interior of British Columbia, they generally made it. I gave up on the canyon after a few years, though my stubborn father wanted to keep trying.

Hummingbirds judge when to migrate south by declining insect and flower populations. Some ornithologists speculate that hormonal changes induced by the decreasing or increasing hours of sunlight also influence them during their southern migrations. All of this means big trouble with climate change. Hummingbirds are impressive little migrators, and they can gain between 25 to 40 percent in weight before they move out and migrate north. If the seasons distort and there aren't enough insects, they will die on their migration, or at best, change their migratory destinations and habits, but that is always dangerous. Hummingbirds, unlike many species, are solitary migrators, which makes them less of a target for predators, as they are so small and fast. Many fly north via continental Mexico. Other varieties make the big leap across the Gulf of Mexico. They are often reported resting on oil platforms and fishing boat rigging, as much as 200 miles from land. They can travel 450 miles in a single day. Sometimes they will fall out of the sky and die from exhaustion. The males usually move north first so that they can establish a territory before the females arrive. Their arrival is always a day of excitement at our farm, as with the swallows, though the arrival of the swallows is tempered by the recognition that every year fewer swallows arrive. Twenty years ago, we used to look out over our ponds and see hundreds of barn, tree, and cliff swallows. Now, we are lucky if there are a dozen, despite our adding nesting sites over the years. Although they don't visit us, the swallow's relative, chimney swifts, are also declining in number, like so many other migratory birds. According to *On Nature* magazine, 98 percent of chimney swifts are now gone.

TUCO IS LOOKING down on me from his perch with some contempt, while defiantly gnawing the marrow out of a chicken bone. He knows which side of the species wall he lives on. His side. In the end, we can only guess what complicated thinking goes on in that walnut-sized brain. Tossing the finished chicken bone over his shoulder, he decides to become obnoxious because he's bored, so I flash the dreaded photograph of the leopard at him. He scrunches up and hisses at it (so much for birds not being able to understand photographs). As with the mink hide, I don't want to use the photograph too often. That might dull its impact or, worse, give him a complex, and I've had a firsthand education in complexes.

When I was a curious baby and a real tub-thumper, I climbed up on a chair while my mother was cooking, and then I slipped and swan-dived onto the surface of the oil stove, instantly frying my belly before flipping back. I ended up with a plate-sized circular scar on my stomach. There it remained for decades. Not only was the scar circular, but as I grew, it separated into circles—yes, I had a target on my belly. How bad can it get? Kids would tell me they knew I needed beating up because I even wore a target.

The shower rooms at the schools increasingly became a place of dread. "Are you a boy or a girl?" That one still hurts in its odd cruelty, especially since it was always said so contemptuously. And the target drew even more attention to my wide-hipped, long-limbed, androgynous body in the showers after gym class.

The headaches peaked in my last year of school, and the weird bone pains I had to suffer along with the pariah universe of being a lady-boy in the sixties, when rednecks would haul long-haired hippies into back lanes, punch them out, and shave their heads. I think they left me alone because I looked more female than male, and that's how I would sneak into the psychedelic nightclubs, such as the Retinal Circus, and see great performances by Janis Joplin and Country Joe and the Fish. Underage girls were not checked too seriously for ID in those days.

Yet I often wore my defiance on my body, the way Tuco will pretend he's ready to fight the leopard photograph. My favourite shirt was a bright-pink frilled shirt with frilled cuffs. It was called a Tom Jones shirt in those days. I loved magenta or bright-green bell-bottoms, which I'd enhance by sewing in a leather or paisley insert to widen the bell-bottoms even more. Sometimes I wore a poncho, Clint Eastwood style. I realize now I was daring the bullies, inhaling the difference in me and inviting a reaction when I dressed like that, though I still miss the day when men could peacock in the world.

Fifty years later, I learned about Pink Shirt Day—a recent annual protest in which students wear pink shirts as a gesture of solidarity with the bullied and a protest against bullying, and I realized I'd instinctively done the same, way back then.

This was also the era when I climbed onto the suicide express, as I called it. I was so full of self-hatred, I would walk the narrow ledges of tall buildings, even though I had a fear of heights after falling out of a three-storey-high treehouse into an enormous blackberry bush. I walked away, scratched to hell, my new green plastic-leather bomber jacket and blue jeans shredded, but I was unbroken after this thirty-foot dive into a cushion of thorns, where I landed lightly on the hollow, rich-soiled, sun-dappled rabbit sanctuary beneath. That was such a rush I almost wanted to try it again.

Those years on the suicide express were probably my worst time. I'd step in front of cars and scare the hearts of some young mother or old geezer behind the wheel. How awful I was in my self-centred pain. It took me a few years to realize I wasn't ready for suicide, and besides, I hated startling or scaring people. I loved life too much, and the suicide express was a misguided testing of my resolve. I stepped off it in a few years. Now I prefer the Hebrew toast—*l'chaim*—to life!

Tuco soon has enough of the leopard photograph and growls his way back into his cage, so I take the picture away. Like most birds, he knows whom to hate. He seems to have instinctively decided, without any education from other birds and without much prompting, who is friend and who is enemy. In fact, if he's wandering around and is startled, he will fly onto the back of our terrified Labrador, Olive, despite his dislike of furred animals. He will stand there defiantly like a Hindu warrior riding an elephant, while the aghast dog remains petrified, gazing plaintively at me for help. Tuco can recognize a cowardly protector when he sees one.

This is where we meet a complex topic. There's been so much said in the scientific community about anthropomorphizing animals—assuming that they think like humans or that they even think at all. In 1904, the esteemed American biologist John Burroughs launched his strident attack on writers of animal stories by some of my favourite authors, including Ernest Thompson Seton and Jack London.

Burroughs was later supported by President Theodore Roosevelt, big game hunter and the man who made America's national parks possible. I've always considered Roosevelt one of America's greatest presidents, maybe because he was so brilliantly erratic yet, in the end, true to the best causes. Both men insisted animals don't think at all but act only on instinct—a stunning stupidity for anyone who studied animals as closely as Roosevelt had. Yet that issue still remains key to the continuing debate about animal intelligence, though the last twenty years have produced amazing advances in understanding what intelligence is, either human or animal, and we've finally begun to question our own intelligence.

Can Tuco think like us? Yes. He can also not think like us. That's because he thinks like himself, and it's our refusal to respect a different kind of intelligence that demonstrates the gap in our own intelligence. It's taken us a long time to recognize our stupidity.

Myths are powerful drivers of human nature, and the accepted mythology of dumb beasts was a fixation until the late twentieth century. Yet tribal belief systems tended to prize animals very differently than advanced agricultural systems—even prey animals, and consider them spirit guides, teachers, tricksters.... That's my Tuco.

John Burroughs and too many other biologists of that era fell victim to scientism, convinced only science and logic can produce knowledge, denying the important humanist component of our thought—the yang to its yin—what's sometimes been called the female or intuitive approach that binds a community emotionally, and us with our environment. Emotional knowledge. It's not always accurate, of course, like many a scientific thesis, but it has also left behind some impressive traditional knowledge.

Perhaps I've always been sensitive to these dual realms because of my childhood and my odd identification with the myth of Tiresias, the ancient Greek who trespassed against the will of the gods by beating two snakes, and was transformed into a woman for several years. He even had children and became the high priestess/

prostitute of Hera. There are several variations on the myth. In each he was doomed to suffer but was rewarded with the gift of prophecy. In one version, he stumbled upon Athena bathing and was struck blind. His mother, Chariclo, begged for the spell to be reversed. It was too late for that, so she was allowed to clean his/her ears, and this gave blind Tiresias the ability to understand the language of birds, which was also the gift of prophecy. Unfortunately, his prophecies were always accurate, and he became notorious for his gift of doom, which usually meant more trouble with the gods. I have no gift of prophecy, except perhaps a need to look at everything from every perspective, but the birds have always haunted me and have now sent me wandering on this misty path between memoir and natural history, while Tuco sits like a little devil on my shoulder.

Because I've walked the fence between intuitive understanding and scientific knowledge, between the male and the female, it always seemed obvious that both must work together to enable us to curb the worst aspects of each.

One of the reasons why Henri Bergson's *Creative Evolution* was such an enormously popular book in its day is because he defied the mainstream and argued that experience and intuition were as crucial to humanity's success as technological advances and science. Sometimes cognitive dissonance can be a good thing. It came naturally to me. I remember myself live-dreaming with my pigeons as a child, standing in the coop, the flock fluttering around—shitting on me, standing on my head, my outstretched arms. Another memory that keeps returning. A weird, private, spiritual moment. A kind of childish Christ fantasy, possibly whispered into me by a few weeks of Bible class, which I soon walked away from. A communion. *Pigeon dreaming,* as I now think of it, my way of becoming pigeon, even before I understood the concept of becoming an Other. Empathy. It came naturally. I was pigeon, and I felt a calm happiness... yet I also was not a pigeon. Obsessed, I read every book on pigeon keeping and mercilessly interrogated other pigeon breeders for both traditional knowledge and the latest science and techniques. Although my mother was aghast every time I came into the house splattered with pigeon shit, I was beaming with private joy.

Birds have always been teachers, leading me to those years of research, whether about chickadees stealing songs from competitors or watching my chickens being trained by the rituals of the dogs on the farm. Living with birds you learn how close we are, how their behaviour echoes ours, and how our behaviour echoes theirs. When our chickens are on the loose and terrorizing the garden, I can call out the window to our border collie, Bella. "Chickens! Bella! They're in the garden!" Bella will come whistling out of her doghouse at high speed, and the chickens will race out of the flower garden and down the road, like kids caught in a farmer's berry patch. Then they usually fly back over the fence to their chicken yard before the scary dog arrives. After a while, it's like a comedy routine. In the office, Tuco, watching, will cheer and shout and comment on the action. Surprisingly, he's on the side of the dog, and I often wonder if it's because he knows the chickens are being bad or, more likely, because Bella's impressive herding skills awaken the predatory instinct in him.

These are heritage fowl and thus retain the intelligence we've bred out of factory-raised meat birds. I call them "the thugs" or "the vandals," because that's how they often behave, like teenage vandals. One day, going for a walk with the dogs into the forest, I noticed a line of chickens, cartoon style, one head above another, peering around the corner of the back coop, spying on us. I suspected what was going to happen.

By the time we returned twenty minutes later, the chickens had run around the house and across the front yard and were in the vegetable garden, a distance of almost a hundred yards. As soon as they saw us return and the dogs break into a run, they scattered like a bunch of punks caught at a gang rumble by a police car. They not only understand the rules but also understand when they could break them.

That's the way I behaved in my childhood during those lonely school years, and even for several years after I started treatment. More than four decades later, I remember a house with enormous, beautiful sunflowers lining the front yard by the sidewalk. I was in my early twenties. Around midnight one drunken weekend, I liberated the largest sunflower and kept it in a jug on the table, admiring it like a real poet. A few years following this event, after learning how much work goes into growing my own extra-large sunflowers, I suddenly recognized the horror of what I had done—the insult to that hopeful gardener and his generous sunflowers lining the sidewalk.

Birds also have a sophisticated knowledge of who's bad and who's not in their environment. For instance, if an eagle flies over the mallards and pintails in our front ponds, the ducks will immediately fast paddle into the cover of overhanging shrubs. However, an equally large osprey can soar twenty feet above their heads without them showing any apprehension. They recognize the osprey and know it is a fish eater. They will float calmly in the pond even as the osprey smashes into the water beside them, seeking its fish dinner.

AS WITH MAMMALS and insects and reptiles, natural selection has created a stunning diversity in birds around the world.

The smallest bird, the bee hummingbird, weighs .063 of an ounce and is at best 2 inches long, half of which is beak and tail. Often mistaken for a giant bee, it's a busy bird, taking most of its nutrition from insects, yet it can drink from as many as 1,500 flowers a day, sucking up half its weight in nectar—its little wings beating so fast they are a blur to the human eye. The hummingbird is the only bird that can fly forward, backward, and sideways. The "chip-chip" cry you hear when a hummingbird dives is an aeroelastic reaction to the wind in its tail feathers, not its voice.

Birds, like seals, can be found on all seven continents. Besides taking many forms and sizes, from the elf owl as small as a sparrow to the 300-pound ostrich, they also employ an amazing diversity of skills. The penguin can dive 1,500 feet deep, hunting squid. There are three poisonous birds. The pitohui carries neurotoxic alkaloids on its wings, the same stuff found on poison dart frogs.

The wild turkey of North America is a smart and agile animal. Benjamin Franklin argued it would make a better national bird than that often cowardly scavenger, the bald eagle. Turkeys are a bragger's prize for hunters. It was once reported that more hunters in Connecticut were injured than turkeys during the annual turkey hunt. A combination of rum and falling from ill-placed hunting chairs high up in trees proved deadlier than the guns of the hunters. The brave, wary, wild turkey has been bred down to today's frightened, stupid, unhealthy, domesticated, white farm bird. Imagine breeding a bird too fat to have sex. I have a few friends who were once employed as turkey fuckers, stroking off the males and then inseminating the females by hand because the males are too stupid and big and fat to climb on. Yecchhh. What we can do to birds. What we can do to ourselves! No wonder I once heard an American comedian declare the turkey had indeed become America's national bird. There are reports of air force pilots flying over fields of modern turkeys, breaking the sound barrier, and causing whole flocks to keel over from heart attacks, though I suspect that's an urban myth.

The largest flying bird, the bustard (followed closely by the wandering albatross), can lift off and propel as much as 28 pounds of solid weight through the sky. The speediest flying bird is the peregrine falcon, which can cruise at 50 to 60 miles per hour and has been clocked diving at 270 miles per hour. This makes it the fastest living creature on the planet, except for its diminutive bullet of a competitor, Anna's hummingbird; though technically not as fast, this tiny creature can fly 385 times its body length in a second, whereas the peregrine can only cover 200 times its body length in a second, and the slow-moving jet fighter might only accomplish 150 times its body length in a second.

Hawks are tough. Consider what a 200-mile-an-hour hurricane can do to a city. Hurricane Katrina took out the city of New Orleans, and its maximum sustained wind speed was estimated to be a mere 175 miles per hour. I've witnessed hawk strikes several times. One of my favourite homing pigeons, Rocky, rested on a telephone pole before returning to the coop from a long-distance flight. All pigeons fear they will be surprised on the landing in front of the bird door. Rocky was a big, barrel-chested pigeon, slow but tough. However, suddenly out of nowhere, a hawk hit him so fast and hard his head flew off like a powerfully driven golf ball. Rocky's body was hauled away and I was left with tears in my eyes.

Although cowardly and mostly a scavenger, a bald eagle is also a powerful bird. While all eagles are powerful, the golden eagles of the North are a far braver and tougher predator, able to club fleeing wolves semi-conscious to the ground with a closed-foot strike and then leap on the head of the stunned wolf, sinking two talons into the eyes and one into the back of the brain.

When bald eagles mate, they climb into the air, lock together and tumble at high speed before they break apart. I've heard reports of dead eagles being found locked together. They couldn't break away before the ground arrived, but again, this sounds more like legend than reality. Besides, their nuptial flight isn't actual mating, despite the misguided beliefs of many. It's more like love-wrestling. The real mating occurs either on the nest or on branches in trees. I've seen a number of courtship tumbles, and they are always breathtaking, yet I've never encountered any bodies on the ground.

The different species of parrots show an amazing diversity of mating habits. African greys take a long time to bond in captivity, three to five years, probably the same in the wild. They also need a large, private enclosure and a nesting box. In the wild, it's a hole in a tree, the same for macaws and most other parrots. Eventually, the male will dance for the female, doing its "Stayin' Alive" wing movements and circling. Occasionally, he will feed her, and there's tongue kissing.

When white-fronted parrots mate, they give major tongue to each other. The male will sometimes become so excited it will vomit into the female's beak. Ewwww. More weirdly, the female appears to enjoy this "gift" of intimacy.

African greys are monogamous, as are budgies and most other parrot species, except for the ring-necked parakeet, where both female and male enjoy different partners over the years. Cockatoos are notoriously raunchy, and both male and female will masturbate regularly in the spring. Not enough is known about the mating habits of the grey, but like most domesticated parrots they need their large aviaries. They might not be distance fliers, yet they demand lots of space and flying room to feel comfortable with each other, as do many couples I know.

In flight, many birds are capable of soaring vast distances. Vultures can fly for hours without beating a wing, and albatrosses use what's known as dynamic soaring, a swooping zigzag flight, to take advantage of the vertical gradient of wind velocity and wave-slope soaring, using the updrafts above waves. Albatrosses fly long distances over the Southern Ocean, as much as four thousand miles in twelve days, almost without flapping their wings. In fact, they use a shoulder lock, which allows them to lock their wings so that it's easier for them to soar than to lift off or land. Wandering albatrosses have the longest wingspan of any bird, reaching eleven feet. It's claimed they can sleep while they fly, but there's no proof of this. They also drink salt water and have a special adaptation at the base of their beaks that allows them to expel a saline solution.

There are twenty-one or twenty-two (some argument here) species of albatross and nineteen of them are endangered. The remaining two are close to being registered as threatened. Introduced rats in colony islands, where bird colonies nest, and industrial longlining for fish are the main threats. Longlining is a method of fishing using thousands of hooks hanging off one line that can be miles long. When an albatross sees the squid bait, it will try to snatch it, hook itself, and drown.

Friends of mine supported an organization that intended to design erotic comics for the mostly illiterate longline fishermen, usually Japanese, who work as deckhands. These politically incorrect comics are intended to show the fishermen they can buy more vodka and more prostitutes if they clip on a special bird-scaring device above the hooks. This device saves them the time they usually spend untangling dead seabirds when the lines are reeled in, so they can make more money. This educationally bizarre and original campaign is an amusing case of lateral thinking. There's more than one way to save an albatross.

Birds also demonstrate amazing abilities when it comes to detecting and discerning odours. Turkey vultures will smell a one-inch hunk of meat from several miles distant.

There's an oil, mercaptan, that smells like carrion, and gas companies add it to natural gas so people will recognize that the normally odourless gas is leaking in their home. Pipeline workers watching a few vultures floating around a pipeline leak got the brilliant idea to suggest the mercaptan be increased slightly, and now circling vultures are used to discover hard-to-find leaks in gas pipelines in rough terrain in the American West.

The uncanny ability of some vultures to smell led to another nasty scientific debate. This one was between the English naturalist Charles Waterton and the esteemed American ornithologist John James Audubon. Waterton insisted vultures detected their food by smell, whereas Audubon was sure they used sight. This argument went on for decades. As is too common with these fierce scientific debates, both sides proved to be partially correct. The vultures of Africa use sight more to detect carrion. The vultures of America have a better sense of smell.

This makes me wonder about Audubon, whom I've always admired. When I watch the vultures floating around our farm fields on the thermals of the afternoon, they are clearly hunting by smell, and for Audubon—who spent much of his life studying birds—not to recognize this is puzzling. Eagles and hawks, who hunt by eye, have different patterns of flight. Another case of belief trumping reality. Lately, we've learned to recognize how common the denial of facts in the face of preconceived beliefs has become. John Gray, the philosopher and author of *The Silence of Animals: On Progress and Other Modern Myths,* notes that facts and values are often confused by those making speculative hypotheses. Another way of presenting nonsense arguments consists in listing a confusing array of factoids that don't necessarily apply, and then presenting the resulting theory as undisputedly correct because it's "scientific," even if it isn't.

Coined by American science historian Robert Proctor, the term "agnotology" refers to the study of the behaviour of those willfully "not knowing" information and "the cultural production of ignorance" by the political strategies of wealthy corporations, such as occurred in the tobacco controversy and is occurring today in the denial politics of climate change. Big business has always preferred profit over facts. And media manipulators have now discovered how easy it is to control public opinion by manufacturing ignorance. After all, if John James Audubon, America's most famous bird lover, can convince himself that a vulture can't smell, what kind of respect for reality can we expect from the rest of us?

As for smell, it's often been noted that parrots have weak senses of smell. We can cook for days downstairs without a peep from Tuco, yet if we fry an egg or even crack a soft-boiled egg, he will snap to attention and start hollering for his share. He likes eggs and his screeching demand for them worries me about his long-term health. Too much rich food is hard on a parrot's heart, just as it's dangerous for us. But what impresses me is that his sense of smell appears to be selective. Certain odours ring many bells. A chicken in the oven is another odour that sets him off. He loves the marrow in the drumstick.

Tuco has sharp eyes, which I'm told is also unusual for parrots, whereas owls can see a mouse from a mile away. It's so much fun to watch Tuco on his perch get in a snapping duel with a yellow jacket, though I have to trust he knows what he's doing. Those wasps can pack a real sting. Aside from supervising the farm through the window beside his cage, he loves sitting on my shoulder, observing the computer screen.

Tuco has three things of major interest as he sits on my shoulder—the events on screen, my actions, and the items on my desk—and maybe I should mention a fourth. In his snakiest moments, if I am distracted or focussing on a manuscript, he will crap on me and then release his standard pirate's laugh: "Har... har... har...." This is infuriating, as well as tough on my shirts, so I've developed a kind of sixth sense related to his perching and the way he moves, and I can usually startle him into sealing up his sphincter. Even in the cover photograph for this book you can see us duelling. He's just about to shit on my shoulder, but I wheeled around and lifted him on my finger so that he could shit, with some disappointment, into the wastebasket. However, Sharon had been sharp and lucky enough to snap the photograph of me suspiciously recognizing his intent. He doesn't enjoy this cleaner, more civilized strategy. I can tell it pisses him off, as it were. Caught! The sneak attack and the guffaw are much preferred.

And sometimes he meanly withholds the guffaw so that someone will mention, while I'm shopping in town, there's a streak of dried green parrot shit dribbled down the back of my shirt. Once, when I was in a panic, about to drive off with a friend, Patrick, to another friend's home in Saskatchewan, I let Tuco sit on my shoulder while I rushed about packing and then transferred him to his cage, which he didn't appreciate because he knew I was going on a trip without him. He hates my trips and splashes all the water out of his dish, and I'm stuck with perpetually refilling it while he cackles away—another reason why I learned to keep him on my shoulder until I go. Patrick and I didn't stop until we reached a café in Drumheller, Alberta, where I removed my jacket and ordered breakfast. The waitress started trying to dust junk off my shoulder. "What have you got on your shirt?" she asked, imperious as only an aging Alberta waitress can be. "Dried parrot shit," I answered sheepishly, glancing at the shoulder of my shirt as Patrick broke into laughter.

When Tuco and I are eye to eye, he will sometimes display his third eyelid. I think that's what it is. He flashes it so quickly. This is the nictitating membrane, a lid that moves sideways and protects his eye in flight or when he's rummaging through a rotting fruit in the wild. Nighthawks like peregrines and many fast-moving birds have their eyes protected by this same membrane in their mighty dives so that no fleck of wood or drifting object or blood spatter can blind them. It also protects the eyes of diving birds, ducks and swans, and dabblers, who spend much of their time upside down in the water, and it can even correct their underwater vision. The nictitating membrane has different uses in the different creatures that have them, whether it's sharks blinking so that the bones of their victims don't injure them or crocodiles diving for underwater prey, the eyelid protecting against meat and blood and bone. Woodpeckers use theirs to protect their eyes from retinal shaking injuries. Woodpeckers also have a specially designed brain/skull relationship that protects them from brain injury when they are hammering at hard chunks of wood. Unlike guys like me, they are physically designed to crack their heads against walls.

The avian eye is a complex instrument and is tetrachromatic in many birds, meaning they can see a greater array of colours than us, including ultraviolet light. This is a companion to their gaudy display feathers, not all of which we can see. These displays allow them to more easily differentiate sexes in the jungle, so it can be a mating tool. It also aids raptors in detecting the uv-reflective urine marks left behind by rodents.

Tuco's eyes give away his moods. If he's excited, either frightened or ecstatic, I get the look. The pupil shrinks and then blows up and then shrinks again. He'll often do this several times if he grows inflamed over some event. As he's grown older, there's a yellow tinge to the iris. I've noticed what seems to be a red flash, which is not common to all parrots. It signifies you are in deep trouble, so back away. Parrots, like almost all animals, use physical gestures, including eye gestures, along with their voice, to communicate nuanced information to each other. In a few parrots, the eyes outweigh the brain, and since they can swivel their heads 180 degrees, they have a 360-degree field of view.

This is tough to beat when Tuco and I play hide-and-seek. He loves it when I duck under his cage and try to peek up behind him from the other side. Although he can't see my face under the cage, he can see enough of me to figure out which way I'm moving, so it's hard to catch him by surprise. Sharon and our friend Lorna play this game with him for several minutes at a time, and both actually beat him, probably because they're smaller and have fewer body parts sticking out from under the cage.

A friend, Susan, once arrived spontaneously at the house, discovered the radio was on (I don't want Tuco to feel lonely), and heard a voice telling her to "Come in... come in.... I'm up here." It was only when he informed her it was "party time" that she realized she'd been talking to Tuco and we weren't home.

Another favourite practice of Tuco, and most birds, is grooming. He can fuss over himself for many minutes, cleaning every feather, one by one.

Out in the fields after a day of heavy rain, our resident blue heron will take advantage of the sunshine when it arrives and stand on the bridge between ponds and spread his wings droopily, like an old man, his feathers spread and drying, allowing the breeze to flow through them. Turkey vultures occasionally engage in the same leisure practice, and I've seen several at once on our giant maple, perching on the dead branches sticking out from the foliage and taking in sun and wind, their wings draped like a cloak, their necks stretched to absorb the gentle air. It's a creepy sight.

On occasion, with Tuco perched across from me, I'm sure his preening is also a form of exhibitionism. He goes wild, dusting up his feathers, rubbing his beak through that uropygial gland at the base of his tail. Then he scrapes every feather through his beak and even embarks on pretend chases in his feathers, as if he's hunting an invisible louse. This can turn into a hilarious Chaplinesque performance. It was only when I took to collecting his moulted feathers that I discovered they would eventually crumble into nothing due to feather-eating bacteria if not protected by his preening and the glands that kept him bright and healthy. I had to use a preservative spray.

In his younger years, he was thrilled by the vacuum cleaner and would even surprise me by sticking his head into the hose for a real rush. That scares me too much, and I have become adept at dodging him. If I become distracted, he still sticks his beak up the roaring hose while I'm vacuuming. I guess it's like a dog sticking its head out of a car window.

That parrot beak is a mighty tool, strong yet capable of the most delicate dexterity. I've seen him clutching a thin rice wafer while hauling himself up a chain by the beak—without cracking the wafer. He can handle all kinds of food, a ripe orange slice or a safflower seed, never losing control, even while hanging upside down and inspecting the bottom of his cage as he's snacking.

We seldom eat Oreo cookies, but when we do, he gets one because his behaviour with them is so fascinating. First, he will split the cookie and huck the dry piece over his shoulder; then lick the icing off the other side, before eating the rest of the cookie. After that, he climbs down to the bottom of his cage, picks up the dry piece he hucked, and dips it in his water dish, savouring it as it melts into nothing. For years, we've talked about videotaping this and offering his endorsement to the Oreo manufacturer, but we never have the heart to sink to using him commercially. Besides, I worry about giving him too many cookies.

He can also snap a pencil in half without much thought, though that doesn't near match the brazil nut cracking of the mighty macaw. Tuco can adeptly pick a tiny feather out of the air (or catch a wasp), and he can strike like a hammer. Or bite me twice through the lip before I can react to the first strike. Each bite is always my fault, as I noted earlier. I startle him. This has happened several times, echoing memories of my childhood fights as I rush for the bathroom, my mouth full of blood. Over and over again. You'd think I'd learn. This speed is why parrot lovers will say that if your parrot gets in a fight with a cat, pity the cat. However, having suffered once from cat-scratch fever, I also know that the claws and jaws of cats are notoriously bacteria laden and can be deadly long after a fight.

The evolution of the beak—especially the widespread differences in the beaks of the finches of the Galapagos—has often been noted as a source of inspiration for Darwin's theory of natural selection. As with most great myths, this is incorrect. On his return, he recognized he didn't keep enough good notes on the finches, even though they were even better examples, but his notes on the different mockingbirds of the islands allowed him to illustrate more rigorously the concept of natural selection. Beaks are diverse. The crunchers of the parrot clan are a world's difference from the delicate nectar feeders like hummingbirds and lories and sunbirds. Shorebirds have long bills they use as probes. The big goofy bill of the toucan is perfect for fruit. Dabbling ducks graze either on land or by dipping their heads underwater, using their wide flat beaks with lamellae (notched plates) to make harvesting vegetation easier. My Toulouse geese used to rip out our water lilies and bulrushes with glee. Other ducks, like mergansers, have serrations in their beaks that allow them to grip wriggling victims. The upper mandible of falcons has a sharp point that tightly overlaps the lower mandible and can sever the vertebrae of their prey. The longest beak today is the dip-netting bill of the Australian pelican, which can be up to 18.5 inches long.

Tuco has a tongue with more nerves than any other part of his body, and it even helps him navigate when he uses his beak for climbing. He has a varied sense of taste and preferences in diet. Not only does he crave junk food, but like wild parrots, he'll feast on seeds, nuts, fruit, vegetables, and bugs if he can catch them. Wild parrots will also rob eggs from nests and eat carrion and small lizards if they can catch them. They are opportunistic feeders.

The tongues of a number of birds can be baroque as the parrot's, such as woodpeckers, whose tongue tips are barbed for impaling insects, which are also held in place by a sticky saliva. Some nectar feeders have tongues with a brush at the end, or they split into two tongues that can be used as insect feeders or nectar pumps.

Flamingoes are filter feeders and have large meaty tongues to sift food out of the mud. Unfortunately, this made them gourmet items for Romans, and any feast worth its name had a dish of flamingo tongues. Crow and magpie tongues have suffered a worse fate, as people will split them to make the birds talk more clearly. I imagine this practice is now illegal, but that doesn't always stop people from animal cruelty. And since birds use their syrinx, not a larynx, to speak, the tongue is hardly of any importance in the clarity of their speech—though I've met crow and mynah companions who insist it makes the birds' voices more clear.

Hummingbirds are the owners of naturally split tongues. I have rescued countless exhausted hummingbirds trapped in my greenhouse and stuck their beaks in the feeder, then watched the first signs of life seep back as they absorb the sugar water, and soon their tongues are sucking it up at an astonishing rate. Their split tongue and the lamellae it contains allow them to lick up the first sip of nectar and roll it back into the beak, and the rest works by capillary action. It's complex to explain, but it's a brilliant, simple example of the accidental design genius of natural selection. However, if they're too exhausted to move, I have discovered you can tilt them at the correct angle and the syrup will slide down the beak. I had one I thought was dead, but after almost a minute, I detected movement. The tongue began working, and as the bird lay on my outstretched fingers, its tail began to move, acting like a little pump allowing the beak to open and close, creating a vacuum for the sugar syrup until the bird revived.

A few have died, but it's almost too emotionally thrilling to watch a survivor shake itself alive as I open my hand and watch it fly away, usually to a nearby branch, where it will recover its strength and stare wondrously—I like to think—at the giant rescuer. They have just undergone their first alien abduction. It's always gratifying to save the life of a hummingbird. And we have learned, over the years, to regularly patrol the deceptive trap of our house's built-in solar greenhouses, which are accessible from both stories.

Tongues have evolved wondrously to meet the needs of their owners. When Darwin was shown a unique orchid from Madagascar, the *Angraecum sesquipedale*, with its incredibly elongated spur, he predicted there must be a moth with a long proboscis that pollinates it and drinks its nectar. The moth wasn't discovered until twenty-one years after his death, and the orchid is called Darwin's orchid to honour his celebrated prediction.

Another famous tongue belongs to a species of parrot in Hawaii which has a tongue tipped with a little brush-like structure that allows it to feed on flowers also.

As I follow the lives of birds through my own life, I keep encountering fabulous information about the feathered kingdom. The diversity is so spectacular it often leaves me stunned. Yet despite the general availability of the knowledge of this diversity and beauty, our slaughter of domestic and wild birds is increasing exponentially.

Birds have been with us, naturally, since long before writing was invented. Archaeologists have found the wing bone of a griffon vulture carved into a flute. It is 40,000 years old. In south Germany, there's both a mammoth bone flute and a flute made from the leg bone of a mute swan around the same era. In Xinle, China, a 7,600-to-8,000-year-old wooden sculpture of a bird was discovered. The oldest wooden sculpture known to exist. Birds have appeared in our art since cave painting, up to the installation art of today, such as Marcus Coates's marvellous *Dawn Chorus*—videos of people brilliantly recorded singing birdsongs, hung on screens in the air of the gallery in the way that birds occupy trees.

When Sharon and I decided to marry after twenty-seven years together, our friend Sean organized a flight of pigeons as a wedding present, one of the oddest wedding presents ever given in Canada, I'm sure. The morning after the wedding day, we trooped, along with the remaining guests, down to the dovecote and the birds' owner opened the doors. The pigeons didn't lift off immediately, always checking out the sky before leaping into it.

Every time I witness a pigeon's leap, I think what a rush that must be, bursting from the landing into the barely tangible air, and it makes me remember my childhood pigeons. The pigeon fancier who owned this dovecote had discovered during his travels that the Javanese were also avid pigeon fanciers, and they make tiny little flutes, each with a different tone, which they tie to the middle tail feather of each pigeon, so as not to disrupt its flying skills.

This was a great flock with many varieties, including the rollers, who suddenly break into several rolls like fancy fighter planes, along with those most spectacular of pigeon fliers, the tumblers, who climb high into the sky, stop mid-flight, and then just tumble as if they were shot out of the sky, taking their thrill from the fall, before they suddenly level out and climb back up to join the flock. This mixed flock flew around the dovecote in an ever-widening circle, with the occasional acrobat showing off, discordantly whistling as it rolled or tumbled. But meanwhile, a fine hum was building in the air, a symphonic movement of pigeon flutes, playing a number of different notes, hundreds of them sounding at once. It was a grand, haunting present for Sharon and me and our wedding guests.

Then, as the birds began to slow and a few returned to the dovecote, a bald eagle erupted out of the trees and dived into the flock, striking a sudden fluttering chord of discordant music, which seemed to so distract him that he never caught a pigeon, and the flock returned home safely. What a wondrous combination it was—bird flight, with its joys and dangers, and human musical innovation. Sometimes I am made breathless when considering what innovative creatures we live among. I slept well that evening, despite the pain in my crumbling joints caused by walking down to the dovecote in the morning. But the nights are usually always good at the farm.

The epic night songs of the migrating geese are another pleasure of the darkness for us as we lie in bed on our lonely farm where we can't see another home, listening to their echoing honks and then the silence once they've passed, often followed by a goofy, ironic, sometimes lonely goose honk in the dark of Tuco's room. He's hilariously sympathetic.

Some summer evenings, Sharon and I stand in the field as night rolls across the pasture and the ponds, especially if there is a moon or the stars are bright, and the air is sweet with the warm breezes of summer. The nighthawks bring their fledglings down to feast on the mosquitoes rising from the ponds. And like the swallows of the day and the bats of the night, they are satisfied with the supply of mosquitoes and the few dragonflies that rise from the summer ponds at dusk. Although not enough mosquitoes survive the goldfish and the frogs to molest us seriously, they still provide ample feed for the birds. Some species of birds devour an enormous number of insects. Spotted flycatchers alone eat an insect every eighteen seconds.

Like bats, the nighthawks enjoy buzzing us at close range, either because humans attract mosquitoes, or because it's a game similar to the way hummingbirds plunge at us when we walk down our long entrance walkway during the day. Here in the blue gloaming of the early night, the whirring sound of the nighthawks is comforting—their joy, their feeding, their delight in their flight. Their dark, almost black, one-striped, V-shaped underwing is always a thrill. Then suddenly, one rushes directly at my face, veering off within inches of a direct hit. It's unnerving yet welcoming, a kind of suicide game crossing the boundaries of the natural world by a brave jet-winged little bird who knows who is enemy and who is not enemy.

The nighthawk is so fast it has no fear of the Other. *Yellowbird...
Yellowbird... fly down the hill... into the wall of fear....*

The nighthawk's dive accounts for the greater part of its noise.
It puts its wings together and plunges, before opening them and
creating its humming boom. When I was young and healthy and
my knees and feet weren't full of bone chips, my friend Sean and I
would walk up a local mountain among the manzanita and arbutus
and stand on the naked peak in the blue dusk, enjoying the moon
for company and light. We were great targets for the twilight aerial
dances of these birds, and they zoomed around in joyful numbers
and crazy geometric patterns, making us feel connected with the
world, blessed by the moon-glistening flights of the nighthawks.

Chapter 6

BIRDS AND US
AND A BLUE PUNK

S O WHAT DID our ancestors see when they first saw Tuco and his kin? After all, the birds have been waking us up for millennia. Like all stories, this one has many versions. Food? Naturally. But wouldn't it soon prove difficult to eat an animal that calls out your name? Ornament? Pet? A totem, if not a god or spirit guide? In the jungles and forests of Africa, Asia, America, and Australia, gaudy birds swarm, calling out, breaking branches, dropping fruit, shitting long green-and-white streams from the treetops.

One can imagine warriors festooned with their bright feathers, or singed squabs on sticks over fires. We have to remember that an Australian tribe coined the word "budgerigar," which means "good to eat." We're bird-eating creatures, and there aren't many birds we've passed up on the plate—though when I ate my squabs, I found them rubbery and tough, as well as tasty. This makes me contemplate how many thousands of bird dinners I've consumed in my life. Pheasant, quail, pigeon, duck, goose, peafowl, and so on. I've never eaten parrot; nor do I know anyone who has.

Over time, we've found many uses for birds. Necklaces of beaks. Feather fans waved ritualistically above the gasping, prone bodies of the fevered. Bright cloaks. Spirit pouches of parrot skin. A naked child wandering between campfires, trailing a wing-trimmed macaw on a leather cord the bird could snap without thought but doesn't.

Birds have captured our imagination in so many ways, not only the birds surrounding us, like the bald eagle I recently discovered peering at my chickens out of a tree cascading with double-flowered bright-pink cherry blossoms, but those we admire in the bird feeder, those we admire for their beauty, their conduct, their song, the taste of their meat—and the birds of legend as well—often imagined out of a few scattered giant fossil bones.

From earliest history, the story of colossal birds inhabited our imagination, and the flying dragon probably rose out of the rock beds of German quarries, the stones of Africa, Argentina, the flaming cliffs of the Gobi Desert, or the plains of America; these kinds of fossil treasure-hoards undoubtedly led to thunderbirds large enough to carry off children. Although it's equally possible the modern condor is the more likely ancestor of the thunderbird story. It's been claimed a condor will fly up to goats on cliffs and crack its wings together so hard a goat will startle and fall off the cliff, and then be consumed on the ground. I have seen no verification of this anywhere.

We will never guess the true origin of some birds—the firebird, the Persian Huma, who never touched the earth except to self-immolate and be reborn like the phoenix and whose mere wing-shadow gave grace to human lives. The phoenix itself remains forever rising, like many of us, out of its own ashes. Horus, the Egyptian falcon-god. The Fenghuang and the Vermilion bird. The sky-darkening wing of the Peng bird of China—the cause of storms. Even the sun was depicted as a bird, albeit three-legged, in Chinese mythology. There's the Iranian Simurgh, so old it has witnessed the destruction of the earth three times. It sleeps in the tree of life.

The Aztecs's Quetzalcoatl, the feathered serpent, might be the most genetically accurate bird-god when we consider the dinosaur and bird controversy—his totems were the spectacularly colourful quetzal bird, rattlesnakes, macaws, and crows. When he's in his morning star form, he's depicted as a harpy eagle. He was known to the Mayans as Kukulkan.

The Incas also had their power bird, a giant stone raptor overlooking their great cities—and too many minor bird gods to track accurately here.

Garuda of the Hindu faith exploded out of a great egg so powerfully the fire matched the fire of the creation, and the gods had to plead with him to reduce his power. He stole and traded the elixir of immortality in a complex deal with the ferocious Vishnu, one that let him perch above Vishnu at home yet be his mount when they travelled—a killer of snakes and the father of the six races of birds, who were born to hunt their relatives, the snakes. I keep a statue of him behind my desk; hanging from his wooden wings is a small bag containing the last dust of the ashes my father left behind.

Then there is Kamadeva, Hindu god of love, armed with his magical bow and love arrows made out of flowers, his vehicle a parrot.

The fearsome roc of Sinbad, the blue crow of Brazil, the sun-blocking bar juchne of the Talmud. The mare-eating griffin, with the head and wings and talons of an eagle and the body of a lion, and its offspring, the hippogriff, with the body of a mare. And the once-lovely harpies driving blind Phineus off his food until the Argonaut Jason, and the sons of Boreas (the north wind), drove them away. Our lives, planet-wide, are impossibly rich with bird gods.

The Greeks also wrote about the amazing man-eating Stymphalian birds. Their beaks were bronze and their metallic feathers flew off like deadly arrows. Even their excrement was fatal.

Aside from a few grandfathers with a knack for farfetched storytelling, we can assume the majority of these myths sprang from fossil sightings and the rumours that would spread through such a storytelling species as ourselves, as well as a few exaggerations of natural skills in real birds. The parrot received its share of power myths, whether it was a parrot with a woman's face who survived the flood, married, and became the mother of the Jivaro people of Ecuador, or the important Parrot clan, who own the rights to the mysterious blue flute cult of the Hopi. In the earliest records of the East, the Upanishads, a parrot appears as a word to illustrate the colour red. Cinnabar. In the fourth *adhyaya*, there is this fond description of the Brahman of unchanging reality—existence itself: "Thou art the dark-blue bee, thou art the green parrot with red eyes, thou art the thunder-cloud, the seasons, the seas. You are the one without any beginning; you are omnipresent; all the worlds are born out of you."

Superstition, assumptions, visions—these filled out the myths. We're imaginative creatures, and birds that talk especially fuel our imaginations. I like to think of Tuco speaking Latin, Spanish, Senegalese, Sanskrit... Asians were among the first to be thrilled by the knowing behaviour of parrots.

Parrots flit through the pages of the *Rigveda*, one of the oldest texts in the world, where the yellow plumage of a parrot is mentioned in a hymn to sunrise, echoing the bright yellow of the sun. They appear again in the *Kama Sutra*, where one of the womanly arts is teaching a parrot to speak. There's also a sexual pose called the Parrot, involving a chair, which is probably as hard to describe as perform and is apparently a recent addition to the ancient canon, since chairs weren't used in India when the *Kama Sutra* was compiled in 200 CE out of previous texts. Tuco has definite opinions about sex. He still likes to rip up my manuscripts and make a nest for Sharon if she walks by our office. He's also a real pain when pretty girls come into the house, and he starts howling and wolf whistling. Movie time is trying with him, because if a sex scene erupts, he sticks his neck out like a voyeur and starts whooping and cheering, especially if it's a noisy sex scene. He does the same when he hears anything that sounds like sex happening anywhere in the house. The only time sex upsets him is if it's too close, such as if a couple are bunking for the night in the office. Then he gets scared and starts screeching and flapping about his cage. In that case, I think he fears it's two animals fighting in the dark.

Birds are often used in sexual texts; not only is there a sexual position in the *Kama Sutra* known as the congress of the crow—a sixty-nine position with both participants lying on their side, but the ancient Chinese referred to cunnilingus as "eating the crow." This was long before the Brazilian, or the "landing strip," as some would call it, when the mount of life was a little bushier—a bird in the bush? The *Kama Sutra* descends from the *Kama Shastra*, a vast synopsis of the great declamation on love by the sacred bull, Nandi, Shiva's door guard, who'd obviously spent too long listening to the lovemaking of Shiva and his wife, Parvati, inside their home. This was first recorded more than three thousand years ago. One of its famous passages describes a philosopher, Shankara, seeking another famous philosopher to debate. He is directed to the house of Mandana with these words:

> You will find nearby a house at whose gates there are a number of parrots in cages, discussing topics like: 'Do the Vedas have self validity or do they depend on some external authority for their validity? Are karmas capable of yielding their fruits directly, or do they require the intervention of god to do so? Is the world eternal, or is it a mere appearance?' Where you find this strange phenomenon of caged parrots discussing such abstruse philosophical problems, know that to be the gate of Mandana's place.

One of my favourite Asian legends is when Buddha was reborn as a parrot that became so distraught by a fire in the forest it dived into a lake, filled its beak, and rose up and shook itself, emptying its beak and the water on its wings onto the fire, hopeless against the flames but returning again and again. Finally, a heavenly god saw this compassionate action and wept so hard at the actions of the parrot the tears turned into a downpour and doused the fire.

Compassion can be dangerous also, especially when it's fed by anthropomorphism, inflicting human emotions and thought and skills upon an animal. This is easy to do. I do it often with Tuco, despite suspecting I behave more like him than he does like me.

For almost a decade, we had a lovely canary named Zero in a large domed iron kingdom of a cage. He sang like an angel, from dawn to dark, graciously, and we loved him. But Sharon became worried that he had no mate, that he was all alone. I thought he was fine, but I could see her point, so we bought a female canary. A close relative to anthropomorphism is the pathetic fallacy, where we assume other creatures have human desires. More often than not, they don't. The mating needs of canaries are complex, as we learned. The female canary was larger, older, more aggressive, and she proceeded to henpeck the little guy mercilessly, chasing him off the food dish and all around the big cage, yelling at him in canary speak. The poor boy was so crushed, so beaten, we had to find another home for her. And Zero never sang again.

Kwan Yin, or Kwannon as she's sometimes known, my favourite bodhisattva, the beautiful one, is the bodhisattva of compassion, who considers it her mission to save everyone before she becomes a buddha. In paintings, she sometimes has a white parrot flying above her shoulder with a white pearl in its beak. That's my kind of parrot, and I look upon it with the same sad sympathy I have for the misguided emotionalism of anthropomorphism and the pathetic fallacy.

Life's dances with birds go back further than the written record. They were here long before us. For a number of years, it was claimed the oldest verifiable parrot flourished 40 million years ago. Being human, we named him *Paleopsittacus georgei*, which roughly translates into Ancient Parrot George. He was named after the farmer who found his fossil in England. Our species has a tendency to name everything around us, living or landscape, after ourselves. This bird's authenticity is now disputed, as so much bird prehistory is.

For some reason, there's a real hunger to date parrots with dinosaurs. Many confused people also want to claim that people also walked with dinosaurs, including a Canadian cabinet minister who ran for prime minister, and American politicians too numerous to count. Although our bird/dinosaur, archaeopteryx, appeared about 165 million years ago, it took millions of years before the first true bird species of today emerged. The odds, however amazing, are looking good for an actual parrot (unlike people) walking among dinosaurs before they went extinct, especially since it's now claimed (based on the inch-long lower tip of a fossil bill, which seems pretty desperate evidence to me) that a 70-million-year old Wyoming fossil was a parrot. This would recast parrots into survivors of the great Cretaceous extinction that destroyed the dinosaurs 65 million years ago.

The so-called terror birds, land-walking predators, also survived the extinction, until historians claim they were wiped out by human hunters. Based on their musculature and body structure, it's speculated these giants, who resembled an eight-foot-high parrot, picked up their prey and then flogged it to death before eating it. This is not hard to imagine when I see Tuco beating a rag to shreds just for fun.

Another species, known casually as demon birds, survived until almost fifty thousand years ago. It's believed the last "demon duck of doom," as it was dubbed, an eight-foot-high omnivore that resembled a goose on steroids, capable of dining on wombats and kangaroos mixed with a salad of coconut and fruit, was killed off by the first human invaders of Australia. Large herbivores, like the twelve-foot moa, survived until the Maoris arrived in New Zealand. These birds were considered extinct around 1400 CE. Fortunately, the last giants, the ostrich and emu continue.

We're as argumentative creatures as Tuco, so there's disagreement about when the parrot was first mentioned in Western writing.

I'm voting for Ctesias of Cnidus, a Greek mercenary and physician. Upon his return to the corner of Greece that is now Turkey, he took to his unreliable memoirs and wrote the *Persica* and *Indica*, which were said to be short on organization but fascinating, as well as spattered with whoppers: "A perfect farrago of extravagant and incredible tales," according to Plutarch of Chaeronea. Now lost as whole books, fragments of the *Persica* and *Indica* are much quoted, allowing scholars to piece together the general ideas and even suggest some of the farfetched stories weren't so far off the map after all.

Ctesias wrote around 397 BCE and was much enamoured of parrots. He mentions them several times, and talks of their ability to speak "Indian." He described one accurately enough—sparrow-hawk size, blue-green and vermilion general colour—it also had a purple face and a blackish beard. The description is good enough that this bird can be recognized as the plum-headed parakeet.

Parrots arrived with a bang into Western consciousness with Alexander the Great's rampage across the Middle East and into India itself, and the parrot now named after him, the Alexandrine, was the first parrot sent back to the West. Two centuries later, these extraordinary birds were flooding into Greece, and the rare birds first marvelled at by one of Alexander's commanders, Nearchus, had already become common.

Arrian of Nicomedia's book, also confusingly named the *Indica*, describes the incredible expedition of Nearchus, who was a commander equal to Alexander. He sailed down the foreign waters of the Indus River and up the coast to meet Alexander again in Babylon. Written in 108 CE, Arrian's book dismisses parrots as being unworthy of note due to their ubiquity in his era. Not surprisingly, they remain common in Rome today, like the feral ones I saw in the garden of the Villa Borghese.

When Alexander died, Ptolemy inherited the rule of Egypt and as part of the ceremonies paraded cage after cage of parrots in his procession, and the city of Alexandria soon became the hub for the ever-growing parrot trade, a trade that continues planet-wide today.

The prestige of parrots reached a high point when, after defeating Mark Antony, Octavius was greeted by a parrot shouting, "Hail Caesar, conqueror and leader!" The emperor immediately bought the bird for a princely sum. Another clever bird trainer tried to do the same with a talking raven. This trainer, not taking any chances on the war, had also trained a raven to say: "Hail Antony, conqueror and leader." Alas, his partner, whom he cheated by keeping the twenty thousand sesterces reward, complained and revealed the second talking raven. Octavius, who had a sense of humour in those early days, saw the funny side of this swindle and merely insisted the trainers share the reward.

Talking birds were much admired in Rome, and both Petronius and Martial taught parrots to sing complex Latin praises. And when rich Romans died, their bird companions were sometimes slaughtered and buried with them. Ravens were also much loved. In 36 CE, according to Pliny, a popular raven was given a public funeral. Pliny also had this to say about parrots in his *Naturalis Historia*:

> A parrot's beak is so hard that if you throw down the bird from a height on a rock, it saves itself by landing on its beak with its mouth tight shut, using the beak as a kind of foundation for the shock. Actually its whole skull is so thick that, if it has to be taught anything, it needs to be admonished with blows. Although it really does try to copy what its teacher is saying, it wants an occasional crack with an iron bar.

I've often thought the same about Tuco. He probably has had similar thoughts about me.

The parrot and its gossipy relatives had an obvious impact on the ancients, considering some of the greatest writers—including Callimachus, Ovid, and Catullus—wrote about them. Ovid devoted an entire elegy to "Corinna's parrot" in his *Amores,* shortly before he wrote another erotic book, *Ars Amatoria.* That cheeky classic got him banned for life on the margins of the empire, ancient Romania. Ovid never explained how he annoyed the emperor, only admitting that it was "a poem and a mistake."

There are numerous surviving portraits of parrots from the Roman era, including a pair of parrots harnessed to a cart full of farm implements in the Dionysus mosaic. Those who consider this image a flight of fancy can check out the numerous modern photographs and videos of macaws pulling carts and riding bicycles today. Macaws enjoy playing with toys. Tuco, alas, enjoys destroying toys.

Harnessing Tuco to anything would be both dangerous and destructive. A few victims would have chunks missing from their ears and fingers, and he'd have that cart in pieces within minutes. All architectural objects fascinate Tuco and he considers it his duty in life to render them into their components. I've spent years hearing the crash of objects falling to the floor in the office, soon followed by his nefarious Long John Silver cackle. He can even unscrew bolts. In terror of his skills, I designed a Houdini-proof chain for hanging his cage and all its heavy toys from the ceiling. Despite even that, I live in fear of his talent for destruction.

Parrots weren't admired enough historically to completely dodge the dinner table, as I mentioned earlier, and throughout history, cooking parrot was up there in the realm of show-off cuisine, except in India, where the idea of parrot pie would be horrifying. In the medieval European era, serving exotic birds was regarded as a sign of wealth, such as in a dish where a peacock was skinned and its head removed; then it was baked. Afterward, the plumage and head were sculptured around the baked bird on a platter served to the table. This feast and its presentation would lead to the spectacular dish being peppered with crawling bird lice, but that wasn't a problem because the pretentiousness of it was more important than the reality.

I have only cooked a couple of peafowl, including one disruptive cock that had to go before it crippled another bird. Curried, it was one of my favourite curries ever, and everyone at the table agreed, despite being unhappy about its death, and that was the last peafowl we ate. The taste reminded me of pheasant, and it was a little chewy, as wild birds often are due to the density of their muscles. It was delicious, yet felt immoral.

As the medieval kingdoms of Europe grew, parrots continued to be prized and kept by a few, but they also became more mythic and were often portrayed in fabulous bestiaries, where they were commonly illustrated with various numbers of toes.

In *The Marvels of Rigomer,* an errant parrot dodges an archer's arrow and then chastises the archer for not realizing he serves the greatest knight of all, Sir Gawain. And in another Arthurian romance, the parrot Willeris even acts as a matchmaker for Arthur, though this romantic bird was also a coward in battle. Already, the modern trickster vision of the parrot was surfacing.

This is most likely due to a growing familiarity with parrots as they spread across Europe in increasing numbers. Almost every parrot I've met has a special fondness for tricks and hoaxes. Even if they've been taught a trick they don't understand, they can sense the trickiness and delight in it. Our neighbours have a hyacinth macaw. All you have to do is bark: "Check for weapons!" He will snap his wings up into the air, ready to be frisked for guns. He obviously likes being felt up, and the routine, I suspect, is merely an excuse for a little stroking and people preening.

Parrots fascinated a whole string of popes—several popes kept elaborate aviaries crammed with exotic birds, many of which had special handlers. The yoking of parrots with popes led to more than a few unflattering references, hence the word "popinjay," which eventually become a derogatory term for a mouthy person.

In 1593, English seaman Richard Hawkins was the first to officially identify the African grey, off the coast of West Africa.

"In [these parts] also are store of... Parrots, but of colour different to those of the West Indias; for they are of a russet or gray colour and great speakers."

In the New World, gaudy parrots were regarded as so astonishing and plentiful that one of the earliest explorers named a country, Papago (the Portuguese word for parrot), after them. Only later did it become Brazil. The discovery of parrots in the New World caused clueless speculators to cite that as proof it was connected to India.

Then Columbus confusingly reported on the Carib tribe, the root word of Caribbean, which somehow also became the source of the word "cannibal" because a few Caribs were reputed indiscriminate eaters of flesh. Historian Peter Martyr set the pot boiling, as it were, with his description of a Native household in Guadeloupe: "... and in a large cooking vessel they discovered boiled human flesh along with that of parrot and geese, and other body-parts skewered on spits." This is probably near the same location where the intrepid explorer Giovanni da Verrazzano was killed and eaten on the beach within sight but out of gunshot range of his ships. There's no mention of a parrot garnish.

In the Americas, bird feathers, along with gold and jewels, were always regarded as treasure. Feathered cloaks were especially valued—and still are. In 1998, a six-foot-long Inca cloak woven from alpaca wool and 560 parrot feathers was stolen from the Arequipa museum, and a cloak of dyed chicken feathers was substituted. This cheap switch was quickly discovered by the curators, and when the theft became public news, the real one soon showed up in a church confessional.

Feathers weren't only used for cloaks. Mesomericans adorned golden armlets with feathers and wore jewelled diadems combined with jaguar skin and pheasant feathers. The Florentine Codex (a vast sixteenth-century ethnographic history of the Nahuatl people in their language and Spanish) describes a fringed and painted vest with "feathers as delicate as foam." Bird wings and eagle-feathered bonnets featured highly in Indigenous cultures of the North American plains, and eagle down remains sacred among a number of Native American tribes. The Aztecs's prized headdresses made of rare quetzal feathers remain resplendent today in their crowns of macaw feathers.

Feathered clothing has featured worldwide, from the ostrich-feather shoulder capes of the Zulu to Freya's magical cloak of falcon feathers to the Maori feathered cloaks of authority. The Hawaiians, though, are the real masters of this art. The making of the yellow cloak of Kamehameha continued through eight reigns of kings and eighty thousand finches before it was finally completed. The yellow mamo finch that feathered this cloak is now, as you would expect, extinct.

Then there's the legendary story of Aka (sometimes known as Laka), a great traveller of the Marquesas, who set off on the voyage to Aotona, later known as the Cook Islands and now known as Rarotonga, for the red feathers of a special parrot, the kula. Of his 140 rowers, 100 died of hunger, but the survivors filled 140 bags with parrot feathers, including bags for the kin of the dead. A few versions of the story claim they plucked them off living parrots, because it would have been improper to kill them. They did this by building a large house of palm leaves and then cooking coconuts inside. The birds, lured by the coconut, flew down the smoke hole by the thousands, after which the smoke hole was plugged. Then their best feathers were plucked and the birds released. The kula birds weren't so lucky when the first settlers arrived on the Tonga islands. They are now extinct on those islands.

Parrots were so intriguing to Europeans that Columbus brought back "fortie" and more on his second voyage. Stories of bondings between parrots and collectors soon became common. Pope Martin, as long ago as 1418, needed two travelling attendants to mind his Indian parrot. London's Birdcage Walk is named after the famous aviary of Charles II. His mistress, Frances Stuart, was said to have possessed an African grey for forty years. It died four days after her death. It was stuffed, of course, and is thought to be England's oldest stuffed bird.

The dedicated companionship of parrots is notorious, and they often bond so closely, as Tuco did with his previous owner, that their friendship becomes a problem. Not only are they amazing vocal companions, but they can engage in the full panoply of human behaviours, including jealousy, shame, deceit, and drunkenness.

Years ago, I came home from my night shift at work and discovered Sharon sitting in the TV room, looking somewhat stunned, with the parrot staggering drunkenly along the back of her cushioned rocking chair beside the wall, his wings outspread as he reeled about like an incompetent tightrope walker. Not even thinking about what had got Sharon into this state, I shouted: "What did you do to the parrot!" At this outburst both snapped to attention, attempting to look sober and normal. That didn't last long, as Sharon sagged back into the chair, precariously balancing a cup of coffee. I took the cup from her hand and sipped it, suspecting it was laced with Irish whiskey, which wasn't hard to guess due to the half-empty bottle of Jameson's on the side table. It tasted very strong indeed, and Sharon is a cheap drunk, as they say. She has a low threshold for wine, and a couple shots of whiskey would definitely be the end.

Tuco started banging his head against the wall, as if trying to drive the alcohol out. It didn't take much to realize that Tuco, who had a taste for sweet coffee and cream, had been sneaking sips of her fully loaded coffee while she sat foggily in the chair. I picked him up and took him back to his cage. He was grumpy for days afterward and hardly said a word. It didn't take long to winnow out of poor Sharon what had happened.

She's a nurse, and while she was on shift at the trauma ward, a man was wheeled in, already dead from a car accident. Protocol demands the emergency staff attempt to revive incoming patients, no matter what their condition, in case they've been misdiagnosed or they suddenly come out of the shock caused by an accident. Every blue moon this happens. As they began working on the man, she suddenly recognized he was a close friend, so she had to identify him for the records.

We were told later he'd been out at the nearby pub. As he was crossing the road to go home, a drunk driver suddenly roared over the hill and he barely had a chance to turn to face the car before he was hit. He was struck so hard he flew right out of his shoes, and for some reason, no one had the forethought or nerve to pick them up and they stayed there for hours, a little monument on the road. Life unfolds in strange ways in this scattershot world. I remember those shoes—side by side—a strange memorial that has haunted me for more than two decades.

In 1665, painter Jan Steen portrayed the first parrot being offered wine in an allegory on intemperance in which everyone on the street was smashed, including the parrot. Parrots were by then long rumoured to have epic drinking skills. Aristotle said they are "outrageous after drinking wine." Drunk parrot stories are legion today, though parrot enthusiasts insist parrots are poor drinkers. It makes them ill and they can pass out. This clearly isn't the case with Tuco, but still, I keep him off the sauce, though, to my shame, I offered him a sip of beer a couple of times in the early years and learned he preferred the foam to the liquid, thankfully. However, over the years, mischievous guests have snuck up to our office and tried to con him into drinking beer when I'm not looking. This is how he came to address visitors with: "Wanna beer?"

FOLLOWING THE RENAISSANCE, the mistreatment of parrots and birds grew, especially as an industrial-style approach to trade in animals took hold, and they came to be treated like widgets in the cargo hold. Collecting birds is a devastating business, killing massively more than are captured. It's estimated that up to 80 percent of parrots collected in the wild will die before they reach the pet shop. Then the pet trade sells the many thousands of surviving birds to people who will mistreat them.

By now, just about everyone knows about the horrors of the chicken factories. We are equally cruel to most birds. It constantly amazes me the methods we invent to abuse each other and animals. Take this centuries-old cure for gout: "Skin a fat puppy: and stuff him with cucumber, rue, pellitory, juniper and the fat of a goose, fox and bear, equal parts. Then oil him and add wax to the grease that floats on top, to make an ointment that could then be applied...." The rancid fat of pet cats was also a cure. The cruel fantasies our species has!

So-called scientific experimentation on birds eventually began, and Bruce Thomas Boehrer in *Parrot Culture*, an informative history that has been indispensable to this chapter, discusses an astonishingly nasty painting: Joseph Wright's *An Experiment on a Bird in the Air Pump*, in which the family pet cockatoo is sacrificed to demonstrate to the children how oxygen is necessary to life. Although it's doubtful any father would be that cruel and willing to pose for a painting of it, one never knows. But the attitude illustrated by this painting has chillingly become common to our relationship with birds.

More than a century after this painting was created in 1758, a slightly less brutal image appeared in the first colour movie ever made (created by the father of colour film, Edward Turner, in 1902). It portrayed his daughter and two little sons using sunflowers to bash a goldfish bowl with the unfortunate goldfish inside. It also portrayed a scarlet macaw calmly turning its back to the camera. It was Turner's fate that his advanced studies with film came to an abrupt halt when he died at the age of twenty-nine in 1903. It's also interesting that our earliest films would illustrate animals being abused. Maybe this tells us something about ourselves.

Our species has lived alongside domesticated birds like macaws and Tuco and farm fowl for a few thousand years, but we've also lived among birds as diverse as condors, penguins, ostriches, passenger pigeons, and hummingbirds. And we have not lived well with too many birds. Not only are we responsible for the physical extinction of a number of species, such as the dodo and moa, but we also kill millions of them every day. Millions and millions; 8.6 billion chickens were slaughtered in the USA alone in 2011. That's a lot of dead chickens.

Our extinction skills reached their apotheosis with the passenger pigeon. In Saginaw, Michigan, on April 8, 1873, a continuous flock of passenger pigeons flew overhead between 7:30 AM and 4 PM. Another flock, a mile wide, flew overhead for four or five hours. They were so thickly packed, thirty or forty birds could be brought down with one shot. It's estimated there were about 5 billion passenger pigeons then, nearly the number of all birds in the U.S. today. As everyone knows, not a bird survived.

One of the common hunting techniques was to tie a captured pigeon to a stool, knowing that it would lure a flock of the gregarious birds down to the waiting guns. Thus, the term "stool pigeon" was coined. No wonder it's such a nasty term.

It's been suggested that passenger pigeons were originally a major food of Americans. The indigenous population of what is now North America was vast when the first explorers arrived and spread their diseases. By the time the colonists arrived, there was only a vestige of these once-great civilizations, and the colonists discovered the majestic forests were spookily quiet and open (from the extensive undergrowth burnings that the lost Native American people had practised to increase game and make hunting easier). With the Native Americans so diminished, the passenger pigeon population, minus its major predator, grew to enormous numbers. The destruction of the indigenous populations in Latin America unrolled differently, with the conquistadors and their diseases.

Abandoned, spooky forests didn't only occur on the East Coast. When Captain Vancouver named Desolation Sound, he did so after travelling through miles of deserted, silent coast. Something dark, something evil, something very contagious had moved inland along what was called the Oolichan Trail, the trade route for coastal Natives. Whole tribes disappeared. The forests were silent and empty of human life, and of course there would have been few birds calling in the old-growth coniferous forests.

In the animal kingdom, the birds are one of the most prolific in their variety of species. There are about ten thousand species of birds in existence. From ostriches to condors to motmots to honey guides. Their variety is spectacular, though except for a few ubiquitous bird clans with impressive survival skills, like sparrows and starlings, there's cause to fear for the future of many.

Evolution's worst blunder is humankind. We are reaching the level of comets, ice ages, volcanoes, and other planetary disasters in our unintentional and intentional slaughter of everything from insects to apes. Evolution also has its tools for correcting its mistakes (such as climate change). The number of bird species we are responsible for destroying is enough to take the breath away.

Like a circling flock, the birds I have killed keep returning—the arrow-pierced robin forever falling out of that pine tree. All the chickens I have slaughtered, the ducks I have shot out of the air and water, the ring-necked doves in our "fly" in the forest, the pheasants, the grouse.... All this guilt, and yet I know I will eat a bird this week, like most weeks.

We've exterminated at least 190 species since the 1500s. The news gets worse—more than 1,200 species of bird are considered endangered today. Some of them are doomed already. Originally, there were the famous and mindless slaughters of birds as diverse as moas, passenger pigeons, auks, and dodos. Other extinctions were caused by habitat destruction and, lately, by introduced species and predators—including the brown tree snake in Guam, which wiped out 60 percent of that island's native birds.

Torture crosses all species, and I've seen it in various creatures, whether it's a cat torturing a mouse, or an osprey holding a live fish like an ice cream cone while it slowly, meditatively ate the head off the still-squirming fish. Tuco is a master of torture. Not only does he love to torment and trick us, but he also takes it out on any Other. His favourite prey are the cats, but the dogs receive their share. Although he likes them, he's often cruel, yet he throws them food when he can and as I mentioned earlier, flees to Olive if he feels threatened. In many ways, his mistreatment of other creatures reminds me of children abusing animals or each other... a mob of kids surrounding me like crows as I scooped up that handful of gravel... Cruelty has evolved within the animal kingdom, inhabiting every creature, humans included, I've spent time with, despite the Disney World concept of nature held by some pretend ecologists. You just have to look and you will eventually recognize Othering everywhere—whether in hummingbirds or sheep. Children are natural masters of cruelty—my robin dropping out of the tree....

Every predator kills and every carrion eater consumes the flesh of the dead. Some, like dinosaurs and eagles, eat both carrion and live prey. Tuco would kill a smaller bird without qualms. Birds in captivity will kill or peck each other into bloody messes in the confinement of today's chicken factories. That's why the operators melt down the beaks of egg-laying chickens.

Eagles, ravens, osprey, crows, starlings, and goshawks will casually eat still-alive fish, birds, and reptiles—the victims squirming or screaming as they're being chewed up and dismembered like that fish in the claws of the osprey.

I still have emotional difficulty recollecting a pack of evil nine-year-olds, including me, and our experiments with soup cans, cherry bomb firecrackers, and frogs. Nor can I bear to describe our test launchings of frogs and frog parts high into the air, perhaps because its cruelty was so casual. Oh yes. I don't have an idea what possessed us, or me, going along with this and even enjoying it. I just wanted to be a member of the pack on my first and last night of frogonauts.

I got myself into far worse trouble in those wild years, becoming a sidekick, on occasion, to the rough boys a few years older than me. They could be a rowdy bunch, and since there was an ongoing war between gangs on opposite sides of Boundary Road, between Vancouver and my community, Burnaby, I typically managed to get caught and slapped around by the Vancouver boys on one of their forays to our side of the road. As word of this passed around and became increasingly exaggerated, it grew into a huge gang challenge, and by the arrival of Friday night everyone knew about the coming rumble. There were hundreds of young hoods and little brothers and girlfriends, all waiting for the Vancouver toughs to accept the challenge and cross the street.

This was a classic "next valley" scene, where the people in the next valley, next tribe, next nation are always evil—cannibals or rapists or dirty scoundrels. They are the Others, and I, an Other, ignited a challenge to Others. Suddenly, I found myself being defended by the same toughs who regularly beat me to the ground. The craziness....

Naturally, nobody showed their face from Vancouver, and a foray was suggested and seemed likely, until one of our toughs asked me to describe the ringleader. I announced he had blue hair. Hey, it had been dark and his hair grease glistened in the streetlights. I could hear the words "blue hair?" sifting through the suddenly restive crowd of wannabe gang fighters. And then the cops arrived and the crowd dissipated. My fantastical perceptions had kicked the heart out of them, and I forever felt guilty about that incident for a slew of obvious reasons. I also eventually took a few more beatings because of it.

Another time, my older brother, Leonard, was talking with a few of his friends in the back lane where Father had a sandpile for some building project that kept being delayed. I'd taken over the sandpile with my toy cars, making freeways, bridges with boards, and so on. It had become elaborate over the months. The younger brother of a friend of Leonard's, Terry, a handsome boy with a perfectly oiled pompadour roll over his forehead (better than Elvis's) and a greased-back ducktail, was also there. I liked Terry until I noticed he was running his fingers unconsciously through the sandpile, wrecking my elaborate racetracks and highways. Enraged, without even complaining, I snuck behind him and cracked the back of his head with a rock. This shocked everyone, including myself, and poor Terry was bleeding all over his glorious hairdo and his face. I think he ended up receiving stitches, and I was banished to my room again, after a lot of yelling. Nobody could understand what had caused me to silently do that, and neither could I, and I remain unhappy more than fifty-five years later, recalling what I did to a guy I liked. At least after that incident the local toughs bothered me even less—the psycho outlier.

Tuco has always had a similar troublemaking quality. He arrived with attitude and never lost it. One night, we were in the television room, and Tuco was on his television-watching perch with his popcorn bowl, when Tara, our first Labrador, wandered in. I could see the gears going around in Tuco's head. From the way he was eyeing the dog, it was soon apparent that mayhem was being planned. He grabbed a piece of popcorn and flung it toward Tara, who caught it in mid-air. A few more popcorn tosses in this game and he had the dog directly beneath his perch. That's when I twigged and yelled: "Tuco, don't do it!" But Tuco was definitely doing it, and he was too quick to stop. He's always been faster than me. Now that he had the dog in close enough range, he whipped around, lifted his tail, and shat on Tara, directly between the eyes. It was an impressive splat, and the aghast dog ran out of the room. We had to catch up with her and wipe the shit off with a paper towel, while Tuco cackled on his perch, raising one claw triumphantly, as he does when he's having a howler.

After a few years, the cats, accustomed to his terror attacks, would usually slink out of a room if he arrived, but there was the time when he flew from the office and miscalculated his landing downstairs, hanging awkwardly off the back of the wooden rocking chair, before righting himself with much fluttering, until he was perched on the chair back. A classic parrot landing. This attracted the attention of our champion rat-catching cat, Wu, who slowly began stalking him. Tuco almost did a double take at the nerve of Wu and rose up on his legs, wings spread wide, fluttering his wingtips slightly, like a biker boy inviting a fight. Wu stopped and began thinking twice about this. Then I yelled from upstairs, distracting the cat just as Tuco lifted off, straight for Wu. This was all too much and the cat fled to hide in a bedroom, under the bed.

The animal kingdom has its many brutal moments, yet we've achieved a clinical cruelty disguised as science or manufacturing that exceeds in scale and devilishness almost anything the natural world has invented so far, outside of volcanoes and asteroids. Not only is the scale and style of factory farm bird production horrific, so is the collecting and "accidental" slaughter of exotic birds for pets (more about that later). Even bird lovers have done their share of damage. Although gathering birds for museums and natural history exhibits may seem to be relatively benign, there were an astonishing estimated 9 million stuffed or skinned birds in collection in the United States and Canada by 1994.

Bird hunting remains popular, but it should never be called a sport. It's hunting, and Native traditions provide a great guideline for any hunter. This is all part of that crooked path up the mountain that our species is taking, the path I am following erratically in these pages. Respect your victim. Treat it with honour. Ask the body for forgiveness. Thank the prey you have killed. It also needs to be said that all trophy hunting is sick and usually involves endangered or rare animals, or taking the most prime creature out of an ecosystem, rather than predating the weakest as other predators do. To kill for bragging rights is depraved in our era of diminishing wildlife. However, hunting for food where a species is plentiful—or worse, ecologically out of control, such as the environmentally dangerous deer populations of North America—needs to continue.

Like Roderick Haig-Brown and Jim Corbett, Aldo Leopold also hung up his gun, except for a few plentiful game birds he hunted occasionally until old age—a kind of life lesson he thought it wise not to forget. In his book, *A Sand County Almanac,* which remains a classic of the conservation movement, he treats bird hunting with some wisdom and irony, as is clear in his well-known quote about autumn hunting among the "smoky gold" tamaracks: "This is written for those luckless ones who have never stood, gun empty and mouth agape, to watch the golden needles come sifting down, while the feathery rocket that knocked them off sails unscathed into the jackpines." The more I read that sentence about the joys of a missed shot, the more depth I find in it. You have to see all your world in order to see the parts clearly, and how they work together.

It was the initial shooting of a wolf that he'd stalked, assuming it was killing the deer he wanted to hunt, that turned him into a conservationist in one of the most famous descriptions in naturalist literature: "We reached the old wolf in time to watch a fierce green fire dying in her eyes. I realized then, and have known ever since, that there was something new to me in those eyes—something known only to her and to the mountain."

After this incident, now known as the "thinking like a mountain" story, he stopped hunting big game and eventually limited himself to his few birds. He still liked to eat meat, and wild meat is the best meat. I've been eating it ever since I was a child and continue to take my two deer a year.

The arrival of the twentieth century was America's apex of bird hunting. Along with sport shooting and the addictive behaviour of the passenger pigeon hunt, our passion for fashion was also responsible for the monstrous slaughter of a multitude of birds. The rage for exotic feathers in hats and other decadent clothing items (even purses) led to the age of the plume hunters. According to *The Bird*

Collectors by Barbara and Richard Mearns, it has been estimated that between 1870 and 1920, "twenty thousand tons of ornamental plumage" entered Britain every year. That's a lot of dead "birds of paradise, cock o' the rocks, parrots, toucans, trogons, hummingbirds, and especially egrets." In one nine-month period, William Hornaday, a former taxidermist at the Smithsonian, calculated that London alone had bought and sold the feathers of more than 130,000 slaughtered egrets. Peter Matthiessen describes this plume trade with unrelenting authority in his epic *Shadow Country*.

Along with the factory farming of domestic creatures, our beauty industry has been mighty toxic to animals. In 1971 alone 700,000 rabbits were tortured and killed. All for new lipstick colour, skin creams, eye shadow, and so on. Some animal testing has been crucial to human health, so the issue can be nebulous when it comes to real science. Nevertheless, science has its share of cruel experiments. Here are just a few of the tests itemized in Peter Singer's magisterial *Animal Liberation*: designing a "well of despair" and a "tunnel of terror;" then there's always psychological death in monkeys; malnutrition in kittens, and pain in cat testes. And so on.

WHAT HAS CLEARLY become essential to the survival of our species is the need to evolve beyond cruelty into imaginative identification with the Other. At the rate of climate change, and the disappearance of the earth's resources, it's now unlikely we will evolve quickly enough to prevent social collapse among the human clade of the great tree of life. Yet the human race has proven remarkably innovative and shown an even more remarkable ability to survive the worst messes it can get itself into. Besides, evolution is not necessarily a slow, stately process. More than a few modern scientists argue for a punctuated evolution—a creature might remain the same over thousands of years, and then suddenly evolve into another. Physical changes, like mental changes, can occur quickly when an environment suddenly changes.

Paradigm shift has become a hackneyed phrase, yet it accurately identifies an important aspect of human behaviour. These shifts in attitudes have blown through entire cultures in a few years, and sometimes they can instantly occur to an individual, as happened to Aldo Leopold (who also made his own bow and arrows) with his wolf and to me when I shot that robin out of the tree with my little yew bow. That was the click—the insight that strikes like an inevitable revelation—first named by feminists discussing the moment when they suddenly understand the need for feminism, or the click that poets get when the overwhelming knowledge they are poets consumes them—the recognition they are poets and always will be poets. Margaret Atwood describes it beautifully as a giant thumb coming down out of the sky and pressing on her head. The "I can do this" moment. The moment that teacher dropped Rimbaud's book on my desk, the moment that led directly to these words and this story of our Othering.

So here we are, living in the sixth great age of extinctions, the Anthropocene era, when human impact on the planet has become dominant. We're the killers now. We are why the massive losses of songbird migration is increasing exponentially, spurred by everything from climate change to hunting, increasing storms on the migratory journey, vast forest fires, food disruption due to early hatches of insect prey or feed for the seed eaters, habitat loss due to the consolidation of farmland, the unending amoebic sprawl of suburbs and malls killing habitat, and millions of tons of pesticides poisoning birds—a bycatch from the impossible quest to eliminate insects we don't like. Many pesticides now banned in North America but still manufactured at the same factories are sold around the world, and with the increasing globalization of food production and lack of environmental controls in the majority of nations, they are not only killing birds like bobolinks and swallows by the tens of thousands in the southern part of their migrations where the toxins are still used, as well as returning in produce to the U.S.

and Canada, where those chemical-blasted tomatoes sit fresh and tempting on the store shelves.

Meanwhile, our relationship with birds—especially tricksters like parrots, crows, ravens, and magpies—remains multi-faceted. I can think of no other predator that loves what it kills as much as our species. While the cruel numbers of bird slaughter increase, more and more people are devoting themselves to the protection of birds and admiring them in the wild. In 2001, a U.S. Fish and Wildlife study claimed as many as 46 million Americans considered themselves birdwatchers.

For Alexander, the popes and nobles of Europe, and the lords and princes of the Middle East and Asia, owning exotic birds—ravens and parrots and raptors—was considered essential to their prestige. Peasants imitated the lords with their split-tongued crows and mynahs and their caged finches and nightingales. One of the most tragic sights I've seen was bird alley in Beijing, with its chilling clamour of thousands and thousands of caged birds up for sale as pets, and/or dinner.

In the Victorian era, the veneration of pet animals reached an apex after the death and elaborate funeral of Queen Victoria's beloved royal husband. The population of the nation, empathetic with her great mourning, soon began burying their favourite pets in a similar manner, and before long, parrots were given spectacular send-offs and honoured with carved monuments on their graves. By the end of the nineteenth century, the "royal cult of animal death" raced across Europe as well, though it had long been common in the Arab world. Usama ibn Munqidh, the twelfth-century Syrian poet tells of a pasha who gave an elaborate public funeral for a beloved hawk.

Coincidentally, this is where the European fascination with parrots expanded wildly. It didn't help that in 1883 Robert Louis Stevenson published his inspired *Treasure Island*, forever associating pirates with parrots, though there's no documentary evidence to match Long John Silver and his sugar-eating "swearing blue fire" and "pieces of eight" parrot, whose longevity Long John exaggerated by declaring it "may be, two hundred years old." This bird instantly became legend and led to another leap in the public awareness of parrots.

Parrots were also often associated with American presidential households, and the White House has seen its share of legendary birds, from Martha Washington's singing parrot to Dolley Madison's macaw and Andrew Jackson's hard-swearing presidential parrot, which, according to rumour, had to be removed from Jackson's funeral, because it was shouting obscenities in the manner of its deceased master. President Jackson's ill-tempered parrot was followed by parrots owned by William McKinley, Teddy Roosevelt, and Calvin Coolidge. Roosevelt, though a noted big game hunter, was not always thrilled by his macaw, looking upon it with "dark suspicion." I think it creeped him out, as parrots can do.

The trickster nature of parrots almost demands jokes, and there's no end of them. Each throws more light on our behaviour than that of the parrots themselves, as if they are the perfect foil to reveal our weaknesses and faults, and I've often felt the same way sitting in my room with Tuco, day after day, year after year. Here's one that made me smile:

A woman noticed a beautiful parrot in a pet shop. It was only $100. When she asked why it was so cheap, the shop owner explained that it used to live in a brothel and it could say some mighty powerful words. The woman, being modern and liberated, thought this was funny and purchased the parrot.

When she took the bird home and set up its cage it said, "Oh wow, new digs." She liked this. When the woman's two teenage daughters came home together after school, the parrot immediately said: "Oh wow, new tarts!" This cracked up the woman and her daughters.

Then her husband came home a few minutes later, and the parrot eyed him for a few seconds, before saying: "Oh wow, hello Mike, I haven't seen you for weeks."

Lewdness has been long known among parrots, and it's not alien to Tuco, who picked up his legendary wolf whistle from somewhere I don't want to know about, as well as those distracting cheers, whistles, and whoops during sex scenes in movies. I've never heard any rationale for this behaviour among parrots, yet it's common enough to cause a whole repertoire of sex jokes.

The intelligence of parrots, long questioned by scientists yet long believed in by people well acquainted with the birds, remains controversial, though modern science and research continues to close "the gap" between the human and animal kingdom it has advocated for centuries.

Parrot jokes are without end and of great variety. It seems to me the diverse body of jokes and lame stories signifies our nervousness about these birds... and their powers... long recognized by the Indigenous peoples of Central America, who, according to the writer Paul Bowles, believed "the parrot can be a temporary abode for a human spirit."

One day at an auction, a man bid for a parrot on a whim. The price began low. But the amount kept going up in the crowded auction house, and the man, captured by auction fever, was now determined to buy the bird. Finally, after he bid way too much, the other bidder quit. Later on, as he paid for the parrot, he remarked, "This bird better be a good talker for that kind of money."

The auctioneer smiled and said, "Oh, don't worry. This bird talks pretty good. Who do you think was bidding against you?"

There are thousands of variations on cursing parrot stories. Tuco picked up a few swear words from me, and I can hear my voice in them. I suspect it's the heightened tone common to cursing that attracts parrots to foul language. Tuco knows when Sharon and I are going to have a quarrel before we do, and if we start shouting out at each other from opposite rooms while looking for something, we're toast, because Tuco will intentionally shout contradictory, often rude, comments, until we become so confused we have to stop yelling and start laughing. Parrots are so sensitive to emotion it's almost scary, and it's easy to understand why people have the common belief they possess ESP.

Tuco is a professional tormentor, and there's nothing he loves more than turning the tables on some unsuspecting victim, especially when there's swearing involved. I've never understood why people love to teach a parrot to swear, yet they do. My good friend Patrick, who could be naughty indeed in his younger years, was staying with us, along with his wife, Lorna, and it developed that when I wasn't looking he was sneaking into my office and trying to teach Tuco to say "asshole." As with most humans with agendas, Tuco was having none of it and remained impeccably silent. This, we learned later, went on for several days.

Then Patrick had to go for a morning radio interview at some ungodly hour, and everyone immediately announced we weren't driving him all the way to Vancouver during rush-hour traffic. He'd have to take the bus. This didn't please him.

That morning, around 5 AM, the household was gradually awoken, one by one, to the sound of walking and showering and slamming doors, and I kept hearing Patrick go into my office, looking for one of his books or a manuscript he'd left there, saying, "Sorry, Tuco," and the light would flick on and off. This happened a few times.

Finally, with the entire house awake, Patrick shouted: "Okay, I'm going now!" to everyone's relief. Then a voice called out from the dark of my office, "Bye, asshole," and the entire household burst into laughter as the door slammed. For some reason, Tuco had a little trouble with the double *S*s of the word, which found its way into my blue macaw dream twenty years later.

Since then, when leaving the house after a visit, Lorna has made a habit of saying goodbye to Tuco and then points out: "Notice he doesn't call me asshole." Tuco, enjoying the laughter he got as Patrick departed, kept "asshole" in his repertoire for Patrick, every once in a while, usually when Patrick was least expecting it.

In the parrot kingdom of the curse and blue air, the oldest living parrot was reportedly hatched in 1899, which makes her 117. A female blue-and-gold macaw, she is falsely reputed to have belonged to Winston Churchill during the war and is legendary for her explicit anti-Nazi curses. Cursing parrots also have their share of comeuppance stories, and for reasons I've never understood, there's an abundance of parrot and freezer jokes. Here's one that has both these attributes:

> A hard-cursing parrot nearly drove its owner out of his mind. At last, the man vowed if the parrot swore again, he was going to stick it in the freezer. You can imagine the parrot's choice reaction to this threat. Before the cursing even slowed down, into the freezer it went.
>
> After a half hour, the worried owner relented and opened the freezer door, and the chattering parrot leaped out and onto his arm. "I'm sorry," it said. "I'll never swear again." The owner nodded proudly and back to the front room they returned. Once the parrot was on its perch, it eyed him for several minutes, until it finally asked: "By the way, what did the turkey do?"

This story has an impressive echo in *The Parrot's Lament* by Eugene Linden. A woman owned an African grey named Bongo Marie, along with an Amazon named Paco, and a number of other birds. Due to space limitations, Bongo Marie had her cage next to the dining-room table. One day, the woman unthinkingly baked herself a Cornish game hen, put the dish on the table, and picked up the knife to carve it. Bongo Marie, who hated Paco, glanced at the little baked game hen and with "great enthusiasm" mischievously called out: "Oh no! Paco."

In more than 4,300 years of written culture, the parrot has gone through many changes. Rare and revered bird-god, beautiful trickster, gourmet delicacy, ubiquitous pet, commercial opportunity, guide on the eternal, confused, foggy path up the mountain. The biggest change in our relationship with parrots is only beginning to appear—the recognition of bird intelligence, the intelligence of the Others. It's difficult to describe all I've learned from Tuco after spending twenty-five years in the same room, learning in my left-handed way from a left-handed bird. Yes, parrots and polar bears, like poets, tend to be left-handed.

Meanwhile, a new generation of thinkers and scientists is reversing the paradigm of our relationships with our environment. This is the new story. The new path we'll encounter later. In recent decades, Tuco and his kin, creatures that were once considered mindless automatons, have begun revealing all kinds of secrets about communication and intelligence in a wide variety of studies of the animal kingdom that includes us. We are finally learning we are mere mystic creatures among mystic creatures in the scattershot world of evolution.

Chapter 7

BIRD WATCHING,
BIRD KILLING, BIRD RESCUING

WE ROSE EARLY under a damp, gauzy sky on Pelee Island in Lake Erie. Sharon and I felt lost among a clutch of old-school birders, professional ornithologists, naturalists, writers, and artists who delighted in inspired sightings of the feathered gods who lure us into their forests and fields and shrubs and lakes. I've never been a birder. I tell people I prefer living with them rather than looking for them.

I like my birds to find me in the magic of the day, the craziness of event, the whims that lead us to the unexpected; Tuco is a master of this art, striding on my shoulder, studying my computer screen with great intensity, hoping for dinosaurs or gunplay or glimpses of hot women.

He's got me into trouble more than once. Years ago, our son set the kitchen on fire while deep-frying potatoes. There was lots of smoke damage throughout the house, and the insurance company hired several people to redo the wallpaper and clean up the dozens of artworks, prints, and paintings, including the large number of ceramics I'd made over the years. So it took the cleaners a week.

After a few days, I noticed the young and pretty black-haired woman was giving me strange looks and even turning back in the hallway so that she could enter the room behind me by another entrance, through the kitchen. Something was wrong, but I didn't want to be rude. Then, one morning, as she walked down the hall-way, passing my office door, Tuco erupted with a particularly loud wolf whistle and she rushed quickly past the doorway. Realizing instantly what had been going on (I often don't pay attention to his games), I leaped out of my chair and yelled, "Hey, wait. Wait! Come back. I didn't do that. It's the parrot. I can't even whistle. I don't even know who taught him that."

Suspiciously, she peeked around the door. Tuco noticed her immediately and, believing he had succeeded, gave her a perfectly naughty extended wolf whistle, which made her smile.

"See, I'm totally innocent. He came with that whistle, and he likes girls." It didn't take long for her and Tuco and me to make friends, especially because he obviously assumed he'd lured in a hot lady and pulled out all the stops, performing acrobatics and various conversations with her. Tuco always loves the ladies. At least this time I was off the hook.

PELEE ISLAND WAS an altogether different experience with birds for me. I'm not a bird counter, and our two sets of binoculars are so old and dirty and useless we usually don't bother with them.

I'd somehow ended up the featured speaker at the annual fund-raiser for the Pelee Island Bird Observatory (PIBO), and I was way over my head. This is a well-known annual event, sponsored for many years by a core group of serious naturalists and writers. I'd never done any bird watching like this. It was fun yet intense. Before we knew it, Sharon and I were out bird watching with two carloads of extreme birders. Since we weren't aware we'd be doing any bird sighting, we hadn't even brought our dirty and cheap binoculars. I knew that was a lucky move as soon as I saw the array of optical artillery our friends owned, so we took turns borrowing their binoc-ulars, and I was soon like Goldilocks with the three bears.

One set of binoculars was so expensive our friend said they were his last birthday present, ever. These enormous self-levelling mil-itary binoculars were almost powerful enough to detect missiles being launched in Russia, though you had to be the size of the owner, who is very tall, to hold them up. Their great bonus was they locked in on the image you were examining. If your hands got the shakes, the lenses didn't. Very impressive. Another set was so tiny and powerful and had such a narrow field of vision that I couldn't actually find birds using them, though when I tried to peer at a tiny warbler maybe fifty yards away, I managed to stumble across it and was practically able to count its neck feathers. The most extra-ordinary binoculars for me were illuminated around the rim. They had a vast field of view and were so bright I could find birds easily. Being the fool I am, I suddenly pronounced these the best, a tactless remark among birders, which inspired everyone except the owner to gaze at me with annoyance. These birders took their equipment seriously, and I'd just demonstrated, clueless kid that I am, my pathetic knowledge of optic politics.

In the end, the binoculars weren't a problem, because I did bet-ter without them. And although Sharon enjoyed looking for birds, she much preferred feeding orange slices to the brazen orioles on the picnic table near our cabin. She almost had the orange-addicted birds eating out of her hand by the end of the visit. She preferred bird socializing to bird spotting.

My father had raised me to be a hunter from my youngest days, another of his strategies for making me a man. We still-hunted for deer together, duck hunted in a dinghy, or slow-walked, dogless, for grouse or pigeons. He had the gun. I became the dog—a pointer.

Still-hunting taught me how to sit motionless. When you're still for long periods of time, your ears become almost superhuman, and a leaf falling will sound like a rock drill going off. You also learn to look for what is foreign, some shade, some tiny movement. By the time I was a teenager, I had a hunter's eye. I always saw the deer first, just as a good botanist's eye will pick out one strange green plant among a thousand. The writer and ethnobotanist Wade Davis claimed his teacher, the father of ethnobotany, Richard Evans Schultes had such an eye for plants he could walk into a clearing and recognize instantly, among those foreign plants, any that were previously undiscovered.

Strangely, my hunter's eye turned out to be quicker, on average, than the eyes of these lifelong birder friends. One in the all. All is in the one. History finds its reasons to make us go to strange places and form into a whole. By the end of the afternoon, I noticed a few of our crowd were almost unconsciously waiting for me to spot something. I had become pointer dog to the crew and would rapidly point to birds lurking in the brush or high branches. I'd have no idea what the bird was but its presence would leap out of the foliage for me. Then the birders would shout out the species name, and the naming became an unconscious, good-natured contest. The painter among us, impressively, was the fastest caller in this high-grade clutch of birders but not always and not by much. It was fun, and falling into the mood of it, I soon understood why birding has become the most popular outdoor sport in North America. Once again, I thought of the great Japanese proverb: "Time spent laughing is time spent with the gods."

Then I suddenly realized that while my friends were watching the birds, I was watching my friends. Once again, my years of outsider training had sprung into the moment.

Bird watching didn't exist until the last century, and if an eighteenth-century peasant encountered someone who wandered all over the world to just look at and add birds to their life list, they would consider the birder crazy. You lived with birds. You didn't count them. In fact the term "bird watching" was only first coined by Edmund Selous in 1901. He was the bird-watching younger brother of the world famous big game hunter Frederick Selous. Edmund eventually came to detest game hunting.

This new subspecies of the human species has grown into its full plumage over the last fifty years. One faction has turned it into a competitive sport that invites obsessive-compulsive birders who will do just about anything to add to their life list. These people are called "twitchers," and the epic ones are often referred to as "chasers." My bird-watching friends are ironic yet kindly about these people. "They could do worse with their lives" is their attitude. And it's true. As we grow further from the natural world, we feel a need to participate in it, if only as a tourist, counting birds. But bird expeditions now involve mapping and the new citizen-science of tracking migratory routes; plus, they're an enormous voice for preservation. Despite their nutty foibles, even the twitchers should be encouraged. There's an amusing book that skewers British birders called *Bill Oddie's Little Black Bird Book*, and it's a fun read, defining the sport of bird watching and its participants, as well as many of the terms that have fluttered over to our continent.

The very first bird lovers were brutal. They not only studied birds but they also slaughtered them by the thousand, stuffing or skinning crates full for museums and collectors.

We comfortably forget that John James Audubon, the god of bird fanatics, was perhaps the best bird killer of his era. For instance, to prove the now-nearly-extinct (but populous in his day) reddish egret was easy to slaughter, he shot twelve in a half hour. This savage man and monumental bird lover, regarded by many as the father of modern ornithology, and a father of the conservation movement, also created the most legendary bird book in history.

Modern, serious birders are not entirely different creatures. Their obsession can become life-consuming, except they only "shoot" birds with a tick mark on a life list.

Birding has evolved into what we call ecotourism. According to a 1996 study, there were 51 million birdwatchers in the U.S. alone.

A more recent National Audubon Society survey estimates there are now 71 million. Another survey, the 2001 one I mentioned earlier, claimed there were 46 million. These are mighty elastic numbers, yet they do illustrate there are millions of people out there who consider themselves birdwatchers. Birders have their own language, complete with different dialects, and some terms that can be humorous and colourful.

According to the famous Bill Oddie and his very British viewpoint, a "tick" is a mark on the life list of a twitcher looking for an "LBJ" (little brown job) in "sum plum" (summer plumage), or it can be a "megatick" (a rare LBJ), or even a "crippler" (a megatick that gives you a heart attack) that is a "sibe" (normally summers in Siberia but got lost). It's not on a "vis mig" (visible migration), and you once "dipped out on it" (missed it when everyone else saw it), or even, horrors, considered "stringing" it (megaticking a dubious sighting).

I encountered my first cluster of twitchers two decades ago in Coba on the Yucatan Peninsula. Driving down a lonely road, we saw a crowd of people staring intently into the jungle. Curious, we stopped the car and walked up behind them. They didn't acknowledge our existence.

Someone was playing a taped birdsong, attempting to lure an LBJ into the open. I noticed the birdwatchers were wearing their own fine Abercrombie & Fitch plumage and guessed their field clothing was worth more than our entire three-week holiday.

Barely ten feet into the jungle was one of the largest bromeliads I've ever seen, in full spectacular flower. It was awesome. "Hey, look at that great bromeliad," I called out instinctively.

They dropped their binoculars and stared at this glorious cascade of flowers, then turned as one and gave me a dirty look. Not only had I interfered with their bird watching, but I'd also pointed out that not one of them had noticed the bromeliad. They couldn't see the forest for the bird they couldn't find.

We beat a hasty retreat to our hotel, where they soon also appeared. I tried to make amends over the next few evenings in the bar, where they invariably appeared after another hard day's slogging while enraptured by their handsome young guide whose jungle stories had them swooning—the coral snake on the path and the jaguar in the tree, etcetera, they followed him around like a gaggle of lovestruck geese.

One night, I learned their real reason for visiting Coba was to megatick the rare double-tailed motmot, local to the region. These are people who will fly to Madagascar to tick a single bird.

Without thinking, I blurted out I'd seen a motmot that very morning, while sitting on the toilet in my bathroom and staring out the window. It was perched on a nearby branch, staring back at me. This arriviste news so enraged the birdwatchers they refused to speak to me evermore.

The incident made me consider the nature of birders. The obsessive ones tend to be city folk. For real twitchers, birds are a mathematical, accumulative thing. It's a collector's act, not a communing one. Yes, Othering, once again. They snottily refer to birders who merely go to "beautiful places to perhaps see beautiful birds" as "dudes"—amateurs.

The deliriously cranky but great writer Jim Harrison opens one of his essays with a description of himself lying on the floor of his cabin, his shotgun trained on a pretty little songbird. His desert cabin was surrounded by annoying life-listers who'd been pestering him for a week due to a sighting of this lost bird. He relented, of course, and didn't shoot the poor creature, an irritant only because of the irritating people it attracted.

I've been lucky enough to have several great birders and naturalists teach me a few things about how to watch birds in a real way.

I must admit I now often jot down a bird sighting, the date and place, in my near-destroyed field guide, not to count it, but as Wayne Grady pointed out—the notes make a fine memory tool, evoking long-forgotten journeys and incidents. A birder's bible can open marvellous doors into the secret traps of memory.

At the same time, I've always preferred observing, say, hummingbird territorial wars (these aerial tigers use such impressive jump-jet tactics) or mating displays, rather than attempting to distinguish between a rufous and an Allen's hummingbird at a distance.

I couldn't imagine seawatching for hours beside a telescope, staring into the horizon on a stormy coastline, hoping for a long-distance tick of a rare oceangoing bird, though I was astonished and smiling when I saw many hundreds of rare-to-the-region puffins off Qualicum Beach one year—nothing like the thousands Sharon and three friends had spotted a couple of years before. It was wondrous enough, as wondrous as the collection of bald eagles in late winter near the little town of Campbell River. They line the beach for miles, along with seals and Steller's sea lions, all awaiting the feast of April—the schools of spawning herring. Sometimes the eagles are packed barely a few feet apart as far as the eye can see.

Perhaps living with the wilderness around our farm has made me a different kind of bird enthusiast. Our twenty-five years of planting our version of a migratory bird sanctuary in our yard, with its food plants and protective tangled shrubs, has had great success in recent years, and now I suspect flocks pass the news along the migratory route. "Hey, there's this meadow on Salt Spring Island..." First a single goldfinch pair arrives; the next year we have a hundred. Sometimes I wonder if this is like a meme that passes through our species. An idea, a word, a place that becomes "hot." According to Richard Dawkins, this is similar to the way genes are passed along.

One of the pleasures of today is learning about the explosion of parrot watchers making descents into hidden valleys, or camping by jungle rivers, or booking into luxurious eco-resorts built out of sustainable wood and recycled windows, paying impoverished locals to lead them to a sighting of a hyacinth macaw, or flocks of the many varieties of Amazons or even African greys in the midst of modern war zones, or parrots in the groves of Australia or along-side the Ganges River. This is so much more civilized than owning parrots. And there are parrots on every continent except Antarctica. Parrot watching has become a worldwide phenomenon. Ecotourism might have its drawbacks but what a benign way to love the parrot, to witness it in its wilderness. Besides, it can be fun watching the birdwatchers watch birds. They're part of the wildlife, too.

The idea of parrot watching makes me recall a day paddling dug-outs up a lonely little river in Costa Rica, past crocodiles and a big snake, and suddenly witnessing the antics of an enormous flock of parrots flushing like grouse from tree to tree, all with the joy of jun-gle birds that have encountered a ripe crop of fruit. How my heart fluttered with the thrill of witnessing wild play and delight among parrots. Wild—yes, it was wild.

THE NEXT DAY on Pelee Island, we all clustered in the grey morning, the rain drizzling down sporadically, though not enough to disturb raincoasters like Sharon and me. The group divided into a couple of vehicles and drove to the observatory. This was more complex than I assumed. Despite being a public institution and open to the public, the observatory didn't encourage random visitors. Too many wor-ries about vandalism or distraction or disruption of the rituals of an observatory, which is a kind of simultaneous religious and scientific process, performed with casual grace in the temple of the woods.

The Pelee Island Bird Observatory is only little more than a decade old, but it's important because the island is a major migra-tory stopover, allowing the observatory to conduct "intensive migration-monitoring research and breeding bird studies" during the great migrations each year.

There are several sizes of mist nets, but the standard is usually about forty feet long and approximately eight feet high with a one-inch mesh. They are hung in small clearings—stretched so that their bottom is a few inches off the ground. At their base, some old planks were laid so that the earth didn't turn into gumbo. We watched Sumiko, move along these nets like a slow dancer, graceful, beautiful, extricating the small birds ensnared and slipping each into its own soft-clothed bag with a pull tie. Once she had accumulated a few of these bags, she'd bring them back to the observatory, where Graeme, the observatory manager, would withdraw the bird from its bag, uninjured, call out its identification, sex, relative age, and health (blowing on the feathers of its chest and exposing the skin beneath, he could discern whether the bird was fat enough to survive its migration). His talent and gentle care were even more impressive than the bird-identifying skills of our *über* bird-watching group. Then he banded it and slipped the bird onto the ledge of a tiny bird door, which was a channel through the wall, open to the forest, a passage where the stunned bird could regroup before flying off.

The first recorded case of banding was in Europe around 1595. Henry IV's banded peregrine got lost chasing a bustard in France. It was captured 1,350 miles away, in Malta, after twenty-four hours, having travelled at an average 56 miles per hour. That's flying.

By 1902, the scientific banding of birds was underway, and a man named Jack Miner, who had built a water bird sanctuary in Ontario, began banding thousands of birds, including twenty thousand Canada geese. Thoughtful hunters brought the bands back to him.

The little birds Graeme released into the door bird shook themselves alive, facing the natural world before bolting into the sky. They made me recall the remarkable recovery talent of birds. I've seen birds smash into windows, struck by a hawk, and snatched by a cat. If they are rescued, they will lie immobile and death-like for a while, and then suddenly snap back into this world, as if they had decided they were dead and then decided they are now alive. Shock is a state of mind fed by the chemical body. Because of my condition,

I've long been sensitive to chemical rushes. Shock is why accidents shift into slow motion, a trick of the mind that gives us more time to respond to the potential death hurtling toward us. I've had several near-death moments, rolling a truck off a cliff, a runaway log sliding down the mountain straight toward me in a gyppo logging show. With the truck, I was still trying to steer while rolling seventy feet down, over and over four times, crazily attempting to straighten it out so that I'd stop rolling, until I landed right side up on a driveway beneath the main road, almost having speared the truck and myself on the sharp points of an iron gate. Stunned, I was bleeding profusely from the skull, picking up the spare tire, broken-off mirror, and tail gate and calmly throwing them into the back of my flattened truck, when the ambulance and fire truck arrived and a medic shuffled me gently onto a stretcher. I had no idea I was hurt. I couldn't see the blood pouring off the back of my head, though it felt wet. That was a classic case of concussion and shock. It took thirty-six staples in my skull to stitch the wound together.

When the log on the northern Nisga'a hill came roaring at me, I heard my name shouted by the bicameral voice, as it's known, the god voice, the angel voice, and I looked up at the stump end of the log, and it almost stopped, I swear it, and somehow I took one long step, and then I was ten feet back, as if I had psychically transported my body out of danger; then the log whistled past, a few inches from my face. Later, I learned nobody had seen the log coming, no one had shouted my name. I realized that in the sudden moment of awareness of the rushing log, I'd shouted my own name inside my consciousness. Sometimes our bodies and brains are more alert than we are.

I looked at one of the tiny warblers in the observatory release box. After it recovered from the shock and flew off, I wondered how it felt, finding itself in that box, the free world returned to it. And I began to imagine little warbler legends of alien abductions. "Then the wingless giant flipped me on my back and blew on my chest until it tingled, and suddenly my leg was cuffed with a metal clamp I can't bite off...."

Or did it consider this just another part of the dangerous world, the animals always coming at you, one after another, every bird spending a life alert and on the run, carnivorous tooth following tooth, beak after beak, winged devil raptors like incomprehensible bullies, diving out of nowhere and stealing companions, or following them through the leafy shrubs of their short lives.

I thought of my rolling truck going over the cliff... and a doomed bird snapped out of the air by a glass wall, the fat, healthy flicker I found broken on our deck. He'd smashed into our house window: beautiful scarlet streaks so bright—his tongue hanging. A tongue that reminded me of Tuco's grey, sensuous tongue. This bird's tongue, narrow and long and pink, filled me with sadness—the horror, the beauty, the confused merging of the one into the everything, life roiling and life joyous and life strangled, life smacked against the invisible wall we merely identify as a window or a mist net or a truck going over a cliff.

Young Graeme withdrew a bird from its bag, dead. Sometimes there are casualties at migratory bird observation stations, and with Graeme and Sumiko, you could see the anguish. Even those who dedicate their lives to birds still find birds dying in their hands. Already weak from long migrations, they die of shock when they hit a net. Their heart gives out. Others break a wing. Hawks, owls, coyotes, or dogs will sometimes pluck them out of the net—another reason the observatory doesn't encourage tourists.

This incident made me curious, and I asked Graeme if there was much of this. He thinks there was for a while, and there were suspicions that some banding organizations were more careless than others in their eagerness to develop big bird counts and thus achieve higher funding. Oh yes, even the bird advocates! It's a dread subject for all the organizations, because nobody is going to admit to accidentally killing the birds they are trying to protect, especially through carelessness or greed for funding—putting too many nets up so that the collectors sometimes don't fetch them for hours, stressing the birds even more. But it had become a subject of discussion in bird circles in the last few years, and he thought the few negligent stations were cleaning up their act quickly. On the American Museum of Natural History's website, there is a reference to a recent study that declared that twenty banding sites showed only 0.23 percent of birds perished in the banding process, which sounds respectful and diligent; except when I looked up the original study, I discovered that of the seventy-seven sites where the information was requested, only twenty replied with statistics. Others said they didn't keep mortality data, or their data was not in a form that could be easily supplied to the study. This could be interpreted as suspicious, yet these organizations are there to help birds, so I tend to give them the benefit of the doubt.

These banding sites supply important hard data on both local and migratory birds necessary for protecting endangered birds. But birds continue to disappear at an alarming rate, despite the increasingly desperate warnings—like the 98 percent of chimney swifts that vanished. According to BirdLife International, on its threatened bird website: "One in eight of the world's bird species is deemed globally threatened and the fortunes of 198 Critically Endangered species are now so perilous that they are at risk of imminent extinction. Some of these species have not been sighted for many years and may already have succumbed."

The rate of destruction of migratory songbirds accelerates on a brutal scale.

In the early seventies, troubled and craving to be alone in the woods, I often stayed at a friend's cabin on Texada Island, and from there I used to hike into the heavily forested region of the southern island, past three lakes named with some inspiration: First Lake, Second Lake, and Third Lake—where I'd sometimes fish the clear patches between the dense bulrushes, enthralled by the noise and flights of a multitude of red-winged blackbirds. Following the logging road farther, though I never did reach the logged area, I would be surrounded by swallowtail butterflies and a treasury of migratory birds in the spring and fall. Until then, I'd never encountered so many goldfinches, grosbeaks, and waves of both bohemian (in the early spring) and cedar waxwings. Only once since have I seen such a cluster of cedar waxwings, perhaps ten years later, when I was watering our front garden with a hose because we had just planted a few dozen perennials and annuals. I suddenly realized I was surrounded by cedar waxwings and they were flying through the sprinkle of the hose. I quickly switched it to mist and called out to Sharon, who was weeding not far away.

These dry and dusty far travellers wanted a bath! They lined up systematically, taking turns in twos and threes to fly through the hose spray from one tree to the next. Then I turned the hose on the magnolia, and soon an impressive flock clustered on the branches of the tree, happily bathing and shaking themselves clean. It was an amazing vision, and we both smiled as I supplied a summer wash for the whole flock. They were so obviously blissed. Thinking about this made me realize how scarce the waxwings have become at our farm, despite twenty-five years of planting "bird plants" for attraction and feed. I saw a couple dozen—if that—cedar waxwings about five years ago. I can't remember seeing more than two or three since. It's also reported that the same diminishing numbers are true for goldfinches. Fortunately, the tribe of goldfinches that found our farm apparently returns every year. They're lovely to watch out the window at the breakfast table.

According to the 2004 report of the Audubon Society, 30 percent of North American birds have declined significantly. Some, like the rusty blackbird, have lost 90 percent of their kin. In fact, the Audubon Society has also declared that, overall, the total bird life in North America has declined by 68 percent.

A 2013 Smithsonian Institute study estimates that cats alone kill up to 4 billion birds a year on our continent. Kindhearted "samaritans" continue trapping wild cats, cleaning them up, giving them shots, and releasing them again to feed on endangered wild birds and mammals. These people consider themselves animal lovers.

A few years ago, I listened to an interview with one of these cat lovers and her defence of releasing feral cats into the woods. She called the bird counts and calculations by the Smithsonian Institute junk science and then went through the same spin as climate change deniers and intelligent design fundamentalists. Once again, I was witnessing the triumph of epistemic closure over science. This study has endured a firestorm of criticism by cat lovers. A *National Geographic* article estimates there are more than 70 million feral cats in the U.S. alone, and probably as many domestic cats.

The destruction of European migratory birds is worse due to recent developments in the Mediterranean. Although all the numbers aren't in, massive disappearances in recent years have led bird lovers, such as the novelist Jonathan Franzen, in a 2013 *National Geographic* article, to state the situation is far more dire than the preliminary numbers show. The 2012 bird count, according to the Royal Society for the Protection of Birds in Britain (RSPB), states that 60 percent of all species are declining, and some varieties of birds are disappearing catastrophically—71 percent of turtledoves, 53 percent of nightingales, 44 percent of cuckoos, and so on. The magical grey hour of morning in the forests and fields and shrubby margins of Europe, that hour when the hope of the world, its birds, sing us into sunlight, is fading into silence. I became aware of this while driving through southern Europe two years ago, growing increasingly nervous about the few birds we encountered. We only heard masses of them in sanctuaries, islands of safety where the birds know they can survive. These islands are growing smaller, and there are insufficient green bridges—environmental corridors— between parks and sanctuaries in Europe. Although anecdotal history like this can be considered meaningless by scientists, it wasn't for us.

I was shocked at the quiet forests of Switzerland and Italy especially. They had turned into what's been called green cement by ecologists—ersatz forests. They look good but have become the Disney cartoon equivalent of a forest, silent and relatively empty.

It's hell out there, and to the horror of conservationists, the very mist nets developed to catch and band and enumerate bird populations for their protection have now been turned against the birds on an epic scale. The possession of mist nets is illegal or strictly managed in many countries, yet the black market easily transports them to the major killing sites.

A TV crew from a German wildlife series calculated there were four hundred miles of mist nets along the coastline of Egypt in 2013 (almost the length of Egypt's coast), waiting for the exhausted birds after their autumnal Mediterranean crossing. The only parts of the coastline not netted were the military bases and urban areas. These nets are now augmented, especially since the flood of computer applications allowing cellphones and other devices to play recordings of mating and invitation calls for specific birds to feed, sometimes through speakers, so that even high-flying birds can be lured down to the nets. In Queensland national parks in Australia it is now illegal to play bird tapes, because they disturb their habits so much and stress them. Birdwatchers who use these now-toxic apps have found themselves in the midst of a sometimes hostile debate about ethics, or even verbal abuse in the woods.

A few years ago on Quadra Island in British Columbia, Sharon and I were walking out to the end of Rebecca Spit when I noticed a flock of eagles perched on a dead tree, taking a break from fishing the coho salmon run, no doubt. I never heard of anyone doing this at the time, so it was just on a whim that I took out my cellphone and played an eagle call from the Cornell University All About Birds website. The eagles rose en masse and swung around in the air, calling angrily as they whipped past and away. I felt guilty for disturbing them, and I wondered if Cornell had recorded a territorial threat call from another bald eagle. With my curiosity aroused, I tried the cellphone again when I thought I saw a wood duck on a log, back-shadowed by the sun out in the water. The wood duck has a particularly colourful plumage. I played its call because I wanted to see that bright colour, and the duck soon leaped off its log and rapidly swam toward me. Only when it was about ten feet away did it realize its mistake and swim away. I never did get the chance to admire its colours close up. That was the last time I ever played a bird sound to a bird except Tuco, who loves to hear different birds and sometimes imitates them. It was clear to me at the time that these recordings could be deadly in the wrong hands, and now they are.

Today, the unfortunate migratory birds of Europe have to run the gauntlet of calls luring them to mist nets, hunters with guns, the many traps set in agricultural fields, and the notorious bird lime. This is a centuries-old hunting technique whose origin is lost in the fog of time. Shakespeare mentions it several times. From *The Rape of Lucrece:* "Birds never lim'd no secret bushes fear."

Limesticks are branches slathered with sticky substances such as plum sap, and a bird is stuck as soon as it perches. Since their feet are designed to clamp down and the release muscles are not as strong—like a crocodile's jaws—the sticky sap is sufficient to hold them. Many of these birds end up in a variation of the reverse crucifixion position, upside down, or with their wings also caught. Up to twenty thousand limesticks are set along Cyprus's south coast alone.

It's a sight to see photographs of CABS (Committee Against Bird Slaughter), guerilla bird savers in France sucking on the wings of live warblers and nightingales. CABS is an independent clutch of bird lovers willing to take direct action against illegal bird traps and bird killers. Putting the birds in the mouth is a sweet and convenient way of dissolving the plum sap spread on the limestick traps, and allows the birds to fly out of their mouths, as it were, once their wings are cleaned.

According to BirdLife Cyprus, 1.1 million songbirds were illegally slaughtered in Cyprus in 2008. This mass slaughter is for the cooking pot, in particular for a dish called *ambelopoulia*, a pickled and grilled delicacy. The preferred bird is a robin or a blackcap. A hunter can earn as much as $5 a bird from a restaurant that prepares them. They are a popular meal. The following is a quote of a posting from a Cypriot public forum. What's most fascinating about it is the casualness about death—the wry cruelty within the straightforward description. I first though it was satire, but I now believe it's real. Note how the cook recommends using an official RSPB bird feeder and coating it with glue. Even more horrific is the part about disposing of any extra wrens accidentally caught.

The Cypriot dish is called *ambelopoulia,* and here is my version of it. I think it would make a deliciously festive treat on, say, Boxing Day, when you are sick of turkey. However, you will need to catch your robins on Christmas Day because they must be marinated overnight. Catching them is not too difficult—they are very presumptuous at this time of the year and may approach within grabbing distance. However, best to copy the Cypriots and lime a (low-lying) tree branch with glue or resin and simply harvest them later. Better still, coat an official RSPB bird feeder with glue or resin. You might find the occasional wren or dunnock in the mix, but no matter, give them to the dog. Wrens have a rather bitter taste.

My recipe, for four people, is intended as a starter; so allow two birds per person.

INGREDIENTS:
Eight robins, plucked and with the skin cleaned with a damp cloth and rubbed in salt. Leave the intestine intact.
Tablespoon of olive oil
Maldon salt

Lemon zest
Soft butter

FOR THE MARINADE:
The juice from six lemons
2 cloves of garlic, finely chopped
Four tablespoons honey
Teaspoon of cider vinegar
Salt
Black Pepper
Finely chopped flat leaf parsley
Fresh thyme, chopped finely

Mix the ingredients for the marinade in a Tupperware container. Coat the birds and leave them in the marinade over night, turning a couple of times. The lemon will tenderize the meat.

Next day, shove a kebab skewer or wooden skewer through the arsehole of each bird until it is securely fastened. Wipe the excess marinade from each corpse and rub over a little soft butter. Season with salt and pepper.

Heat the oil in a large heavy-bottomed frying pan. When it is quite hot put the birds in the pan, with the skewers resting on the pan edge like the hands of a clock; you will need to turn the birds once every two minutes, ensuring the outside of each robin is crispy and with the suspicion of charring. You cannot beat slightly blackened robin.

Serve on a bed of garlic, chili and coriander couscous, garnished with rocket. Voila.

I hope that this has been helpful.

Not only is songbird slaughter common to Cyprus and Egypt, but it's consistent along the entire Mediterranean. In Albania, the estimate of bird kills is 8 million a year, though the Albanians don't systematically hunt their local birds and mostly eat migratory birds. When Jonathan Franzen asked some hunters why they were slaughtering the migratory birds, the simple reply was: "They're not our birds." That's right, they are Others.

Franzen tells the story of one migratory flight of fifty thousand geese driven south by a storm from their usual feeding grounds to a valley in Albania. None came out of that valley alive, massacred by shotgun and Kalashnikov, a real bonus for the impoverished Albanians trucking them to restaurants and the homes of the wealthy.

I remember windfalls of ducks in my younger years, especially when hunting with my father. Around my twenty-fifth birthday, my father and brother and I were hunting a harvested corn field. There was a blind at each end. My brother used a single-shot shotgun, and I took my father's pump shotgun with its broken safety and gave him my trusty single-shot. I didn't like doing this, but we knew this combination would be more efficient if we panicked a flock of mallards into what's called "a fly," driving them back and forth in the air above the field.

There were ducks everywhere on this gorgeous autumn day. I was wearing a plaid mackinaw. These wool jackets used to be endemic in the north. They were light yet warm, even when wet, and its several pockets were handy, including the giant back pocket with two openings, one on each side. I stuffed my dead ducks in there, though it became heavy after a few birds. Then, wheeling around, I caught the barrel in the blind and realized there was a twig stuck in it. I pumped out the gun and flicked the twig off. Then something went very wrong. I knew it immediately, but I never heard the shot.

They say you never hear the shot that hits you, though I certainly heard the scatter-gun of my childhood. A shotgun shell had stuck in the chamber, and with no safety, when I pulled the gun back to flick the twig out, I can only assume the trigger caught on the beak of a duck hanging out of my back pocket.

I realized I was in shock. My finger started to squirt jets of blood, so I had to hold it up, above the level of my heart, like a young Renaissance saint in an oil painting, only with no finger and with dead ducks hanging out behind me. I looked for the finger but couldn't see it. I was annoyed, thinking some lucky duck would probably eat it. I'd been shot by a duck!

Since I was in shock, everything moved in slow motion, and the world became even more unnaturally beautiful than it was. I will never see the likes of that blue sky again, that yellow cornfield. I began the long walk across the field to what I knew would be the horror of my brother and father, especially my father, who later bitterly regretted giving me that gun with a broken safety. Yet it was also one of the finest moments of my life, the beauty of it all, the magic of the sky and the field as I trudged through the mud, knowing I had about a half hour before the shock wore off and the pain hit. I had to reach the hospital fast. I would also never live down having been shot by a dead duck.

That was the last duck I shot. Yet sometimes, when I see them out there in the field, my teeth practically start to chatter, like the cat watching the birds at the bird feeder through the window. And I think of all the wild duck dinners I have missed. On desperate days, I go trapshooting and bring down a few clay pigeons.

I guess every duck has its day, and I had learned that I wasn't bulletproof. The first time I was shot it was only a scatter-gun; this one was real. The finger is still missing, and I was mini-seconds from losing a hand on this long journey up the foggy mountain of my life.

UNFORTUNATELY, ONE OF the difficulties in tracking the loss of wild birds—all animals, in fact—is that we are such web spinners. Beautiful liars.

A few bird lovers on the fringes of the environmentalist movement have shown a tendency to wildly extrapolate scientific data, so deaths in the migratory gauntlet have been estimated from a low of 14 million to the more likely 140 million but can run as high as 500 million. Such figures are always suspect unless backed up by a

scientific study by trusted organizations such as the World Wildlife Fund and the Zoological Society of London, whose 2014 study
states that more than 50 percent of all living animals have disappeared in the last forty years. Organizations.like the Smithsonian
Institute and BirdLife International are also excellent, but even they
are responsible for controversial research papers.

The numbers are catastrophic, and not just in the southern coast
of the Mediterranean, where the recent economic downturn had
the already trigger-happy Italians hauling out their guns with a
vengeance. The Italians have a long history of shooting tiny birds
out of trees. In 2001, a truck trailer with 13 tons of frozen birds was
seized by the police—120,700 songbirds, 83 species—including pip-
its, skylarks, and turtledoves. No winged bird is too small for these
crazed hunters and gourmands.

The tragedy of turning bird lovers' tools of protection, such as
mist nets and recordings, on birds is all too evident. Not only are
these birds feeding the impoverished and starving, but they also
provide wealthy trenchermen with platters of songbirds. BirdLife
International estimates the illegal underground economy is worth
10 million euros a year. Year by year, the Mediterranean is eating
the heart out of the great songbird populations of Europe.

One of the most infamous dishes enjoyed these days is ortolan
bunting. It's estimated there are 400,000 to 600,000 pairs in all
of Europe, yet in France alone, CABS estimates 40,000 to 80,000
birds are captured every year, driving this delicate little creature
ever closer to extinction. These are suspect numbers—CABS is a
notably enthusiastic organization, yet there's no doubt tens of thousands of ortolan are being tortured to death every year.

In a grim article in *Esquire*, Michael Paterniti describes the last
meal of the socialist former president of France, François Mitterrand, who was dying of stomach cancer. About forty friends were
invited to this feast. It began with a rare variety of raw oysters.
Then foie gras—a pâté made out of the livers of tormented ducks.

Ducks have no gag response, and in the old days their feet were nailed to the floor so that they couldn't move about, and then a tube was stuffed down their throats and they were force-fed a fattening corn mash. Their diseased livers would soon bloat to an enormous size and make the greatest of pâtés. I've tried this mutation, and I've also eaten the pâté of a healthily raised free-range duck, as well as a pâté made from the livers of wild ducks shot by a Ojibway artist and hunter. The tortured foie gras, I had to admit, was smoother than the pâté made from a normal domestic duck, but I preferred the livers of the wild ducks. There was a richer flavour, and they were honestly collected and killed instantly. In my mind, that added to the taste, the terroir was more real and it sang inside the flesh. There's a tangible difference between eating tortured animals and real food that's lived honestly and been slaughtered honestly. Although this is considered farfetched, I'm convinced we can taste it.

The ortolans featured in Mitterrand's last meal were captured in cornfields in small traps called *matoles,* which lure the birds inside with grain and, lately, those damned recorded birdcalls. The bird steps on a trip bar that slams the cage shut. It's like a mink trap. Then they are blinded, usually with hot needles. The blind birds are fed almost continuously until they are obese little thumb-sized creatures.

Before this expensive meal, they are drowned in a glass of Armagnac, the oldest of all distilled brandies in France. Then they are plucked and placed whole in a dish, where they are roasted in their own fat.

When the ortolan is served, it is the custom to drape a large serviette over your head or to put your head under the tablecloth while you eat them. Some say this is so God won't see your shameful devouring of such a tiny, beautiful creature. The real reason is that by covering your head this way, you can better savour the delicious aroma of the bird as you munch your way through the head and body and feet. Eating this bird requires a lot of mastication. And it's a crunchy, chewy business. For the privilege of this strange feast served by an outlaw master chef you can pay up to 150 euros a bird.

As for Mitterrand, it's said that after this repast he took his cancerous stomach to bed and never ate again.

The hunting of endangered ortolans has been illegal since 1999. Still, it is continuing at such a rate that guerrilla groups of vigilantes from CABS are fighting back, invading cornfields and releasing decoy birds and destroying the traps. This has so enraged illegal bunting hunters that they've insanely threatened to phone the police to report them for trespassing and even waved shotguns in the direction of the CABS defenders.

Reading about this terrible songbird slaughter makes me recall with some shame the exciting hunts of my youth with my father. We had discovered a terrific fly, where we would stand with shotguns and blast pigeons as they flew back and forth between two copses. And then we would return home and have great feasts of pigeon. They were tough yet delicious. I look up at Tuco and think of all his relatives roasted on sticks, and a shiver runs through me as I remember myself belly-swelled, burping at the table, a mound of bones on my plate. Oh, the beautiful bones. Our appetite for the rare or the exotic once led me to check out the night market, Donghuamen, in Beijing, where young Chinese sons of the wealthy impress their girlfriends by eating exotic birds and insects.

I couldn't bring myself to sample the barbecued sparrows on sticks and the deep-fried centipedes of Beijing. Or the stag beetle larvae of Thailand and the deep-fried tarantulas of Phnom Penh in Cambodia. I've turned them all down, yet a certain part of me wants to have known the taste.

I have eaten my share of wild game, as well as exotica, like shark's fin and bird's nest soup before I knew better. In some ways, I regret not sampling the other show-off snacks during the years I didn't know they were endangered, yet I'm glad I passed by these sometimes rare and endangered creatures that are being devoured to pump the egos of young men and wealthy gourmands unconcerned about the plight of the world around them.

There is another point of view in impoverished regions.

As the Egyptian man said to Franzen: "You Americans feel bad about the birds, but you don't feel bad about dropping bombs on someone's homeland." Franzen remarks that he can be horrified at the behaviour of both cultures, and I like that response, but my heart goes out to the poor, hungry people of these regions where tiny birds are desperation food and not a gourmet treat. Living on a subsistence diet on the edge of the Sahara, how many of us would pass on a mist net or limesticks? These are questions we must always understand. It's a peasant tradition (without the mist nets and guns) that goes back to the age of the pharaohs, and probably earlier, yet now must end.

Some birds are more endangered than others, and their destruction is especially monstrous. Golden orioles are regarded as the Egyptian version of Viagra, so naturally, they're popular with the men. Franzen estimated at least five thousand were captured in one location alone. Satisfaction for a lot of raunchy Egyptians.

The other ugly hunt in Egypt, as well as many Middle Eastern nations, is for migrating raptors. A rare saker falcon can sell for $35,000 and a peregrine for $15,000. That's tempting for a poor family. The hunters often sew the eyes shut of smaller, unsaleable hawks so that they are easier to handle and tether them as lures. Fortunately, at the end of the migrating season, the Arabs usually unsew their eyelids so that they can see again and release them back into the wild, as much out of a bizarre kindness as out of practicality, since it would be expensive to feed these hawks during the off-season. They just catch new ones the next year.

The only live creature I've seen sewn up were the iguanas, with their jaws sewn together, being sold for food in a Mexican market. The sellers also break their legs and tie them behind their back so that the big lizards won't scratch or bite the cook. Too bad. These days I'm on the side of the iguanas.

Middle Eastern hawk hunters also use pigeons and turtledoves, tied to a stake and festooned with nooses and traps. Another hawk-hunting technique is to drive slowly around with a hawk tethered to the hood of a truck. If the hawk looks up, the hunters know there is a larger bird high above. They will then stop and leave a trail of tethered or weighted-down lure birds with their traps.

Hunting has become a moral issue today, but what's forgotten is that sometimes it's better to hunt than not hunt. Consider the deer population that is devastating habitat in the U.S. Since the 1950s, according to *Time* magazine, their population has increased 800 percent to 300 million. Deer are responsible for 1.2 million car accidents a year and the deaths of 200 Americans, not counting those suffering or dying from Lyme disease, which is carried in deer ticks. Not only are they dangerous to humans, they're even more dangerous to the environment, contributing to the endangerment of great numbers of rare plants, such as orchids and lilies, some of which, it is claimed, they don't usually eat, but they will in stressful times. Because of their voracious appetites, they are endangering not only several species of plant-specific bumblebees but also migrating songbirds, whose cover and lower nesting shrubs are being devoured.

The fight over culling deer populations is an interesting one. Because we have screwed up the food chain so badly, we have to help correct it, not ruin it, and that's why feeding deer is illegal in Canada. Unfortunately, nature fakers—often known as brown-eyed ecologists or charismatic ecologists—those ecologists who love brown-eyed or cute creatures at the expense of the ecology—appear to believe the Disney green cement of unbalanced forests is a real forest. Sometimes even our love for the Other can make us Other the natural world.

Feed a deer or a raccoon or a coyote or non-migrating Canada goose or one of the other out-of-control but lovely creatures that over-populate our environment, and you might as well pour oil in a creek.

We're all a little stupid.

I only have to remember the stupidity of my wild-pigeon hunting days when we mistakenly assumed they were bountiful. When we moved to our farm twenty-five years ago, there wasn't a pigeon in the local wilderness—though the band-tailed pigeon is not endangered on the continent (lately, surveys are beginning to disagree with this and are considering them vulnerable). I suspect packs of too-enthusiastic hunters like us shot them out of the trees on the coast and diminished their local population extravagantly. This made me sad and guilty. Then, five years after our arrival, I heard a cooing in the high cedars. The next year, I heard a few more. The numbers increased. I was thrilled. It made me feel less guilty about shooting them right out of their feathers in my teen years. Then there were dozens. Recently, they discovered our bird feeder and soon learned that if several landed on it they could fling most of the feed onto the ground, where they preferred eating. This drew a flock of California quail from their hiding place in our shrubby wild quince. It also brought even more Steller's jays, which were now annually massacring our filbert crop. Tuco, meanwhile, ogled the pigeons on the wire outside my office as they waited for their chance to dive-bomb the bird feeder. "What's that?" he shouted, imitating me but adding his own urgent inflection, and they all flew away at the bark of his voice. "Awwww...."

And so the pigeons continued their depredations, but I no longer had the heart to hunt them. Although this many were becoming a pest, it was good to see the population rebounding.

Around this time, an islander imported hundreds of domestic rabbits that had gone feral, with the intent of protecting and sterilizing them. The wildlife authorities noted the fences weren't strong enough and issued a desist order, which didn't make much difference. The islander denied there were any problems with escaped rabbits. However, within a few months, the entire island was mysteriously infested with rabbits. I soon had ten of them in the freezer. But this is where the intricacy of nature impresses me. This invasion of rabbits forced us to erect thousands of dollars' worth of new anti-rabbit fencing at the farm, as almost all our vegetables were destroyed that first summer. It was enough to make us weep.

Then I noticed the growing number of barred owls at night in the surrounding forests, screeching out their territorial disputes. They only screech and growl if they are competing for territory. This means there's a lot of them. We seldom see them. Owls have special feathers that muffle their flight noise, so they are creepily silent on the attack and usually appear only at dusk or in the grey hour of morning. Then waves of larger hawks appeared, and the chickens were soon trembling under the decks or trees by their coop if the peafowl weren't close by to protect them. They were especially frightened when the goshawk dropped by. With good reason. It was faster than my fastest chicken, a gorgeous Egyptian fayoumi, who was so quick I'd ceased worrying about her being killed in the field. The goshawk hit her in the narrow confines of the driveway, before the dogs could even start running to her rescue. I briefly saw the powerful hawk flying away with the corpse of my beautiful bird.

Yet it's good news there are hawks everywhere these days— mostly rabbit hunting—but any inattentive chicken can also be a target, and my unfortunate heritage laying birds have lived carefully for the last year. At least our heritage breeds are so much faster and smarter than the new factory breeds.

This is the second time hawks have taken to the farm, and the results were similar. The first hunting frenzy was instigated by a Cooper's hawk, which usually specializes in small birds. Not only did an entire flock of quail disappear but also a number of those pesky pigeons, most of the Steller's jays, and a few other songbirds we enjoyed hearing or watching, such as the red-winged blackbird.

As of today, with the larger hawks watching our fields, I haven't seen a single rabbit in four months. In semi-natural habitats such as Salt Spring Island, where pesticides are a taboo used only by one or two farmers on the entire island, nature can still protect the chain of life. But we missed the blackbirds and the jays, especially considering the habitat destruction and dangerous migratory gauntlets of today.

NOT ONLY IS the worldwide slaughter of wild birds an ugly phenomenon, the illegal trade in live birds and other animals is almost as monstrous. Italy is notorious not only for its slaughter of birds but also for its smuggling of wild nature, importing $500 million worth of creatures a year for redistribution throughout Europe.

People around the world have traditionally eaten birds (except for a few vegetarian cultures, like the Hindu faith) and caged everything from macaws to tigers.

Next to drug and weapons, smuggling wild animals takes a strong third place. According to a 2005 UN report, it is estimated the worldwide trade in wild creatures is valued at $25 billion annually, and 38 million animals, worth $1 billion, are stolen every year from Brazil's rain forests alone.

Any rich fool can buy a baby giraffe for $22,000, but the bird trade is particularly lucrative, notably when it comes to raptors and parrots. In Europe, where birds are more expensive than in North America, a Lear's macaw was sold for $60,000. Yet the average peasant or finder might make less than $100 for a parrot, slightly more for birds nearing extinction. Small wonder I would have strange dreams about macaws being smuggled while working my way through my research on the smuggling trade. Parrots, as a whole, are more endangered by the pet trade than any other bird species alive today.

Like many caged animals, they can be difficult to keep happy and can even lash out at friends after dozens of years. Almost every parrot keeper I've met wears a scar somewhere.

I HAD BEEN gone several days and I was excited to be home and to see Tuco. I dumped my luggage and burst into our office, and Tuco started bouncing on his perch. I released his cage door and it fell with a crash, and Tuco made one of his gymnastic leaps—from inside to the very tip of the cage door. I stuck my face up close and practically shouted, "How the hell are you?" In my enthusiasm I had stupidly crossed the play boundary again. I was being too aggressive, especially after being away so long, which annoys him.

He punished me with a retaliatory and instinctive bite through my lower lip and then quickly retreated back into his cage. He knew what he'd done. Meanwhile, I was bleeding like a hemophiliac. Again! Not again!

He shuffled guiltily in his cage while I held a napkin to my lip. "Sorry, Tuco. It was my fault."

"Baaaad birrrrd," he said, utterly contrite and now pouting. He didn't want to hurt me; it just happens. This is why parrot fanciers often have small scars on their fingers and face. Mistakes. One wrong move, and we change someone's life. Holding the napkin to my lip, I knew I had to cheer him up, so I started dancing, since he so loves to dance. I did my best one-handed John Travolta salute: "Staying alive! Staying alive!" He soon threw himself into his acrobatic Swan Lake/rock and roll fusion stretches and bobs. Standing on one leg, nodding his head, and unrolling a wing, Cambodian Apsara dancer style. That bird can rock. And he rocked hard because he felt guilty, and that was readily apparent in his movements.

Why can't I learn? Why would I startle him like that again? I've always been at fault. Blood gushing everywhere once more and holding the paper towel to my lip, I go look at myself in the bathroom mirror as I've done so often over the years.

I must have been fifteen years old, and there I was holding a bloodied paper towel to my head, given to me by one of the kindly staff in the cafeteria at the bowling alley when I walked back inside, looking for a bathroom where I could staunch the bleeding.

A few minutes earlier, I had been standing outside the bowling alley with the local toughs, who were actually just suburban teenagers, arguing about where we wanted to go next. I'm sure I was nattering. Then a fist came around from behind, blindsiding me with a haymaker to the eye. The guy's big ugly silver ring gouged my brow. As anyone who's been a fighter knows, the eyebrow and the lips are bleeders, and the ring took out a chunk of my brow. Ever since, if I raise my eyebrows, that one goes into a point. Arched. I can see it now in the mirror as I staunch my bleeding lip.

When you're born weird, if your body's weird, and your mind is weird with all of it, you invite bullying, almost incite bullying. You learn about the bullying of the world. He said something like, "I'm sick of your mouth, Brett." And thinking back, although no one ever deserves to be hit from behind, I know I angered him with my constant nattering contrariness. My "friends" walked away, abandoning me as I tried to rise from the sidewalk, so blinded by blood I couldn't even fight. Worse, this youth was bigger than me and it was a cowardly blow, yet somehow I was the one left with the guilt. That can be the nature of bullying. The injured carry a strange guilt and blood, while the assailant proudly walks away from his coward's hit.

At least Tuco feels guilty about snapping at me. And now the bleeding has stopped, this time.... Still, he demonstrated once again how easy it was to Other him, how I was so full of my own emotions that I startled him, and he reacted.

His swift reaction takes me back to another time—buying Tuco, and all the unfortunate parrots we had seen in our quest for the right one. I thought I had done my research, but it didn't take long with Tuco to realize how over my head I was, and that I was in for a lifetime of work keeping him healthy and happy. The rescue woman who sold Tuco to me thought he was a wild captured bird because of his angry reaction to hands coming straight at him, a reaction he still has, yet lately, I've felt this could easily be a symptom of bad handling at a parrot farm.

Bad handling is why we hear the stories of self-mutilation by captive birds, their screaming, and biting. Instead of helping these birds, their owners apply even more painful punishments. The worst are the dark basements, the spare rooms, the closets. According to Cheryl Meehan, who studied animal welfare at UC, Davis: "What we are now learning is that it's actually very difficult to keep parrots as companions. It's not uncommon to hear about a parrot being put into a corner in a cage with a towel over them for 10 years." That's torture.

International law designates solitary confinement as "cruel, inhuman, or degrading treatment." Yet there are eighty thousand male and female prisoners in the U.S. who are suffering in solitary confinement. One innocent man spent twenty-nine years in solitary confinement before his conviction was overturned. It's better in Canada, though still horrific, according to the B.C. Civil Liberties Association. One in four Canadian prisoners has spent time in solitary confinement. The BCCLA cites studies showing "psychosis, hallucinations, insomnia and confusion." It causes mental illness. This is what our legal system can do to human beings. Now imagine almost 12 million members of the parrot family being raised in the U.S. alone. One can only wonder how many are suffering solitary confinement, as well as being cruelly punished in other ways.

The Othering of domesticated parrots is a grisly business. For a flocking creature, it amplifies the cruelty. That's why we have always moved Tuco around, changed his cages, and watched movies and played cards with him.

That's also why from morning to dark he spends most of his time outside his cage. Barring the very few hissy fits on his part, the door to the office is always open to the rest of the house so that he can interact with what is going down. Everyone in the house soon took to talking to him, even if he is out of sight. He haunts our days, always listening, always fascinated. We are his flock, and he comments on our behaviour at the most surprising moments. In fact, he's usually the one who gives in and calls for quiet in the end. "Time for bed... time for bed...." the cry growing more plaintive the longer he isn't noticed, until finally, I rush up to the office and he scrambles into his cage, and I close his wire door and give him a short good-night conversation: "Good night, good night, don't let the bed bugs bite!" Then I leave the room, shutting the light out, though the door remains open when he is alone.

He can be serious about bedtime. Once, when a young friend of the family was working late, studying his university texts, Tuco, in his front room cage, about four feet behind him and in the study light's glare, grew fed up that his "time for bed" calls were being ignored. Usually, at first, he tries the kitchy-koo variations or calls out with loving, mournful versions. The same as when he's demanding cookies. Then he turns forceful. "TIMMMMMMME FORRRRRR BEEEEHHHD!" If that fails, he turns creepy and starts up his best Boris Karloff scary calls and loud whistles, until someone shuts out the lights and locks up his cage. He always wins in the end. That night he so creeped out Joaquin that for a number of days the lad refused to stay up alone with Tuco.

Not all parrots are as fortunate as Tuco. Although he's technically a rescue bird, his previous owner doted on him. The number of "rescue" birds—only in tougher circumstances—remains high. It's estimated that almost as many birds are being euthanized today as dogs and cats.

Strangely, the Convention on International Trade in Endangered Species (CITES) agreement banning traffic in parrots and other endangered creatures around the world hasn't dented the volume of pet parrots, as vast bird mills, or "parrot farms," grow across North America, producing as many as thirty thousand birds a year, according to one parrot rescuer I know. The smaller, backyard breeding operations are generally run by real bird lovers, and the birds tend to be treated far better than in the big factory farms for pet birds.

Interestingly, many owners of the smaller bird farms are turning them into rescue operations. Their love of the animals overcomes their business instincts, and although some continue to breed to fund their rescue efforts with maltreated birds, others have become charities, scrambling for funds to keep their birds alive.

The size of the big parrot farms is almost designed to raise mad birds (it reminds me of factory chickens), taking them away from their parents, orphaning them for hand feeding to "make them" more human oriented, and delivering waves of neurotic birds into the hands of too many people like me, who know nothing about what they're committing themselves too, which is why I was forced into such a fast learning curve.

It can be relatively easy to discover when you've gone beyond play with a parrot (if you're paying attention). It will usually perform several warning gestures before it leaps for your throat. Parrots can "flash"—a sudden impressive ability to shift eye colour to a bright red if they feel excited or angry. If that's accompanied by some tail fanning, watch out—the bird has gone hostile. They don't all display this behaviour. I think Tuco has flashed me, but I'm not quite sure, because it occurred so quickly.

According to the calculations of the World Parrot Trust, there are approximately 60 million parrots in captivity worldwide, and 6 million in American homes. Whereas the American Veterinary Medical Association found 8.3 million birds in 2012. I've encountered a claim by M.K. Weston, whose study declared there are 12 million, which sounds excessive, though it's a bona fide survey. Bigger numbers, unfortunately, are always regarded as better by those with a cause, which is why I treat them with caution. Readers with similar concerns can find even more complex facts and figures online, but this is a memoir not a treatise. Whatever the numbers, the captive bird population is evidently increasing almost as quickly as the wild population is diminishing.

This has naturally led to overcrowded sanctuaries and rescue stations, which have sprung up since the CITES agreement made the importation of parrots illegal, creating an initial boom in both parrot smuggling and parrot farms. The punishments for smugglers are usually minor, so it's financially more worthwhile than having a kilo of heroin strapped to your belly. Despite the unexpected increase in smuggling and parrot farms, the bans are now having an effect. It's difficult to ascertain the number of rescue sanctuaries, because so many are hidden from the public, due to fears of being robbed. There are more than one hundred recorded public sanctuaries, and there could be five hundred nurturing as many as fifty thousand traumatized birds. Yet again, so many numbers in the mysterious parrot trade are speculative.

Some bird sanctuaries in the U.S. even have armed guards. You can imagine the haul if someone raided a sanctuary with five hundred high-priced birds. A single rare macaw can be worth $10,000 and an African grey $1,000 in the U.S. There are also thousands of small-scale bird enthusiasts who do a little breeding, more for enjoyment than money. These days in England there's been a wave of robberies striking personal aviaries; one burglar targeted a child's collection of budgies. Several chat rooms have appeared, reporting on the trail of thefts and warning bird owners about any clusters of robberies in a region.

Robbery is merely one of the worries of a good sanctuary. To maintain a parrot with an average life-span can cost as much as $36,000. Not all parrots recover from abuse, but a few can, with intensive care. This is where the need for volunteers comes in—finding stalwart people to big brother a parrot back into the flocking, nurturing, companioned world it needs. Sanctuaries and parrot rescuers all have tales of screaming, self-plucking, mate-killing rogues that gradually healed.

The World Parrot Refuge on Vancouver Island is one of the more public parrot refuges, as well as the most controversial around our neighbourhood. Its guardian, Wendy, is an independent thinker and operates it in a way that has horrified a few parrot fanciers I've met. Yet there's much logic in her tactics. For instance, the majority of the birds sheltered there run free. She has enormous chambers for them, and they often fly in mixed flocks of birds that would kill each other in minutes if they were in close quarters. I suspect there are still a few deaths from conflicts. This is one of several strategies that disturb parrot lovers and experts, who always keep the different species separated. Wendy thinks this is unhealthy for flocking birds. Do we know the truth yet about parrots in captivity?

Wendy is a fascinating woman to chat with. She believes parrots have ESP and communicate telepathically. Almost any scientist will tell you this is nuts, and I have my doubts, many doubts, yet I've gone through a lifetime of eerie interactions with birds. Rick Glassey, an animal tamer, tells us he can sense the moods of animals, and the animals sense his. This has to mean they have a theory of mind. Big cat keepers (like Wendy with her birds) often believe their animals can read their mind. Sharon and I have been together for so many years and are so sensitive to our patterns of behaviour that usually our conversations are full of gaps. The conversations would sound incoherent if recorded, yet we know exactly what each other is saying, even when it's not said. Throughout the day, we will make a remark just as the other is thinking the same thing. I believe we've become so sensitive to each other's behaviour that we can read it and act like we are using ESP. Although I'm dubious about ESP, I remain open to being impressed if ESP is ever proved scientifically. I'm sure I've felt it several times in my life and still don't know if it's real. Until it is proved, I prefer to think parrots are smarter than I am in their own parrot way, just as I am smarter than a parrot in my human way—still, they are the real masters of emotional intelligence.

Tuco has often given us the chills, such as on the morning Sharon and I were lying in bed late, listening to a farfetched radio program about testing parrots for ESP (a study whose methodology was later denounced as claptrap by other scientists). So Sharon, laughing, held up a finger and called out to Tuco down the hall in my office: "Tuco, how many fingers?"

There was silence for several seconds; then a clear and defiant bark: "One!"

We lay there flabbergasted. Worse—after that—no matter how many times we tried, he'd never call out a number again. In fact, that's the only time I can ever remember him saying "One."

I asked Wendy how she ended up running a sanctuary with nine hundred birds, especially after our provincial government ceased funding her operation. She told me the banning of the importation of parrots, despite good intentions, has led to new problems. Importing parrots has been banned now in Canada for ten years and for twenty-five years in the U.S. The U.S. State Department says 2 to 5 million birds are illegally trafficked every year. That might be an underestimate. The new laws could be killing even more parrots than before. It's estimated illegal trappers in Mexico yearly ship 65,000 to 75,000 birds within Mexico or to the U.S. Between 60 and 80 percent of these birds die while being smuggled. Various bird organizations believe it's closer to 80 percent. The yellow-headed Amazon population has been reduced by 90 percent since the '70s. Twenty-one percent of African greys, like Tuco, are wild caught, 359,000 from their diminishing habitat between 1994 and 2003. In Cameroon, a real hot spot of African grey smuggling, 1,000 birds were discovered in a single illegal shipment in 2010. Cameroon also allows the legal export of 12,000 threatened African greys a year. There's a terrible video on the Internet of African greys flocking around clay pits. They like eating this clay because it's full of healthy minerals. All of a sudden, large hoop nets fall upon them, and then the smugglers move in and grab the screaming, distraught birds and box them.

Of the 372 species of parrots approximately a third are threatened with extinction. Usually, it's the largest and most attractive, like the Spix's macaw, which is now considered extinct in the wild. The blue-throated and the red-fronted macaw populations are down to about 150 birds. In Europe, before 2005, more than

2 million wild birds a year were being imported. Not just parrots, either—hummingbirds, barn owls, hawks, falcons, eagles, the whole gamut. Along with snakes, turtles, monkeys, crocodiles, and wild cats.

However, Stacy at the Raptor Centre, a rescue organization devoted to hawks, vultures, eagles, and so on, tells me the breeding of birds like parrots and hawks tends to create fewer rogues than thirty years ago, because the breeders, being bird lovers, are better at confirming customers know what they're getting into, and their birds are more socially healthy than wild-caught birds. I'm sure this is true in many cases but obviously not in the bird mills.

As disheartening as it can all become, I take a lot of heart from the many bird rescuers, whether parrot or raptor or stork and crane. And I also know that behind me there is an army of bird defenders—millions of people worldwide. I also love the sheer diversity of bird-helping enterprises. Crowd sourcing and the new citizen-scientists, or "biological sensors," as they've been called by one lab, are tracking birds everywhere, planning for migratory events, scheduling bird-healthy changes for wind generators, and persuading the managers of tall bright buildings to turn off the lights at night. BirdTrack has an arsenal of tools for everything from weather models (to better predict migrations) to microphoned buildings (to warn birds of danger) to radar tracking of large flying birds in flocks entering airplane routes. Ducks Unlimited, a hunters' organization, has proved magnificent at preserving habitat for numerous wetland creatures as well as their beloved duck populations. What began as an offshoot of the Boone and Crockett hunting club turned into the most prominent wetland protector in North America.

Still, bird smuggling remains unchecked. According to the Animal Law Coalition website, birds are transported in containers ranging from "... toothpaste tubes, stockings, hair rollers, and toilet paper tubes to thermoses, glove compartments, hubcaps, false compartments in dog crates, and tire wells. The birds are drugged or given alcohol such as tequila to keep them quiet during the trip. Or their beaks may be taped shut. Sometimes their feathers are pulled out to keep them from flying."

There's almost every kind of parrot in the flyways at Wendy's. Many are mutilated, and I think this is where the real revulsion at Wendy's methods among fellow bird lovers begins. She believes the birds can heal themselves best with a good community and a good pet doctor, and she will not personally authorize any bird to be euthanized, though she will allow her vet to make the decision. She just doesn't have the heart to order it herself. Because she also lets the rogue birds run with the healthier birds, there can be fatal fights. And it's grim to walk into this sanctuary and see mind-sick and stricken birds everywhere. Birds dragging useless wings across the floor, birds so self-picked they leave a trail of blood behind where they walk. Flightless African greys like plucked zombie chickens, aggressively chasing guests across the floor and trying to bite them. It's not for the faint of heart, yet in its own savage way, it makes visitors most aware of our cruelty to birds when they witness these damaged birds in her sanctuary.

When I asked Wendy how the sanctuary started, she told me that two decades earlier, she'd been robbed. Men broke into her house and stole four expensive parrots, and several others were injured in the attack. This might be one of the reasons she preferred to do our interview in the parking lot, even though she makes it clear her World Parrot Refuge is both well guarded and well alarmed. Besides, with nine hundred birds under her wings, there would be such a ruckus if anything happened that not only would the neighbours know, but the police in the nearby station would be right on it.

Eventually, a couple of her parrots were returned but at least one died due to the trauma, and one returned to good health. However, the newspaper coverage of the event attracted a host of callers offering their birds up as replacements. She soon realized this was because they couldn't handle their birds. So she took them in and quickly found herself nearly buried under a tsunami of unwanted birds.

Wendy is one of those natural, independent thinkers who earn their stories—maybe because she's on the periphery of bird management due to her unorthodox approach. Toward the end of our interview she told me the story of her eagle attack. She was walking along with her African grey bouncing along on her shoulder, when suddenly, a bald eagle struck her and snatched hold of the parrot. But this parrot wasn't going lightly, and it latched onto the eagle and her, while still managing to scream like a banshee. Wendy turned and started trying to pull the parrot from the eagle's claws. At this point, everyone was screaming and scratching or biting, including the eagle, which quickly realized it had taken on more than it expected and left Wendy with her shaken parrot and nine talon holes penetrating her skin.

Her grey's ferocious reaction reminded me of that other grey encountering the hawk on the ground and Tuco's ferociousness if someone points at him too closely, yet if I come in sideways, he will leap onto my forearm and then crawl up to my shoulder or sometimes, dubiously, let me scratch his head.

There's something in the minds of parrots, as well as many other birds, that makes them consider themselves heroes despite their size.

It's only when they give up that you realize how frail they are. I once saw a video of a peacock showing off in a zoo enclosure when it was suddenly grabbed from behind by an annoyed bear who began eating the offending peacock. The bird quietly submitted to being devoured alive. It wasn't a pretty sight. Yet peacocks can be amazingly brave and were originally domesticated in places like Sri Lanka due to their reputed (and disputed) fearlessness when facing poisonous snakes like cobras. Peacock feathers found in a Sri Lankan home are considered a curse, because it means peacocks have been stalking a snake in the house. Their Sanskrit name is *mayura:* "killer of snakes." And the *Ayurveda*, the classic text of Vedic medicine, lists several uses of peacock parts as cures for snakebite. Ours have shown astonishing bravery on a number of occasions, such as standing beneath an eagle perched on a branch, honking, daring it to come down and fight. And I saw our peahen, Blanche, jump on the back of an eagle on the ground when it was trying to figure out how to reach some wild ducks. She latched her beak onto his neck and began beating him with her wings, while riding him like a bucking bronco, until he finally threw her, and she harrumphed her way back to her chicks while he lifted off the ground and fled.

One of the joys of my time in Cambodia was wandering around the food and curio stalls in Angkor Thom near Siem Reap and discovering a sign and gate at the back. It was a sanctuary, the Angkor Centre for Conservation of Biodiversity (ACCB), where extremely large birds were walking in the distance. This sanctuary and rescue centre is only open for limited guided tours. A good idea perhaps, since they recently discovered two deadly pit vipers on the grounds and shipped them off to deep wilderness. Tourists are a pain, as they are for most rescue centres, but they are necessary for education and donations. Following a brief guided tour of the centre, they let me wander on my own for a while.

I soon found myself in front of the wise eyes of a young scarlet-headed sarus crane almost as tall as I am—or watching adjutant storks on their nest. The adjutant gets its name from its pretentious, gawky demeanor, which reminded witty birdwatchers of the administrative assistants of senior military officers in India. Some of the birds, who could never be rehabilitated and were kept for breeding, walked stately among the visitors. To stand face to face with a greater adjutant stork is a rare magic in today's world and a reminder that I was facing an imposing creature so damaged it couldn't be wild released, yet there were no sign of wounds. A century ago, this species was common. They used to feed on the partially burnt corpses of Delhi. This horrific habit helped reduce diseases. Vultures, despite being unrelated to storks, have equally strong stomachs, and they can even digest anthrax and render it harmless, along with other virulent pathogens.

Discovering sanctuaries and rescue stations like our secretive, nameless Salt Spring Island parrot sanctuary run by an old friend that I stumbled upon, and other magical sanctuaries, such as Greyhaven in Vancouver, ACCB in Cambodia, and even the disorienting pain of World Parrot Refuge, almost makes me feel good about our species, though I can never forget it is us who made these birds so endangered. Nor can I forget our many tortures of birds.

Those wasteful plates of flamingo tongues. Ducks with their feet nailed to the floor and force-fed. The cruelty of humans, the cruelty I have accidentally dealt out in my own lifetime, the cruelty of all of us, not just the young Egyptians with the hawk whose eyes they've sewn closed. Passenger pigeons shot out of the sky with a cannon just for fun. The corporate farms melting off the beaks of millions of day-old layer chicks for their egg factories. We have such bizarre notions. A medieval rooster burned at the stake during the Inquisition for witchcraft: "the heinous and unnatural crime of laying an egg" that would be hatched by a toad, creating a demonic cockatrice—a two-legged dragon with the head of a rooster. Right. Sure. The priests also prosecuted sparrows for blasphemy, because they were "chattering in church." The list of our foolish sins is endless.

Those that we inflict on others and ourselves ... and these crazy stories of prosecuted roosters and sparrows drag me back to my troubled years in the early sixties, my lonely walking everywhere, hauling that big radio over the log piles on Quadra Island, sometimes thirty feet high on the beaches in those days of wasteful logging, a lonely boy with a rocking heart, wounded like the eagle. "Are you a boy or a girl?" Oh, the terrible question that helped drive me into my loneliness. Yet I didn't know then it would lose its burn over time and become a kind of badge, while the target burned onto my stomach faded away.... And for a moment I am in the sky. I am my eagle and I am me, both of us healed, soaring above the beach, above the gun; then I hear the bang and the snap of my wing, and I'm hurtling back down to the ground again, hitting hard, lying there, until I hear in the fog that old voice: *Get up. Get up and go back and get your books.... Be a man! Yellowbird... Yellowbird... fly down the hill and then up the mountain path.* We're all in Pandora's enormous jar of the world, with the wispy invisible rush of a butterfly of hope fluttering around us. *Fly, Yellowbird, fly.*

Chapter 8

SPEKE, PARROT

"WHAT'S THAT?" a woman's voice said from my office. There was a pause: "It's a parrot!" replied a much higher voice, obviously excited.

I looked in the room as I strode down the hall. Nobody was there except my little devil friend. There usually isn't. This was a conversation Tuco had picked up from last night's epic party, and he liked it.

I've been trying to teach him phrases since we first met, and he continues to look at me as if I'm mad, barely tolerable because I feed and entertain him. In fact, I'm sure he thinks he's merely allowing me around for his entertainment. It's more fun tormenting me than repeating a dumb phrase. Like most African greys, he has a large vocabulary as well as a rudimentary knowledge of grammar. He has spoken, I estimate, close to five hundred words in our years together. Some only once and never again, some repetitively. I'm told you are considered fluent in Chinese if you know three hundred characters. That great intellectual among parrots, Alex, had a larger conceptual grasp of human intellectual requirements than Tuco, yet his researcher claims he only knew one hundred words, but he used those words well. Tuco's five hundred words would be sufficient to consider him fluent, though I don't know if I do. He speaks his own language, and English is merely additional slang for him.

He also utters gibberish, lots of gibberish. He loves gibberish, noises that are almost words yet not quite, like someone faking another language. Maybe with good reason. The French word *"jargon"* derives from their word *"gibber,"* which is said to be a term for the chattering of birds. Yet when I am talking to Tuco, I often wonder if he considers English a form of gibberish, fun to imitate yet otherwise uninteresting.

It can hardly be mentioned enough times in this ramble through the world of friends and Others that the limits of human intelligence, spiked with our arrogance, have caused us to spend a lot of time attempting to explain our superiority to our animal relatives. That gap again. Now philosophers and scientists are finally recovering from the "animals are automata" delusion, which only illustrated that many a brilliant thinker spent too little time in physical contact with animals.

Animals have always been "brute beasts" in the histories of Western thought. In the Eastern universe, the wall between the natural world and human world remained ambiguous or transparent for centuries, and creatures that blended sexes, or even several creatures merged in one body, were not always monsters. In fact, many were beneficial—and tribal cultures worldwide also generally exhibited a similar attitude to their relatives in the animal kingdom as well the universe of plants.

THE GAP CONCEIT, as I've previously noted, is everywhere evident in Western thought. First in the need of Christian fundamentalists to find gaps in evolutionary theory and between the human race and the rest of the planet. "And God said, Let us make man in our image, after our likeness: and let them have dominion over the fish of the sea, and over the fowl of the air, and over the cattle, and over all the earth, and over every creeping thing that creepeth upon the earth." Similarly, scientists have attempted to separate our species from all others—animals don't use tools or have intelligence, empathy, language, and so on. All of these validations were consciously or unconsciously designed to put us atop the tree of life.

The tool wars have ended in the last couple of decades—too much evidence of too many creatures using tools, from ants to elephants. Language and intelligence have become the last crumbling walls between human and animal. Only humans have language. Right.

This is where the brilliant and deliciously hardheaded linguist Noam Chomsky enters the story with a vengeance. He built his claim to fame as a linguist with his impressive theory of a "universal grammar" in humans, a genetic trait that no other animal has, which led to some linguists calling him an Einstein of language and others considering him the leader of an unhealthy cult. This theory also doesn't account for the recently discovered "language gene," F2, which is also evident in animals.

Universal grammar practically made a god out of Chomsky in linguistic science, and he laid down a daring pattern of reasons why our language is different, why it is a real language no animal could duplicate. Couple that with his political writings, and it's no wonder a 2005 poll voted him the "world's top public intellectual." Chomsky insists our language separates us from the animal kingdom. We are naturally born to create languages with grammar, with recursive traits, and this generative grammar is our badge of honour, what makes us superior to animals, and that's the gorilla in the room, the assumption of superiority, rather than difference.

His theory threw down a gauntlet of concepts that are difficult to deny, if one wanted to deny them, until we reach his conclusion that only humans have language. However, this theory tends to define language as human language and fails to account for the supplemental forms of communication animals have outside of grammars. If you define language as human language, it automatically eliminates animal language and can treat it as inferior.

Jules Michelet, a French historian who lived in the era of Darwin, has a more benevolent version of bird language and song: "Winged voices, voices of fire, angel voices, emanations of an intense life far superior to ours, of a fugitive and mobile existence, which inspires the traveler doomed to a well-beaten track with the serenest thoughts and the brightest dreams of liberty!" A quote that makes me remember young swallows learning to fly, their exuberance, their beauty, their reaching for the sky. Their ability to inhabit a close-to-unconscious joy—the joy that our religions promise but only deliver to a few of us.

I'm so on the side of Roland Barthes: "Language is a skin: I rub my language against the other. It is as if I had words instead of fingers, or fingers at the tip of my words. My language trembles with desire."

Over the years, the gauntlet Chomsky threw down has taken a stomping as scientific studies have chipped away at universal grammar, until it's been reduced to its last bulwark—recursive language, which he claims animals don't have. Recursive language is the ability to insert phrases within phrases, which I've caught Tuco doing once in a while, though he prefers stretching out the words if he wants something and embellishing them with various, often screwball adjectives until he gets his way, rather than by inserting other phrases. Chickadees can insert different syllables in a call or create longer strings of symbols as shown in sonograms. By illustrating their notes, that miracle tool of the 1950s, the sonogram, allows us to view them as shifting symbols, often inserted inside other symbols, which sounds close to recursive grammar to me, though without a chickadee dictionary we know not the meaning of these extra syllables and notes.

On the human front, Henry James's novels are an exquisite example of recursive language, with sentences that seem to go on forever. Proust, though he used less recursive language, could still spend thirty pages at the beginning of *Remembrance of Things Past* to evoke the complexities of trying to fall asleep.

I could never imagine an animal creating novels like Proust wrote. Yet I am one of those lost boys who keep wondering what stories animals tell in their own animal languages—like my returning memories of peering over the crossbeam at a baby barn owl in its nest. I'm sure both the owl and I were wondering: "What creature is this?" The gravel against the window, the boy with blue hair; I keep wanting to think outside the past, outside the assumption of a linear world. A world of creation and destruction falling like stardust on all of us, going way back in time from the origin of the universe until now. Of course only humans speak human language, but is that the pinnacle of language or merely one variation on a planet of many languages?

We have to remember that linguists, like most scientists, are incredibly territorial about their theories. The advocacy of a specific theory tends to lead to the Othering of differing theories, sometimes an aggressive Othering. It took decades for American Sign Language to be accepted as a language among linguists (and some still don't). You can imagine their difficulties with accepting the multiple structures of animal language. Myself, I think of this kind of pedantry as similar to claiming a horse can't run because it uses four legs instead of the two we use.

There is hope in this confusion. Phenomenology is the modern science of studying the world without preconceptions, a way of turning the subjective into the objective through reflection. It's had a rocky road, yet it's necessary for finding a new way to break the barrier between the scientific and the intuitive world, the yin and the yang of things. Intuitive and anecdotal evidence need to find their niche alongside statistical evidence.

David Rothenberg, in his inspiring *Why Birds Sing*, quotes Don Kroodsma, a famed and obsessive student of birdsong for forty years: "The whole field is full of people pushing their own pet theories." Rothenberg goes on to say they only "cite the evidence that supports their views and ignore ideas that are too tough to prove." He discusses Wallace Craig, the brilliant (yet now barely known) bird ethologist of the early 1900s who Konrad Lorenz—one of the most respected students of animal behaviour in the twentieth century, the author of the legendary *King Solomon's Ring*—declared was his teacher. Rothenberg tells us "Craig heard music where other scientists heard *units of production* and *packages.*" Craig also noted on the subject of birdsong that "art is a fact," contrary to the scientists who still think it's merely a "release mechanism" for emotions. Yes, release mechanism—think of that the next time you hear one of the reputedly twelve thousand songs of a hermit thrush or an elegant composition by a nightingale, and then remember that nightingales also steal the songs of other nightingales. And how do these release mechanisms differ from "Greensleeves" or "La Vie en Rose"? Release mechanisms filled with both subtle and obvious emotion. European marsh warblers sing wildly complex songs they've stolen from African birds. The red-eyed vireo is claimed to have more than twenty thousand songs. Not only is it an artist, but it's also as obsessive as many artists. Craig considered the wood pee-wee daybreak song the most artistic of all birdsongs. The composer Olivier Messiaen, in his notes for *Quartet for the End of Time,* says: "The birds are the opposite of time. They represent our longing for light for stars, for rainbows, and for jubilant song." And I'm betting these linguists don't consider Beethoven's "Ode to Joy" in the Ninth a glorified release mechanism.

Parrots also have an uncanny ability to know what's important. There's a scene in *Robinson Crusoe* where Poll the parrot shouts out: "Robin, Robin, Robin Crusoe, poor Robin Crusoe, where are you, Robin Crusoe? Where are you? Where have you been?" Crusoe recognizes that is what he had been saying without thinking. The parody makes him realize how pathetic and self-pitying he has become, and he resolves to change his ways.

Noam Chomsky has proven as stubborn and clever in the language wars as in his fascinating conflict with American governmental policies. Still, more and more linguists have come to question universal grammar, especially when Chomsky's no-holds-barred style (and that of his disciples) tends to dismiss most differing opinions as the misguided notions of quacks and charlatans.

On the subject of universal, it's been observed that bird calls at the sight of a hawk are similar, crossing species barriers, so that all understand the predator is here. Now there's a universal language. Then there are the tanagers, whose alarm signal is one of the quickest among birds. The sneaky little devils also occasionally use their alarm call to distract another bird from a choice insect.

Under pressure, Chomsky's definition of universal grammar has grown misty—a shifting cloud that can't quite be nailed down; nor can most of the general scientific methods of proof be applied to it. If we consider that the assumption implicit in universal grammar is that it's perfectly designed to contain our physical and conceptual needs in communication, wouldn't that be the same with animal communications in general? Isn't the whole theory a tautology? Wittgenstein noted: "If a lion could talk, we would not understand him."

Since his theory of universal grammar, Chomsky has also proposed what's called a minimalist program (MP) of language. This is so complex I'm not going far into it, but a rough paraphrase of the theory, one that might give a few linguists heart attacks, is that we have an innate ability and desire to create grammar and, in most speech and writing, stick to the heart of what we want to say and not wander too far outside the rules of grammar. But there's also a pretentiousness inherent in this theory. Here's a Wikipedia quote on the MP: "The MP appeals to the idea that the language ability in humans shows signs of being incorporated under an optimal design with exquisite organization." Say no more. Tell me no more of our superiority.

Yet Tuco's language suits Tuco just as the bee's dance suits the bee. They also have an "exquisite organization" for what they need.

I don't want to argue with someone I admire as much as Chomsky, and besides, that would take us into a boring, complex, science-speak debate uninteresting to all but a few readers. However, it does lead us into the realm of how language works for us and how language also manipulates us. And just what are those birds saying, anyway?

The legendary Sapir-Whorf hypothesis theorizes that every language changes every culture. It was originally denounced, mostly because Edward Sapir's more enthusiastic student Benjamin Whorf tended toward an all-or-nothing approach and used a lot of interesting facts about the Hopi language to illustrate this theory. Unfortunately, his understanding of Hopi was distorted. The Hopi people are a slippery lot. They've learned how to survive almost two centuries of American oppression by keeping their major secrets underground and sacred. Also, as tellers of trickster stories, they have spun more than a few tall tales for gullible linguistic researchers and anthropologists.

Whorf's stiffer interpretation insisted that language is the shaper of thought. However, Whorf's mentor, Edward Sapir, had more moderate and accurate opinions on the influence of language and how it can make us behave in certain ways—sometimes. Eventually linguists split this hypothesis into two, a weak version and a strong version. But it still remains controversial. What's most special is that they never constructed this hypothesis themselves, and knew nothing of it during their lifetimes. It was drawn from their writings and has tended to cause more than a few deranged linguists to attribute facts and suggestions to them that neither made.

Just as a happy song cheers a house and laughter proves healing, so does language motivate us. This makes me think of the happy songs of birds and wonder if they are as truly happy as their songs.

Wilhelm von Humboldt, the brother of the flamboyant naturalist, explorer, and co-founder of the Museum für Naturkunde in the nineteenth century, noted with near-perfect simplicity: "The diversity of languages is not a diversity of signs and sounds but a diversity of views of the world." This applies not only to us but to all animals, and especially to birdsong and communication.

THE POPULAR SCIENCE writer Steven Pinker, originally a Chomsky devotee, considers language no different from any other complex abilities, like echolocation—and that the development of language progressed like the evolution of the eye, a mysterious and changing organ that began from simplistic cellular roots and turned into the complex bee's eye... the protected eye of the shark... the eye of Leonardo da Vinci... and the hawk's eye scanning the field below. Yet evolution, like communication, is not linear, even if its roots are genetic; it's often convergent with different creatures evolving similar abilities in our scattershot world.

As for language being hardwired into us, it's clear that normal children usually begin acquiring grammar and language at two years old—the same age people typically identify as matching a parrot's general speech and behaviour. But normal children do not acquire language if there is no human contact. And if there's no language before puberty, it seems impossible to acquire with any facility after that—as a few "wild childs" have taught us. Our language is our gift to the young, and unless you've learned several languages by puberty, different languages become tougher as you grow older. Yet people who have learned a number of languages when young can keep on inhaling new languages. Language is a strange brew indeed. Teach your children a second language. Like music, it will alter their minds. Parrots apparently have a lifelong ability to acquire words and are not fussy about language.

Other linguists, such as Umberto Eco, go astray in different ways than Chomsky. Eco, a best-selling novelist and semiotician (the linguistic science of signs and our reactions to them), argues that animals are incapable of lying, because they have no concept of symbols. But as anyone who has worked with wildlife or domesticated livestock and pets will tell you, animals constantly lie, some as smoothly as a pool shark in a pool hall. Their tricks can be especially cruel. Coyote packs will send a female coyote in heat into a snowy field, where some dumb male dog will follow her scent, until she goes around a copse of birch and the rest of the pack leaps out and devours the dog. This tactic involves not only the female's deceit but the strategizing of the entire pack.

Symbols and lies and variations on tool use (such as a imitating a phone ringing) are built right into animal stories, as they are in our stories. Tuco, like many of the higher parrots, can construct some mighty farfetched stories, usually at the expense of Sharon or me. Sharon is a classic victim. She's more susceptible to simple tricks, because she's so trusting. Once Tuco figured that out, he would wait until he saw her out the window, gardening in the flower beds. Then he'd do a pitch-perfect rendition of the phone ringing and imitate my voice hollering out the window: "Sharon, it's for you!" She is such an innocent that she'd stand up and rush into the house to pick up the phone. Then, when Tuco heard her entering the house, he'd break into his nefarious laugh: "Har... har... har...," a vocalization I'd often unconsciously do when I pulled a sneaky one on him.

This happened every few months for a couple of years before Sharon learned to double-check by shouting back, "Who is it?" That's a real question, sneakier than it sounds. He couldn't go beyond the next stage. He couldn't think of who'd be calling. All he had to say was Roben, and she'd come running, but he couldn't make that further link.

Although Western history and myths have had their characters who speak with animals, their numbers are not great. Melampus the Greek soothsayer, who conversed with vultures and termites. Orpheus, who charmed the birds. The Pied Piper, who appeared to regard children and rats in the same way. Tiresias. And the saccharine Doctor Dolittle, who learned the languages of animals. Although once we consider ahistoric societies (cultures without written texts), almost every tribal culture has one or more individual who speaks with animals and has animal guides. Often, their oral history is a history of what the animals have given them, or taken away. Us, we spend our time teaching parrots our languages. Talking dogs, bonobos, chimps, and Koko the gorilla—rather than being spirit guides, they're all considered inferior, because they can't fully learn sign language or human grammar, yet we've never figured out a single animal language, or an animal grammar. Despite our arrogance about language skills, we're not smart enough to speak gopher or dolphin. But we might mature yet. A new generation of linguists is growing very close.

Tuco can even take human phrases and apply them as metaphors and thus form impressive mental associations. Take "time for bed," his announcement that he wants his light out so that can sleep. Years ago, we were watching a Western melodrama that climaxed when a crooked police officer was shot at close range with a sawed-off shotgun, and the director opted for the standard slow-motion-gun-death scene in which the sheriff falls endlessly, slowly backward, and the dust rises up around his body as he hits the ground. Tuco, neck extended, studied this scene with interest and then announced with great authority: "Time for bed," forever ruining the dramatic impact of that moment.

Tuco constantly reminds me that each of us, parrot and person, is trapped within our own history, our own stories, going up our own mountain, and sometimes we have to keep returning to the same stories, looking at them in different ways, before we can visualize their complexity, walking the same foggy trail over and over again until we understand the route, and this is what I've found myself doing in this trilogy of memoirs. Over and over again, I "hear" the silence of the shotgun and my finger disappearing in a cornfield under a vast sky of mallards, or my own inarticulate response as I watch myself losing a good friend without any real reason, like the way my thoughts keep returning to my inability to repeat the simple, elegant song of the golden-crowned sparrow. The blessing is there's our special need to revisit the unresolved, to walk the mysterious mountain path without logic or even destination, or maybe to assume the destination is the path itself, to understand the difference between want and have, here and there, the journey and the mountain, myself and the Other.

I have my own ways of communicating with myself and others. Tuco has his. Other creatures have theirs.

A few linguists have even rejected bee dancing as communication, because supposedly there is no feedback; however, if you study the dance and the reaction in the community, there is immense feedback, even if it's not as complex as the dance itself (as it usually is with speaker and listener), possibly because it's more questioning than delivering. Sometimes we use our science to excuse our own inabilities to see, hear, smell, understand. Meanwhile, semiotic theoreticians usually demand that with true language the listener mix her experiences with the transmitted experiences. As if we know what the experiences of a bee are!

The uproar over how bees find their life-sustaining nectar is a great example of scientists not only Othering bees but each other. Even before gorillas learned sign language and parrots learned to count, the question of animal language practically turned into blood sport when a pioneering ethologist, Karl von Frisch, devoted himself to the language of the hive. He spent years studying swarms, painting bees, blinding them, gluing up their scent organs, calmly but scientifically torturing them in a thousand original ways as he dissected the living body of the hive, until his sometimes diabolically clinical research pointed toward the concept of a dancing language.

After a bee finds nectar or pollen, she will return and dance. The dance is like a fever that travels contagiously through the darkness of the combs from one forager to another, each passing along her description of the sun's position, the variety of flowers, their location, and the quantity of nectar and pollen. These directions are so precise they can guide a bee over lakes and hills and valleys and around trees to the food supply, sometimes miles away. Honey has a direction.

This is how Frisch defined one dance—a bee inhales the nectar into her honey stomach and dusts her legs with pollen—then returns. She is met first by guard bees and then by storage bees. This is where the song begins. If the flower is close, the honeybee will perform a simple round dance, calibrated to the direction of the sun. One of her greatest directional tools is her specialized eyesight. As long as there is one tiny hole in the cloud cover, the bee will be able to take a perfect position from the sun and add that to her location memory. Talk about GPS! Above her two compound eyes, she also has three photocell-like eyes that can tell time exactly by the intensity of sunlight.

If the forager makes it back to the landing, she is greeted by the aforementioned self-important guards, who give her a quick smell and frisk. She will often lift her butt in the air and fan her wings, delivering an odour account of herself and her journey, and regurgitate a treat of nectar to an overly aggressive guard. Approved, she enters the dark hive and passes the pollen to a storage bee, who quickly packs it away. Then she regurgitates her nectar into the mouth of another storage bee.

Once the forager has off-loaded, she begins the dance. If the flower is far (more than a hundred yards), instead of the round dance, she will perform what we call the "waggle dance," figure eights define the direction while she's wagging her butt with the appropriate strut. The bees touch antennae, and the feverish dance sweeps through the hive. Decisions are made. The swarm focusses on a single source. Flower constancy gives them the fussiness of poets, deciding they are all postmodernists this week, romantics next week, until they are glutted with the source and move on.

Using the calibrations from her polarizing eyes and internal clock, a honeybee dancing for thirty minutes is so accurate she will adjust her dance several degrees to allow for the movement of the sun. Determining longitude and latitude is an inherited trait. Studies have found similar displays in the stingless bees of South America and the fierce giant honeybee of Asia, the *Apis dorsata.* These enormous honeybees, almost an inch long, prefer living in the high reaches of the tualang tree, where, 250 feet above ground, they are safe from the honey-seeking sun bear. Notoriously aggressive, their immense and open hives, which can be as large as a square yard, have been used by bandits, who gathered swarms and adorned their treasure caves with them.

Today, unfortunately the giant bees are becoming endangered due to deforestation—their legendary honey harvesters, a dying tribe of brave tree climbers. There were many more fifty years ago, and the *Apis dorsata* were responsible for the infamous "yellow rain" that fell on American soldiers in Vietnam, who were convinced the Viet Cong were using chemical warfare on them. It was only bee shit.

The Asian honey harvesters continue to use wood, hide, and bone; no metal tools are allowed to harvest the nectar of a mythological handmaid who was killed by a metal spear, and they refer to themselves as her handmaidens, or *Dayangs,* hanging in the dark of moonless nights, hundreds of feet above ground, where they hammer the hive with a burning torch, creating a shower of sparks, which the enraged and dangerous bees follow to the ground while the chanting *Dayang* carves out huge combs of honey with the scapula of a cow, gathering as much as a thousand pounds from a single tree in their cowhide baskets, which are raised and lowered by helpers on the ground.

The *Apis dorsata* is the only bee that dances in full daylight. A returning forager lands on the sunny side of the long, wide, flat, single-combed hive, where she dances exactly to the vertical if the nectar comes directly from the angle of the sun, or whatever degree to left or right it lies.

Everywhere in the world, the bees dance their poetry of food and life.

This is where our story begins again. Like any story, it is about more stories and how they build upon each other, since we are such story creatures. Frisch's theory about their dancing language was so astounding that after a few initial years of harsh rejection and disbelief, scientists applauded him. The dancing bee hypothesis was too beautiful to reject. It soon merged with the canon of general thought on bee communication. Frisch won the Nobel Prize in 1973. Yet while Frisch was being crowned, a stubborn scientist named Adrian Wenner denied the dance that was now evident to every researcher who looked into hives. Instead, he claimed each foraging bee rediscovered the flower by smell and the dance was only ornament, not a real language. All right, that was a little outlandish, but other studies demonstrated that released smells from the Nasonov gland, and pheromones also provided clues, along with the high-frequency sounds of the wings of a dancing bee.

Wenner burst upon the scene like a young Cassius Clay, "floating like a butterfly, and stinging like a bee." His theory was greeted with such outrage that most scientific publications refused to publish him or a cluster of other "rogue" researchers and supporters, including Patrick Wells. In the years since, Wenner and his colleagues developed more nuanced arguments for their odour hypothesis, despite the virulent reaction of the mainstream scientific community, which acted as if it had just been stung.

Since they were unable to publish much in the journals, Wenner and Wells artfully produced a classic example of lateral thinking by writing a witty book about the dustup itself. *Anatomy of a Controversy*, published in 1990, was greeted with rage and praise, but slowly, many entomologists have begun to find some truth to their arguments, or at least the importance of odour, which Frisch didn't put much emphasis on. Probably the most alarming aspect of this debate is that for years one lively disagreement revolved around a single study based on the behaviour of a mere thirty-seven bees. If nothing else, the controversy exposes the lunacy that can inhabit scientific research. Us and the Other. The dancers versus the smellers.

Also interesting are the accounts by these writers of similar bitter denouncements of other scientists by their peers over the ages—until history eventually proved them correct. A little more than a century ago, the greatest scientists of France scoffed at the notion that burning lights fell randomly out of the sky. These days we call them meteors.

Donald Griffin, the zoologist famous for his echolocation work, began exploring "cognitive ethology" in the 1970s, and the *New York Times* claimed his studies were "the only reason that animal thinking was given consideration at all." Yet he was fiercely criticized for his research and accused of the dreaded anthropomorphism, notably after he had the nerve to suggest "that even insects such as honeybees are conscious."

Darwin, of course, was on side more than a hundred years earlier. In *The Expression of the Emotions in Man and Animals*, he bluntly stated, "… insects express anger, terror, jealousy, and love."

Arthur Schopenhauer has the last word on this issue: "Every truth passes through three stages before it is recognized. In the first it is ridiculed, in the second it is opposed, in the third it is regarded as self-evident."

As with many heated debates, neither side is entirely right in the great bee debate. The truth takes all of them. It always does. The real answer appears to be an amalgam of dance and odours, not only from the nectar itself but of the bee's own making and includes high-frequency sounds of up to 250 cycles per second. They dance, they sing, they rub their wings, they release strange and wondrous scents, they seek random directions and then define them. The concept of universal grammar pales in a number of ways when compared to bee communication.

TERRITORY MARKING IS another form of communication that's supposedly not communication because it's not symbolic. But what about animals that insist on marking other animals' markings? Besides, when a stray dog rushes up to my pant legs and practically snorts them down, inhaling all the magic and creatures and odours of a rural farm, I can recognize it is delirious with imagined and real stories. My pant legs are a novel to most dogs. As I walk down a city street, I often wonder about the epic treatises written on a water hydrant with the language of urine, and how that story is built upon by every dog that encounters it. What metaphors do they tell, what stories do they spin? Is a fire hydrant a dog's equivalent of an Exodus, *The Odyssey*, a *Koran*, or the teachings of Buddha? Maybe not, but I'm still betting some wild stories have splattered on it.

When Bella, our youngest border collie, comes to the door, nose full of strange and maybe dangerous smells, her ears twitching with the odd sounds of the night, she moans and actually tries to talk human, but it sounds like a hilarious fake, groany speech, and you can see her frustration at my ignorance; then the other collie, Jen, rushes up, obviously understands everything, takes a quick sniff of Bella's nose, and they're off together to deal with the threat or promise, trusting even an idiot like me will understand enough to follow.

FOR ME, WHAT'S most interesting about the dispute over Chomsky's universal grammar is the number of careers destroyed, the invective, the hounding of both sides with picayune arguments. The gap is actually a wall itself. Either it's no big deal to a few of us who see more similarities than differences, or it's the Grand Canyon to those who insist our use of commas separates us forever from Tuco. Besides, their careers depend on it.

It's important for some researchers to believe birds and other animals don't use language. We have language and that's what makes the human animal superior, not merely different, even if we can't sing long, nuanced, underwater rhyming songs, sometimes subsonic and constantly changing. Imagine the frustration when the whales encounter us with our harpoons and canons, our mighty technology, our superior airs, and our absolute inability to communicate with them or even to care that we can't communicate with them.

Not only are there communication barriers, but much of the world's music is beyond our hearing range. Sound waves below human hearing are all around us. Even planets moving through space make a sound (thus, the music of the spheres), and every forest has an individual sound emitted by its unique combination of trees, a sound we can't hear, yet it produces a sense of well-being. Our bodies can act like a kind of cello, picking up inaudible vibrations and feeling them. This explains the religious experience people talk about when they're among giant trees in "cathedral" groves. Birds and other creatures are also sensitive to this infrasound.

The conversations continue everywhere. Or as Joseph Conrad once remarked: "To a teacher of languages there comes a time when the world is but a place of many words and man appears a mere talking animal not much more wonderful than a parrot." I would put it slightly different—"as wonderful as a parrot."

Besides, imitation is perhaps the best learning technique. My adolescence was suffused with books, reading, language, reciting, and memorization—"About, about, in reel and rout./The death-fires danced at night;/The water, like a witch's oils,/Burnt green, and blue, and white."—singing out poems to myself in my lonely nights or dancing along creek beds in my teens, chasing frogs, hiding away from the human bullies who shamed me because I wasn't a man, not recognizing I was practising my own bullying, playing with innocent frogs....

I was also imitating the sounds of life around me as if I was unconsciously inhaling their magic. The power of imitation is what makes great songs and singers—open minds that learn from their environment. I wonder how much Tuco learns from his mimicry—is that what gave him his devil sense of the world? Recent research now demonstrates how important that memorization and reciting aloud is to the development of a child's mental skills and emotional harmony. It's the same for birds.

Birds portrayed in books tend to speak portentously and mysteriously. "Nevermore," says Poe's raven-prophet. Then there's the absurd parrot of *Treasure Island* or Crusoe's parrot, Poll, who loves to remind Crusoe that he is alone and thus becomes a symbol of Crusoe's forlorn situation. Perhaps that is why, when Crusoe wanted to prove the power of his gun to the cannibal he's named Friday, he shoots a wild parrot out of the trees and they make soup from it—the deed declaring they are men and not of the parrot world. They ate birds and not each other.

We also tend to kill off parrots in our art. As a kid, I cried for the beautiful duck murdered in *Journey to the Center of the Earth*. When I watched the movie *Wide Sargasso Sea*, my heart cracked as the household-saving parrot, who screamed out a warning that saved the others, was immolated by the house fire while trying to flee.

Other parrots are far luckier. One of my favourite poems is John Skelton's "Speke, Parrot." Skelton considered himself England's first poet laureate, but he was such a rascal that the verdict is still out, four centuries later, as to whether he was actually crowned poet laureate. "Speke, Parrot" is a masterpiece of non-meaning. Mimicking human interaction with parrots, its brilliant non sequiturs almost... almost... almost... achieve meaning, then meander off into oblivion. It's one of England's greatest satires, because it savages his worst enemy at court, the eminent Cardinal Wolsey, yet there's not a line that makes quite enough sense to hang Skelton and his sly imaginary parrot. Wolsey never forgave him, and frankly, Skelton didn't care much. In many ways, his behaviour had all the surprise and wit of a very smart parrot, and I often think of Skelton when Tuco pulls a fast one on me and sits cackling evilly in his cage.

Alex, that American experimental parrot who was the object of thirty years of study, might have had a relatively smaller vocabulary than Tuco, or the parrot N'Kisi, who it's claimed has a 950-word vocabulary, but it's how Alex used those words to solve complex problems outside the normal realm of parrot behaviour that makes him most interesting.

He could tell his companion, Irene Pepperberg, at the time a researcher at the University of Arizona, to "calm down," or declare "I love you," and also name objects and differentiate them. For instance, he could apply the word "yellow" to different yellow objects in a pile of multicoloured objects. His last words were, "You be good. I love you."

Pepperberg says of Alex and the controversy of animal language: "It's as if parrot brains are IBMS and our brains are Macs. They may be organized differently, but the same information comes out." That's not entirely true. The same amount of information doesn't always come out.

That's why his rudimentary colour-coding or counting skills strike me as much less interesting than his ability to build up a bigger picture of behaviour and thus tell the good scientist to "calm down."

It is well known that parrots (and ravens) have their own signature call used in their conversations, a call that other birds within the flock use when communicating with them. Until a 2011 study, nobody recognized that the parents of parrot chicks "name" them in the nest even before they begin talking. The chick will eventually commandeer this name and then perhaps alter it slightly to suit its taste. Also, the parents use names closer to their own than to those of other birds in the flock. I have a feeling naming within a flock is more important than we have assumed, and I wonder if there is a Polly the Eighth out there. Tuco quickly learned everyone's names in our family, including sons and grandchildren, and identifies them loudly when they arrive at the house. And if he gets angry at me, he will often call for Sharon or Roben, because he has a special fondness for them and he wants me to know he's been slighted.

The main issue is that we define language as what *we* use to communicate. Sure, we have our devilish recursive speech, but there is the recurrent issue of speaking parrot. Why are we so incompetent, so language illiterate that we can't learn what we always assume is a parrot's "primitive" language? If it's that primitive, it should be easy to learn. Yet we are only just figuring out that the term "primitive" is loaded with colonialist and cultural assumptions. As the old joke goes, it's déjà vu all over again. These are the roots of the torments that led me to the gravel on the window and "Are you a boy or a girl?' This is the use of language to Other. Our language and our vision of language suit our species. Even my discussing this will be regarded by most linguists as wriggling out of the animal language issue, but the science is changing rapidly as we study the various forms of animal communication with increasing intensity. New and amazing worlds of communication are exploding into our consciousness and changing the paradigm.

SOMETIMES, WHEN I am lying down, resting in the orchard with my bees humming around me, I watch them dip and seek and dream and hang out at the landing pad, and I think about their language and hive intelligence—how difficult it is to measure. Parrots are notorious for their devious corruption of intelligence tests, and there's a developing branch of parrot studies examining this skill and their need to mess up intelligence or language tests. This can only make me smile.

Almost two decades ago, we spent a few weeks in a lonely cabin in Costa Rica. I was reclining in a chair on the deck on the first day, sweating profusely in the heat, eyeballing the absolutely enormous grapefruit, at least half the size of a soccer ball, hanging from the tree over the deck. What I love about the world is how it shape-shifts, and the sadness of our times is the economic need to force everything into an ugly similarity and reject diversity for the safety of the same comfortable shopping mall with the same stores malling the world—the invention of an ersatz normal even when the world contains my gigantic grapefruit, which I was about to eat very soon.

Then I found myself studying the planks of the cabin. It was mahogany. One-inch-by-ten-or-twelve-inch clear boards. This wood, so expensive and precious in Canada, was the cheapest wood my friend, the owner, could mill locally to build his little cabin in his orchid sanctuary. In Canada, a single board from this rough cabin would be worth hundreds of dollars.

Then there was an eerie sound, a birdcall, a rising note, rising, rising. The crazy note going louder, going higher, rising... rising.... It began to grow irritating. Rising. Rising. Sounding like an ecstatic woman copulating with a god. *Ha...! Ha...! Ha...!*

"Get it over with," I wanted to shout. *Ha...! Ha...!* Higher and higher. What the hell kind of bird was this? *Ha...! Ha...!* Then suddenly the single rising note broke, and following a sigh, the call descended with all the relief of a woman having had the hottest sex of the century—*ahahahahaahaa*.... Sharon and I had just heard our first laughing falcon. It reminded me of some of the special effect sounds Tuco makes when he hears lovemaking in another room. Why would a bird develop a call like that? How? I found myself lying back on the deck, smiling and wondering, grapefruit in hand.

The talking of the earth goes on, everywhere. Iguanas converse using push-ups. They flash the bright skin flaps under their chins, bobbing in complex patterns that probably tell stories of hot rocks and love affairs. They perform manoeuvres awkwardly labelled with dumb, cute terms by researchers—the "funky jerk" or the "shudder bob," a courtship dialogue full of walking gymnastics. Sometimes they, like us, sing soliloquies to themselves. They have regional dialects, too. An iguana from Mexico might not entirely follow the conversation of some sweet lizard from Arizona—though they have a syntax and grammar common to each other—so they can probably make out fine. A sagebrush lizard from California can offer 6,864 displays in combination, though generally about 172 are used and 21 gestures are exaggerated, whereas, ahem, in Utah, those straight-pushing lizards make no exaggerations. And that's no joke.

Deconstructionists, semioticians, philosophers, chemical biologists, behavioural biologists, and neuroscientists are working toward a new vision of language after finally surmounting scientific prejudices, and they are advancing rapidly. In the next two or three decades, we are going to encounter remarkable new theories about language and communication from information theorists like Emilia Martins. I'm not sure I fully understand her scientific jargon, and trying to explain it would take several pages, so I'm only presenting a simplified version of her results. Studying sagebrush lizards and their "broadcast displays," she has gradually begun to recognize grammatical rules decreeing how the three main ingredients of displays can be used. Martins uses standardized measures developed by other information theorists. The measure of organization, which Martins calls "maximum entropy," measures possible words and signals. The lizards' push-ups have 6,864 possibilities for combined signals. When it is all calculated, they "give an index of 13." English has an index of 1,908. The honeybee, 25. Another measurement calculated is "evenness of a communication code," a crude method for deciding on efficiency of gestures or sounds. When this measure is applied to human beings, we are a useless 0.01. The chickadee is 0.14, and lizard language an impressive 0.48. That's talking! What I love most about Martins's work is that she uses a robo-lizard to dance courtship displays. This sets the real lizards to dance-talking back.

Consider Tuco, who can use rudimentary grammar and simultaneously mimic sound. African greys are notorious for their ability to mimic and confuse other parrots in the wild and in sanctuaries. Tuco's control of the audio universe is something to hear. For a while, I was worried he had a lung disease because he was always coughing and hacking, and I thought I'd have to take him off-island to a bird doctor. This was during my smoking years. One day I pulled out a cigarette and was about to light it. He started coughing and gagging, and I suddenly realized he was mimicking me smoking. He thought that's what you do when you smoke, and I guess he was right.

He's even better at sounds than words. He's most amusing when I flash him a bottle of wine. This is where he innovates, or maybe unknown to us he had some wild fun with a house sitter, because neither Sharon nor I have behaved like he does when facing a bottle of wine. He will look at the wine, do a pitch-perfect imitation of the sound of the cork popping, and then mimic the sound of the glugging of wine being poured too fast, followed by an exaggerated burp. On second thought, maybe he picked that performance up from Roben's young friends trying to talk him into drinking. It's disturbingly funny. He can also hammer nails like a pro, and when I'm renovating, the noise from two different directions confuses Sharon. He still drips like that leaky water heater, breaks out into cockatiel every once in a while, or parodies the cats.

Recent work on the Caribbean reef squid, *Sepioteuthis sepioidea*, has shown they conduct conversations using colour. They are constantly talking, wooing, celebrating, congregating. Every night, they disperse into the deep Caribbean to hunt and feed; then they return at dawn to shallow "hot spots"—squid clubs—where they party and yak. They have extraordinary control over their colour, using patterns, hues, intensities—as words. They can hold two extended conversations at once. One side of a squid can be busily threatening a male on the left while simultaneously flashing its elaborate courtship conversation to a female on the right. How many guys can do that at a singles bar?

The dialects of killer whales are readily distinguishable. Each pod has a different accent, like iguanas, parrots, sparrows, dolphins, and prairie dogs. Whales keep returning to my thoughts, maybe because of my years fishing at sea with my father, watching them rise giant and mysterious out of the depths. Leviathans of the green world.

When I was young, the killer whales would come upon me fishing and my brother swimming off the rocks of Galiano Island or would make sport with our wooden runabout, swimming alongside it and showing us their teeth or spy hopping beside me, giving me the big eyeball. Or rising up out of the deep, jaws open, just before swerving away from the gunwales. They used to enjoy teasing people. Now it's the other way around, and they are regularly tormented by whale watchers.

The humpback whales are known particularly for their clans and their click and song patterns. A not-unusual vocalization shocked me when I heard the first recordings back in the whale music days of the '60s. Since then, I've swum underwater in both the Mexican and northern Pacific and listened to the humpbacks calling to each other across enormous bays. Blue whales are also masters of long-distance calls. Their 189-decibel-plus utterances, all below our hearing range, can carry across an ocean basin. It's even claimed the great sperm whales, capable of dropping their voices below twenty hertz (our hearing level can detect sounds between twenty and twenty thousand hertz, but those extremes are not usable for conversation), can transmit messages from the Pacific to the Atlantic Oceans, which I find a little questionable. Yet male humpback whales, 2,800 miles apart in the Pacific Ocean, have been recorded singing identical tunes, and if that isn't difficult enough, they'll sing while hanging upside down. According to the musicologist David Rothenberg, whale songs sped up sound like birdsongs and birdsongs slowed down sound like whale songs! The humpbacks all sing the same song, gradually changing it until it's completely different by the next year. They also have a weakness for cultural revolutions, such as the time two humpbacks from the Indian Ocean showed up in the Pacific, and within two years, all the Pacific males were singing the new tune of the strangers. One waggish researcher commented on the vocalizations of the sperm whale: "Maybe the great white whale *was* smarter than Ahab."

However, these days, we have to assume these mysterious song-stories are fading into the pervasive racket of human machines thundering through the oceans, as well as the sonar blasts that damage the ears of whales, probably killing more than a few (there's a quantity of evidence of this according to a 2009 article in *Scientific American)*, or causing them to beach themselves to escape our warships and sonic ear-destroying electronic warfare games.

I've witnessed entire pods of killer whales being harassed by whale-watching companies with their big, roaring Zodiacs. To bypass the government-regulated distance boundaries now in place, some GPS the whales, roar out there, and park in front of their path, with motors off or running low. Then, when the whales pass through them and swim the legal distance away, the whale stalkers rev up their screaming motors and repeat this procedure. All this follows exactly to the letter current whale-watching regulations. There are usually several boats doing this all day, every day.

Elephants can also use low frequencies to speak from valley to valley and will cock their ears toward the ground so that it's easier to pick up the low rumble transmitted along the surface of the earth for as many as two miles. Asian elephants can speak as low as twenty-four hertz, and African elephants can be as loud as 117 decibels, with a range all the way down to thirty-five hertz, so low they'd be detectable to those among us with good hearing, but, as with whales, we'd be unlikely to know it was elephants talking, let alone understand what they are saying. They can also use their highly sensitive trunks and the pads of their feet as amplifiers to better hear what's being said, which is perhaps why they will listen with one foot lifted and the trunk resting partially on the ground, triangulating the sound. A mock or real charge can be heard from up to twenty miles away and vocalizations and calls up to ten miles. Nonetheless, their many vocalizations are so complex they are gibberish to us.

Then there's the knife fish, *Apteronotus leptorhynchus*. A small nondescript green fish, it uses bursts of electricity not only as sonar but also to communicate with other knife fish. This fish is its own Internet.

Prairie dogs allegedly have different words for different human beings, hawks, and coyotes. One of them is: "He's got a gun!" Ravens also have a call for that. Prairie dogs vary the numbers of a call to define the strength of the threat, and use different speeds of the same calls to further refine the discussion. This is a grammar of warning, among other things, and includes adjectives for colours and sizes as well as verb-like segments for how the predator is walking or running, whether someone has a gun or merely fired a gun earlier. Not only do they use sounds at different speeds, they also often speak faster than we can discern, meaning they can speak or think at different speeds than we can, slower or faster. This was only discovered when a clever researcher started playing with different recording speeds of prairie dog conversations.

This is just part of the flood of discoveries on animal conversations and intelligence during the last few decades. It is science at its finest.

I've heard ravens use their version of "he's got a gun" after they killed one chicken too many at my farm. They disappear fast if they see me haul out the hardware, since they've already learned from other, more aggressive farmers what rifles can accomplish. I just have to flash a shotgun at them and they disappear for days. But I only use that technique in dire emergency, because I don't want them to become accustomed to me with a gun and grow casual about it. Sometimes I can warn off an aggressive chicken-killing raven by merely pointing a finger at it and shouting a sharp BANG. They know what I mean. I've been told a certain staccato call by a crow signifies an approaching hawk or eagle, and that it's higher pitched than their call for a raccoon or cat.

Birds, like the prairie dogs, can separate sounds better than we can, and they allegedly think ten times faster than us when they hear a sound. Think of a movie for a visual equivalent. The birds can see each frame rather than seeing only the moving picture that we see. That's why they can hear more in a short song and don't need excessive length. A sped-up time sense makes what seems like a few notes to us a full aria for a bird.

Not only do Amazonian parrots have unique dialects, but those living on the borders of different ranges can speak in both dialects. It all depends on what side of the river you are on. Bilingual parrots? Sure. Like the bilingual lizards. The contact calls of the yellow-naped Amazon convey both individual information and "tribal" information as they gather in roosts every night. In a few locations there are three dialects, and most of the parrots are at least bilingual. These birds also show gene flow between the dialects; this means the dialects are learned and not inherited via the genes. We use the term "parrot" to signify that Tuco and his relatives are mere copyists and not original, even though they are all very original birds when it comes to adding to a language, even eventually distorting it as Tuco does with his variations on "cookie" and "time for bed."

What I love is the variety of communication in the world. Every species has its own tools, whether it's the homely croak of the crow or the pip-pip cheeky nagging of the hummingbird. What they lack in voice, the hummingbirds make up for with chutzpah and feathers, arranging their tail feathers in a pattern which makes that special chip-chip little bark as they dive, though even the tiny high-speed hummingbird can't match the notorious noisemaker, the club-winged manakin of Ecuador, which can flap its wings at 100 times a second, twice the speed of the near-invisible wings of the hummingbird. As the manakin shakes out its mating call at this speed, two specialized raker feathers rub "like a spoon across a washtub" and create a violin-like sound that vibrates at a high frequency of 1,400 cycles a second. The wings are moving so fast they appear to be standing still. Now there's a musician, even if it is a one-note wonder. Whatever. It works for the ladies.

According to the book *Chasing Doctor Dolittle*: "Animals can produce signals in the form of every sensory modality that we know of—sight, sound, smell, touch, taste—and even some that we as humans don't use such as electrical current, underground vibrations, and sounds produced above or below our range of hearing."

I HAVE THE reputation of being a great storyteller, according to some people. The truth is I am a lousy talker. I've heard tapes and watched films of myself, and I find them embarrassing. Yet I communicate easily. I suspect I caught a lot of it from my father's Cockney gift for language and my mother's enthusiastically Italian ancestors. I grew up on the road, selling potato dreams to people who didn't know they were hungry. When I stand back and analyze my stories, I realize that I, like most of us, use more than words. It's not the stories at all but my inherited unconscious manipulation of the space between people, eye gestures, hand movements, timing—the weighing of emotions among creatures in an enclosed space. I probably change smells when I am talking. These are all the ingredients of a good bullshitter. Yet I am close to inarticulate by linguistic standards; instead, I'd like to think I talk like the bee talks.

Great, invisible stories are being written around us, every day. The language of the world is full of ineffable secrets and mysteries.

The most amazing aspect of the new research is the recognition of the enormous range of communication skills out there. Communication is rich everywhere, not just with birds and animals and insects—from cell to cell, from plant to plant, even through entire forests. For instance, it is now known that stands of birch can be regarded as a single plant, communicating—via their intertwined root systems and fungi—stories of threats or changes in growing conditions. Pine trees invaded by the pine beetle will release chemicals alerting other pines they are under attack.

Communication is world-permeating. It's everywhere and constant. Kangaroo rats stamp their feet, performing a syncopated toe tapping to communicate. They can drum for territory, in mating songs, or to intimidate snakes. It's their own multi-faceted Morse code.

Different birds use plumage displays to "assess and assert" dominance or, like the sunbittern, mimic a bigger predator to scare away hawks. The quail warning system is almost militaristic, the males perch on fence posts and in prominent locations where they can supervise the flock and keep an eye out for predators. Standing sentry is also a dangerous profession. A few years back, I was watching one perched on a fence post, standing proud; then it disappeared, gone, snatched by a hawk. And that's how fast you can lose your life.

Consider all this another way. Natural selection spent millions of years inventing hundreds, most likely thousands, of variations on wings. Every wing evolved into a different purpose, just as every language evolved to suit its environment and purpose. What beautiful diversity. Wings and gestures and sounds.

We usually consider birdsong beautiful, but I've known some bird sound horrors. There's not much worse than sleeping during the spring peafowl breeding season and having Yeats, the mighty peacock, shout out his 4 AM warning call on the deck rail a few feet from our bed. It's enough to lift us right off the mattress and for me to rush out and chase him into flight to his normal roost in the big maple, while stepping barefooted on a wad of the particularly noxious peafowl shit he's left on the deck. The warning cry of the peacock sounds like a woman being attacked and shouting, "Help!" at the top of her lungs. It's scary indeed. Even scarier than his turds.

Almost as scary, though in a different way, is Tuco's uneven taste in music. He's a pretty legendary singer, as I've mentioned. Comic, often right off the musical rails, and also, equally often, spot on. I've never understood what it is that sets him free. A rhythm, a pitch. Certain notes or refrains. Who knows?

Occasionally I play him local birdsongs from a CD. Some he loves; some make him bristle, so I don't do it often, though he generally enjoys chirping along with them. I love the days he picks up a

song from outside the window and then repeats it in his often gar-
bled parrot way, not caring if he mangles the song. It's his now, after
all. Listening to him, I remember my glistening and glorious winter days when my legs were strong and the crumbling joints were
decades ahead, skiing cross-country in the alpine snow of the Sierra
range, singing out to the ravens and them singing back, doing as I
often do with Tuco, mimicking what might be words. The ravens,
those black angels drifting from alpine fir to alpine fir, shouting out
their replies and leading me down the lonely mountain of birds and
a man and snow and trees in the fog of winter.

Music is the true realm of birds, especially the ones, unlike Tuco,
who can truly sing. That's why we praise someone for singing like
a nightingale yet seldom compare birds to specific human singers.
Although a few singers have been linked with birds, like Edith Piaf,
the little sparrow. Humans only use 2 percent of their air intake to
sing, whereas birds can use almost 100 percent.

From my window, I can hear a number of terrific sparrows that
make me think of Piaf, especially the golden-crowned sparrow,
whose short call is sweet and melancholy, and it always snaps me to
attention, no matter how many times I hear it repeated.

Mozart had a starling for a pet. These birds have a notorious
capacity for song and mimicry. They actually pass sounds along
from generation to generation. Naturally, evolution and sexual
selection being what they are, the female prefers the male that sings
longer, more convoluted songs.

In a notebook for his Piano Concerto in G Major, Mozart shows
how his starling revised a passage from the last movement, turning the sharps into flats. Mozart was impressed, and he wrote the
starling's version down as well, declaring, *"Das war schön"* (that was
beautiful). He would have noted that starlings "throw out a sound
to see what happens." The animal behaviour researchers Meredith
West and Andrew King named this social sonar. And according to
David Rothenberg, like Tuco, they would use not only human words
but also "squeaking doors, clanking dishes, barking dogs, smacking

lips and human gulps." Tuco loves squeaking doors, and whenever he sees me shut a door, he adds the squeak, even if the door doesn't.

Mozart's starling died, as all starlings must, and Mozart held a funeral for it, complete with a graveside ceremony, hymns, and a poem he'd written for the lost songster. About eight days later, he wrote his famous *A Musical Joke,* a send-up of pretentious classical music, and many of its tricks are starling-style tricks, abrupt endings, off-key repetitions of passages, tunes mingled together, and so on.

Starlings—like throat-singing Tibetan monks, Inuit, and Tuvan of Mongolia—and several varieties of thrush can all sing two-part music. The thrush and the starling have split syrinxes so that they can sing two different phrases simultaneously. It's a lot more difficult for people.

Luis Baptista, the late ornithologist, suggests Beethoven also stole a tune—from the European blackbird—for the lilting opener to a rondo in his Violin Concerto in D Major. The blackbirds pass along their songs, as do starlings and a number of other songbirds, and it's likely one was singing this little tune when Beethoven was composing his concerto. Baptista was also much loved for whistling marvellous variations on the dialects of the white-crowned sparrow.

Then again, it's claimed the white-breasted wood wren makes a call that matches the legendary opening of Beethoven's Fifth Symphony, so maybe he was at his window in his childhood more than we know, taking music lessons from the birds in the trees outside. Unfortunately, this kind of fantasy attribution can be dangerous. Despite the similarity, the white-breasted wood wren only sings his tune in Central America. Nor, to my ear, does it sound anything like the opening of the Fifth. Another lesson in suspecting my sources on this foggy mountain trail through my purgatory of research.

Although nightingales and thrushes might have more skills than us because their bodies are more built for song, we do a mighty good job with the tools we have; plus, we can use tools and instruments to make song. There isn't any bird that can match Beethoven's Ninth Symphony for structure. Our music, and our ability to also write and record it, gives us further opportunities, almost as many as our written language. Music is one of our greatest heritages. Millions of years were needed to create the amazing songs of the thrushes. It took *Homo sapiens* merely a couple hundred thousand years to create a Bob Marley, a Mozart, a Ninth Symphony. Hopefully, there will be many more, and there will, if we have the courage and smarts to change our dangerous course away from the evolutionary dead end we are rushing toward.

NEUROBIOLOGIST ERICH JARVIS has devoted his studies to the brain structures in parrots, hummingbirds, songbirds, and humans. He makes some interesting comments: "I believe that the difference, really, between humans and songbirds, besides the general brain organization of mammals and birds is that humans have more of what the birds have." And I don't know if even that is correct. How are we better singers than the hermit thrush with those legendary twelve thousand songs, which, although they last generally less than two seconds, can use from forty-five to a hundred notes with fifty pitch changes—issuing from both sides of its syrinx at the same time? Those fabulous yet minute muscles control both the air volume and its position in the bird's throat and beak. That's a lot of voice no human singer can match. And of course, the recent studies in brain structure illustrates that our brains and bird brains are a lot more divergent than we originally thought.

Jarvis's studies show that 70 to 80 percent of genes in a songbird brain have a counterpart in humans and other mammals (what I'd like to know is what those other 20 to 30 percent of genes are doing.). According to Jarvis, "... we humans need to think of ourselves not as inherently supreme ruling creatures on this planet but as privileged members of an elegant web of evolution." Privileged in some ways, deprived in others. Remember the jigsaw puzzle, where there is no "best part."

Language is a question of not only how we define it but also who defines it. New lateral thinkers are moving the goal posts again, rapidly.

Like most writers, I'm a recluse, even though I tend to be hyperactive when I'm out in the world. I've always been private. I like to lock my door. If I'm writing a poem, I will speak it aloud, over and over to myself, until I feel I have found the best words and rhythm. Weirdly, I will often be typing silently, almost grimly, and Tuco will start making remarks or noises that seem to tie in with what I'm writing. It's creepy. The ESP issue again. Then when I find myself stuck, or needing distraction, I talk—me and Tuco. And he whistles and I whistle, and I cluck and kack and click and moan, and he does the same for me, until we build to a crescendo of important but non-linear noise where everything means everything and not much at all, like "Speke, Parrot" or the great "Louie Louie," one of the raunchiest songs written—though its lyrics are a bottomless well of not-quite-meaning-anything. Still, I've heard live versions that can make the gibberish sound so lewd it has had me nearly rolling with laughter. The FBI investigated the song for obscenity for thirty-one months and found itself "unable to interpret any of the wording in the record." Sometimes this is similar to talking with Tuco. What's fascinating when I improvise with Tuco is that every tune I improvise, he echoes, improvising upon my improvisations more with each volley, until he reaches his limit, becomes bored, and shuts up, staring at me like I'm the fool we both know I am.

We make our little operas that will go nowhere and never be recorded, and we are satisfied with them. Sometimes our noise competitions remind me of the famous duelling banjos in *Deliverance*, only they leave me wondering which one of us is the inbred banjo-playing kid of the film. In so many ways, I'm weaker in his realm than he is in mine. Over twenty-five years, we have drifted away from me teaching him English. It took a long time to understand he's been patiently teaching me how to speak parrot.

Chapter 9

KNOW THAT BIRD

ORTY-FIVE YEARS AGO, I was sitting in the backseat of a logger's crummy, slamming over the potholes speckling a rough logging road as we approached our worksite in Haida Gwaii. Bunkhouse living was still common then. I was dozing as best I could before another day when I would walk the cathedral woods, among the standing and the fallen. I had been receiving testosterone therapy for four years by then, and I was beginning to grow not only hair but also height and weight. I was also beginning to present as male. The bullies and rapists were fading out of my life.

Working as a cat swamper and driver during those few years was what turned me into an environmentalist. When they cut down the last of the giant airplane spruce (Sitkas) in the Yakoun River bottom or alongside Phantom Creek, I encountered fallen treasures so big, so heavy that even the mighty steel spars couldn't pull them, and we had to go back and drill these monoliths and stuff forcite into the drill holes and detonate them, destroying most of this magnificent clear wood so that maybe 40 percent of the undamaged tree could be hauled out. It was the destruction of those trees that drove me away from the logging industry. I quit the camp soon afterward.

It was in the fossil bed at Phantom Creek that I encountered the biggest of the Sitka spruces—three felled trees. I laid my six-foot length across their stumps three times and didn't reach the end. That made them at least eighteen feet wide. It was the most tragic graveyard I've ever visited.

For me, these were tree-gods. According to Roman mythology, beautiful forest nymphs lived inside every great tree, and when that was cut down, they died. For the company, these trees were product. That's the way the corporate world Others the rest of the world. It rebrands it. That's why we are no longer referred to as citizens but consumers of government services. Names do hurt.

That morning, I was just bouncing around with the rest of the crew when the ravens appeared. We called them the twenty-two-mile ravens, because they lived at the twenty-second mile marker from camp, and they would raid our trucks as we drove by. We were easy to raid, because every hungry logger always, wastefully, packed extra food—or not so wastefully, because we knew the twenty-two-mile ravens were there. We'd stick an arm out the window and wave the cheese slices, ham slices, oranges, and pieces of pie wrapped in plastic, and the birds would fly alongside, choosing the best snack from among the eight-armed hydra of hands. We were a buffet of hands. They'd snatch our treats without touching us, even at thirty miles per hour, and then stash them and return for more. We'd be cleaned out within a couple of miles along this straight bumpy stretch.

One day, a chokerman had already eaten his chocolate bar, so he folded the wrapper back together and stuck it out for a laugh. A raven snatched it, and there was a loud caw as it fell back, realizing it had been tricked with an empty package. When it started catching up with us, one of the other loggers gave the chokerman a cookie. He stuck it out, but the raven recognized the offending shirt and arm and seized his thumb, delivering a strong bite on the fly, making him drop the cookie. Then the raven dived to the road and ate the cookie pieces.

These clever ravens brought out the devil in us, and to my shame, one day, while a passenger in my cat skinner's pickup, returning after an exhausting shift of hauling steel mainline cable, I realized I only had a bag of three heavy apples. Unconsciously, as the ravens approached, I stuck it out the window. I hate myself for not pulling my hand back, yet I still smile at the memory. A raven grabbed the heavy bag and dropped like a stone. For a moment, I could see him in my side mirror with chunks of apples and feathers flying. Oh, the guilt! It was also hilarious, a scene out of a roadrunner cartoon. Fortunately, the next day, both ravens were back, none the worse for wear, and no doubt glutted with apples. I must have been forgiven the apple treasure horde, though the one flying alongside my window, I swear, gave me the evil eye before accepting a slice of baloney.

The poor bird didn't realize I was going to make it up to him in the worst way. He saw I had more baloney, so he kept flying alongside. I handed him a second slice, which he took dexterously at our usual speed of between twenty and thirty miles per hour. Then a third. There was still a devil in me in those days. A puckish sense of revenge on the world that arose at the strangest moment. Although I didn't want to hurt anything, I could never resist surprises and tricks. Nothing went in a straight line in my mind—then and now. He was working hard to keep up, and his mouth was stuffed. I had him. Ravens are greedy birds, and they'll never refuse that fourth slice, though they only have a three-slice mouth. He took it and the bottom one fell to the gravel as he kept lugging alongside the truck. My driver was dying of laughter and having trouble keeping the truck straight on the bumpy road.

I could tell the raven was silently cursing me, though it was difficult to complain with a mouth full of baloney, so I gave him another slice. Then another. Each time he took one, he lost one. I didn't feel too guilty about this act of chicanery, because I knew he would eventually return and collect his booty when I ran out of baloney, which I saw him do in the mirror as we drove away.

As with parrots, the greed of ravens is notorious, and I could never resist taking advantage of it when I had the opportunity, mostly because they and their smaller relatives, crows, have done me bad with their tricks on more than one occasion. Another day, I was "babysitting" a shovel operator on a solitary task. No worker in our camp was allowed to work alone in the woods, so somebody always lucked into the lazy job of hanging around in case of an emergency. I took advantage of my good fortune to sleep in the pickup, until I was woken by the thump of a raven landing on the hood. It was one of the twenty-two-mile ravens whose home territory wasn't far from our site. It was after lunch and there was nothing left in the truck, only my thermos and a huge apple. I took the apple and opened the door, while the raven flew a short distance away. Then I placed the apple on the hood and climbed back inside. The raven soon flew up, pierced the apple and then tried to wing it away, but it fell to the ground with a clunk. You'd think he would have learned from the last episode with the bagful of apples. However, this bird was no slouch. It circled the apple on the ground, eyeing it balefully; then it walked up and pecked a neat line down one side, turned the apple over, and did the same on the other side. The apple fell into two nearly equal pieces. The raven picked up a piece and winged away. Within minutes it returned, snatched the remaining piece, and flew off with it.

Although ravens might be intelligent, they also can make some extraordinarily dumb moves. After all, West Coast Native mythology depicts Raven forever getting himself in trouble. Reading Raven stories reminds me of some of the trouble my friends and I have gotten ourselves into. Consider the world around us. Even our greatest geniuses can walk into lampposts. All of our switches are not always working. When I looked up "intelligence" in Oxford online, it defined it as: "The ability to acquire and apply knowledge and skills." That sounds good. One of the joys of intelligence is also the way it surfaces, oddly, beautifully, magically—a mighty leap across a cavern in the mind that leaves onlookers breathless. "How did you get there?" I'd find myself saying to someone.

Tuco is on my shoulder again, dancing, awaiting the chance to snatch another toothpick out of my mouth, but I'm being watchful, mostly because there's already a small clutter of broken toothpicks in my lap. Ever since I quit smoking fifteen years ago, toothpicks have been my writing crutch. The cost of toothpicks is nothing compared to cigarettes, both in money and lung power. Besides, I'm glad I no longer have to worry about Tuco snatching lit cigarettes out of my mouth or flying past the overfilled ashtray and covering my keyboard and me in ashes. He knows me well and waits for me to become distracted by what's on the screen, and then moves in with his astonishing speed to make the snatch. That speed, however, can have its drawbacks. Once, when he was being impossible, I rolled up the usual newspaper and pretended to cross-swat him, only he leaped instead of ducking and took it full on, to my horror, and tumbled to the floor. It's so easy to forget how fragile he is, and although he might enjoy rough play, it's not a good idea. But he was quickly on his feet and ready for battle. I gave him the newspaper as a peace offering, and he triumphantly shredded it in seconds.

Tuco has remained enamoured of my computer screen through the years. He loves watching me type and the screen changing or my mouse arrow sliding from window to window. It's all flash and fireworks to him, like watching the fluttering movement of his tribe through the trees or a wasp flying past his perch. Sometimes he talks along. "Yup... hmhmm... uh... no... yup... hmhhh... hmm uh... okay...," parodying me talking on the phone again as he watches the computer. Electronics—computers, phones, music, televisions, and telephones—are all linked in his mind for various reasons I don't understand. He's a curious bird, and I imagine it is the curious birds that survive longest in the jungle.

A few years back, I was working on an essay, typing fast because my deadline was approaching. Tuco's head was bobbing in rhythm to the changing screen and the echoing muscle movements caused by my high-speed typing. Then he leaned forward, peered around at my face, and said: "Whaddya know?" This stopped my typing, and I stared at him on my shoulder.

"So where did you get that from?"

"Whaddya know?"

"Not much. What do you know?"

"Not much!" He cackled and lifted a foot and started doing his stomp dance, knowing somehow that he had gotten me thinking again, though I'm sure he had no idea what the stunt was. Why does he use that phrase when I'm at the computer screen? It may signify lots but more likely signifies nothing. His memory and thoughts don't operate like mine. My mind is rough enough, so it's hard to judge his. I'm constantly inside a non-linear haunted brew of images and questions returning, a go-cart named Yellowbird, a desperate molester with a knife in a car on the freeway I was hitch-hiking, a cornfield with an utterly blue sky and my shattered finger gushing blood—these whirling memories, this whirl of my history, all history, history constantly reforming and remaking itself, as I've noticed with so many of my friends growing older and rewriting their past each time they tell the same-only-different stories, stories growing less painful, often more heroic. Each of us believes our own rewriting of our histories, which is why we can get into so much trouble. I often find myself realizing I've got a memory wrong in that whirl of my mind. It's especially irritating when I discover a mistake in a published book, so I find myself constantly seeking backup interpretations of incidents.

What does Tuco know?

What do I know? I know the one thing that's driven me up the mountain path ever since I was born. Hope, or *Elpis*, as it was called thousands of years ago, trembling in Pandora's forbidden jar. Hope is what drives our world, our inventions, and our lives. It fuels our intelligence, but what even is intelligence? And why does our species need to deny that parrots are intelligent? They're so clearly intelligent, though it is equally clear they don't possess our kind of intelligence. The same question over and over again, endless questions like a bell always ringing. There are as many neurons in our brain as there are stars in the Milky Way. You'd think we could fire a few more of them up. We might have to if we are going to survive this century.

"What's that?" asks Tuco, and I have no idea. I don't know if he knows, or cares either. There hasn't even been a loud crash downstairs. And I can't resist parodying the phrase, Tuco style, as I wander through my days: "What's that!" This still gets me into trouble because it's so imperial sounding, and sometimes Sharon misses the irony, which puts me in the doghouse again.

There is much evidence for parrot intelligence. I have seen so many intelligent actions performed by Tuco that I don't doubt his intelligence. But I'm not smart enough to understand the nature of his intelligence. Instead, I have to engage in the joy of it, the joy in all animal intelligence—a wolf mother teaching her cub to fish, the cats disciplining each other, our border collies analyzing the geometries of loose chickens as they round them up and guide the reluctant flock to the coop.

One of Tuco's favourite tricks is to take a chicken bone, after he's sucked out the marrow, and use it for his private parrot Olympics. He likes to use his beak to climb the chain from his cage to the ceiling and the hook for the chain holding everything up. Only he immediately discovered he couldn't hook his beak in the chain while holding a big bone—though I've seen him climb using his beak with a micro-thin, delicate cracker in it, never breaking the cracker. He soon learned that when he transferred it to a foot, he still couldn't climb with merely his beak and one foot, so he had to pass it from foot to beak to the other foot for every few inches gained. His ascent is so complex it's impossible to describe clearly without confusing the reader. He resembles a mountain climber belaying his way up a steep face. Then he'll briefly transfer the bone to his beak and bring the remaining foot up. This is the tricky part of the campaign, and if he loses his balance in passing the bone, he suddenly finds himself hanging upside down by his feet from the chain with the bone in his beak, costing him his entire body length in the climb. It's practically back to the beginning, and there's lots of growling and hissing, even with the bone in his beak. It's especially injurious when I notice a fall and start laughing at him as he hangs upside down from the chain, clinging to his chicken bone.

The end result is that this short, thirty-inch climb is an epic task. Sometimes it takes him close to an hour to scale his little mountain. On the occasions when he doesn't give up and reaches the ceiling, his triumphant head bobbing illustrates his pride at accomplishing his task. And just to make sure I know about his accomplishment, he'll take the bone in his foot and rap it victoriously on the ceiling, reminding me of the apes' bone victory dance in the film *2001*.

To keep himself amused when he can't lure any attention from us or the household animals, over the years he's developed several more games too complex to narrate. And I make sure I keep adding to and changing his toys, so his cage has become a kitsch junk box of add-ons, with locks and chains, get-the-almond-out-of-the multiple-boxes, etcetera, all bolted on, which provides more opportunity for his regular bolt unscrewing and loud crashes every few days.

We've learned to tolerate his impressive interruptions of movies with his rude comments or popcorn-tossing sneak attacks on the dogs and cats. We, along with our guests, are his toys, and though I'm somewhat immunized, I often find myself dragged into playing spitball hockey with him while he demonstrates his pyrotechnical goal-tending skills. Or he takes pleasure in annoying me with his bell-ringing-bar-smashing-wood-knocking concertos in between noisily cleaning out the junk that accumulates in his cage, wildly tossing through the door the various spoons, toilet paper rolls, stolen and busted pens, and more. He prefers a clean cage to a clean office.

Without his tribe of parrots he needs lots of attention, and he constantly performs ludicrous gestures to attract people into our room, especially doing his best disco dance moves while trying to attract women. They'll talk to him, but he'll be as silent as a stone until they leave the room. Then he will start yakking like a drug user on speed. And if the kids should arrive at the farm, he calls them up to our office with great authority. "Roben, get up here!"

Flocking birds of different species use each other for protection and food finding and amusement. It took only a short few months for both of us to recognize that Tuco was far more social than I am, so it became his task in life to distract me and make me part of his flock.

These are all common parrot tricks. They are also anecdotal knowledge, as some scientists like to sneer. Parrots are not geniuses by our standards, and what we mistake for brilliance or ESP is often coincidence or reading too much into too little. Although traditional knowledge and individual experiences are crucial to life, they can also be false, sometimes fatal guides. We only have to remember that the great Roman advances in plumbing led to the citizens drinking their water out of lead pipes and leaded goblets, and they even sweetened their wine with "sugar of lead." Or that many traditional cures for syphilis prescribed arsenic and mercury, or that the fresh blood of murdered parrots supposedly alleviated gout, even if parrots are susceptible to gout themselves.

Much traditional knowledge will be forever alien to science because it isn't true, and herbal remedies can be as dangerous as some are miraculous, though lateral thinking can lead to great wisdom. Wade Davis, in his marvellous book *One River*, often talks about ayahuasca, how each of its three Amazonian plants doesn't amount to much alone but when cooked together create the legendary hallucinogenic spirit-travelling drug. It's often claimed the ancient shamans dreamed the drug out of the "spirits" of the plants, or the plants instructed them in how to make ayahuasca. According to Wade, it's statistically impossible to discover this concoction through trial and error. It's certainly another good argument for sensibility over science.

And thus it is with much of what we know and what we have learned. Accidents and deductions both have their place. Despite thousands of years of experience, we are still full of conjecture, especially our more reductionist scientists, who believe only that by measuring minute parts can we understand the whole, forgetting the synergy that can make a dozen people act like hundreds in the right situation or that the dreaded anecdote is just another word for story, yet we are born for story, telling them to ourselves from the moment we awake until we fall into the dreams of sleep. It's all stories, including the stories of science.

Our failure to comprehend the complexities of animal intelligence, anecdotal experiences, emotional intelligence, scientific intelligence, and traditional knowledge can lead to many misunderstandings, which is why, I suspect, you'll find obsessive parrot owners believe parrots have ESP without any real evidence.

I remain suspicious about ESP, even though on several occasions I felt I experienced it. I've mysteriously heard my name shouted in more than one dangerous moment, whether it's logs rocketing down a hillside or another car going through a stoplight, straight toward me. The problem with the supernatural is that it is supernatural, and usually impossible to verify, until it is possible, and then it's not supernatural. Our brains are unruly creatures, and they too, like Tuco, delight in tricking us.

So what evidence do we have of the intelligence of parrots? A lot.

The most famous parrot remains Alex, who displayed as much intelligence in not answering questions as he did in answering them. It's obvious how suspicious parrots are of the mechanical reductionism of scientific tests performed on them and how they find amazing ways for blowing them off. This has driven researchers into fits for years. The intelligent ways parrots have made monkeys out of intelligence tests is itself a delightful and funny read, and certainly a grand display of a different kind of intelligence.

Reductionism, as I've often noted, is one of the most important principles of scientific research, and also it's most dangerous. Still, researchers, over and over again, fail to understand that studying each part of a bird won't give you the whole living bird. Thomas Nagel, the philosopher, wrote an essay titled "What Is It Like to Be a Bat?" that changed the rules for studying animal intelligence. He claimed consciousness is subjective. As such, it can't be shared or even fully imagined, yet we can share much of the consciousness of parrots at specific moments. I can "see" what Tuco is thinking. Maybe not all of it, but enough to know when to duck a flying teaspoon or if he's going to crap on my shoulder—usually. More importantly, according to Nagel: "Any reductionist program has to be based on an analysis of what is to be reduced. If the analysis leaves something out, the problem will be falsely posed." Which is why he believes we have to take a chance and mingle subjective logic (another way of saying emotional intelligence?) with mechanical science.

Chimpanzees, dolphins, parrots—each will defy commands that don't make sense and sometimes grow annoyed at dumb questions. I'd add dogs and chickens and a few other animals to that list. A perfectly intelligent question from our perspective is often about the dumbest thing Alex ever heard, which is why I love reading more about what he does to screw up those tests than how well he performs them. Pigeons are also capable of deception, finding a tiny food source and leading other birds to it. Then, while its comrades are distracted, it will go back and feast on the richer sources. Pigeons can also memorize up to 725 visual patterns. This is where the story gets even weirder; they can also discriminate between cubist and impressionist paintings.

One theory of mind argues that animals don't do drugs, so they can't have a theory of self. I have no idea where this cockeyed theory came from (probably some philosopher who was doing drugs). It's evident the few proponents of this theory haven't seen robins and towhees and waxwings falling drunk out of trees, stoned on fermented berries. Some might argue this is accidental, yet it's obvious when you're among them and studying their behaviour. For birds that don't like being stoned they are pretty impressive at seeking out these berries. Siberian reindeers eat magic mushrooms, and because these are distilled by their digestive systems, the reindeers are even more compulsive about licking the patches of yellow snow where they urinated. Bighorn sheep eat hallucinogenic lichens, grinding their teeth down to the gums from chewing it off rocks. Elephants and monkeys also eat fermented berries. Porcupines and gorillas are fond of the psychedelic iboga plant. Goats eat wild coffee berries for a little buzz.

Three years ago, I was the writer-in-residence at the beautiful Whistler ski area, living in a house whose deck jutted over Alta Lake. It was a spectacular location, but one thing bothered me. I kept seeing squirrels fall from the overhanging tree and land with a splat on the deck, before shaking themselves off and fleeing, only I couldn't figure out why. It was a strange autumn phenomenon.

Then, after almost a month of witnessing this behaviour, while walking down the trail to the dock on the lake, I noticed a lot of hallucinogenic mushrooms—*Amanita muscaria*—had been nibbled on. Whole chunks were broken off. There's an epidemic of bears around this area, and I began to worry I might encounter a bear on drugs. Not a good thought. At that moment, a squirrel tumbled out of a nearby tree, practically landing at my feet, and I realized the squirrels were eating the mushrooms—intentionally. When I looked this up on the Internet, I discovered dozens of reports of drugged squirrels performing bizarrely across America. There's even a charming picture of a stoned squirrel that had crawled up a fellow's pants and was hanging onto his belt buckle, staring at him with an obviously befuddled squirrel's gaze. So much for the theory that animals don't do drugs.

Alex's behaviour displayed a wide assortment of thinking skills. For instance, there's a passage in Pepperberg's book *Alex and Me* about Alex supervising an accountant staying late at her job. Growing bored, the bird decided the accountant needed help, so he began suggesting food. "Want corn? You want a nut?"

Each time the accountant politely replied: "No."

This annoyed to the parrot, who probably wanted to sleep. Exasperated, Alex finally said: "Well, what do you want?"

When doing math, Alex would often provide a spate of wrong answers. I think he hated math, like me. Once he was supposed to give the number of two pieces of green wool. He kept answering with the wrong numbers. Growing frustrated, Pepperberg decided to give him a time-out. Carried to his room, he immediately called out: "Two... two... two.... I'm sorry.... come here!"

Alex understood colour, shapes, materials, and whether an object was present. He could use syntax. Tuco is also capable of grammar. He will change "Do you want a cookie?" into "I want a cookie." But Alex could do him one better and count. Pepperberg was clever both in performing her rigorous scientific studies on Alex and in writing a separate personal memoir of life with him. The memoir is often more interesting than the scientific research, and since it's a personal memoir, she can suggest non-scientific answers to Alex's behaviour.

According to tests Pepperberg conducted, Alex also deduced the concept of zero on his own when counting objects. He could even deduce a missing object and announce there was "none" of that object. This is something of a shock to cognitive scientists. Not even the ancient Greek mathematicians were able to conceive of the concept of zero, though it's been discovered separately in Babylonian hieroglyphs, Indian Sanskrit texts, Mayan inscriptions, and several hundred years later in Arab texts. It now appears the Mayan-Olmec nexus created their zero in both a twenty-based as well as a decimal-based math like ours. Plus they appear to have made this discovery a few centuries earlier than all the others.

Parrots are notoriously mischievous, and it seems obvious to me that to be mischievous you need both a knowledge of self and an understanding of behaviour. Tuco quickly figured out my fake pirate laugh. So he commandeered the laugh and reserves it for when he pulls some particularly naughty behaviour. He also retained and uses a normal laugh.

Darwin's mighty theory shivered the ramshackle and often ludicrous barricade between humans and Others. Now science is occasionally shifting the debate in the other direction. It's becoming evident some specific skills are transparently superior in the animal kingdom, notably in memory, especially with some birds, like the Clark's nutcracker—but more on that later. Tool use was once the private preserve of our species. No more. Chimpanzees use straws to fish out termites. Vultures drop rocks to crack open skulls. The Galapagos finch uses a cactus thorn to hook grubs out of holes in trees. Caged orangutans construct makeshift ladders to bypass moats, or figure out how to make insulated bridges to suppress electrified wires, and develop various techniques for opening locked steel gates. Not only can orangutans create lock-picking tools, one hid her tool in her mouth whenever the keeper was about. What's interesting about their escape compulsion is that they seldom want to go anywhere. The escape is the goal. Once outside, they tend to explore a bit and then return to their enclosure, waiting to be let back in.

I know the feeling. I remember after I left home and started receiving my first steroid injections. Experiencing the cyclone of puberty while in my adult years was a rush. I was walking down the street under a blue sky. The wind was blowing. Everything was fresh. And the rush of freedom was upon me. I stopped and for the first time realized: "I can do anything I want." I was a man now. At last. Free. I could go down any road and up any other. Like that orangutan, I didn't want to go anywhere far at the time, but the knowledge I could do it was enough. I could do whatever I wanted, and since I had a knack for tool use, I knew I could make anything I wanted. That was a powerful feeling at twenty.

INTELLIGENCE IS WIDESPREAD in the bird kingdom. Blue tits used to open milk bottles and drink the cream off the open bottles in Britain. Within a few years, their stomachs evolved to take better advantage of this nutritious food. The milk companies grew wise to them and began sealing their bottles with aluminum seals. The blue tits soon learned how to break into even these seals. What's notable is that although they didn't use tools, they passed this knowledge to other flocks. It's long been known that flocking birds have a remarkable ability to communicate and learn from each other. That's one of the reasons why I believe prime locations on migratory routes gradually become crowded with travellers, as I noted when driving through southern Europe and when I look out upon the bird-rich gardens at our farm.

In Bangkok, at a massively complicated intersection, we were in a cab behind a motorcyclist at a red light when suddenly a small dog darted out and leaped onto the back of the motorcyclist's seat. The motorcyclist looked back stunned. The light changed, and with a wall of traffic behind him, he had no choice but to cross the enormous intersection. On the other side the dog leaped off with aplomb and carried on its merry way, safe, while the motorcyclist glanced back with some admiration at the dog who clearly knew how to use a motorcycle.

The real tool users are crows. We should remember that a crow's brain weight to body weight ratio is equal to a human's. In a famous tool test designed by three scientists, maggots were placed in a four-inch tube. Then the researchers left several lengths of wire in the crow's cage. The bird picked up a four-inch piece, slightly bent the end into a hook, and promptly speared the maggots out of the tube. In another experiment a crow went through nine different sequential intelligence tests to reach the wire for the maggot. If it failed one test it would never get the wire.

Both crows and ravens are shifty. If crows are caching food and they notice other crows watching them, they will lurk about, waiting for the intruders to leave, and then move their cache.

There's a terrific YouTube video of a crow in Russia using a plastic lid as a snowboard to slide down a snowy roof. That crow is having the time of its life. Scientists have long insisted that birds have no sense of play. So much for that dictate.

A BBC story early in 2015 tells of a young child who started leaving cookies and treats out for crows on the lawn and the sides of the birdbath and on the feeders. After a few weeks objects started showing up where she had placed the food. Googaws. Little shiny stones. Pieces of glass. Silver bells. Every time she fed the crows they rewarded her. Some of the gifts, such as a small dead bird, were a little icky for her but would be a real treat from a crow's point of view. And when her mother lost a lens cap while photographing an eagle down the road, the cap soon showed up at the birdbath. It appears the crows had decided to get on her mother's good side as well.

In Scandinavia, carrion crows have been seen robbing fish lines, clutching the line with their feet, then pulling with their beak, then holding it (like Tuco and his bone)—until finally they can pull the fish off the line and fly away with it. And then there's Aesop's fable of a crow being confronted with a pitcher half-full of water and dropping pebbles into the pitcher until the water rises enough for it to drink. An Archimedes with feathers.

One of my favourite sights in the Yukon is the ravens of winter. When light-sensitive streetlamps were installed, it didn't take the ravens long to figure out they could manipulate them. So on the coldest days of sub-zero weather, they drape their wings over the fixture and activate the sensor, warming themselves on the light's heat. It's such a lovely image on a snowy afternoon to see the streetlights mantled by clever ravens.

Ravens are as naughty as Tuco and probably as clever. I always think of them as the gangsters of the woods. According to Bernd Heinrich, who has the reputation of being a god among raven researchers, if a raven is dining on a carcass and sees more ravens coming in, it will flip up in the air and drop dead, convincing its fellows the meat has been poisoned. As soon as they are gone, it will get up and start eating again.

Ravens will also manipulate the psychology of other animals. They've killed more than a few of my lambs. If one of our ewes delivers twins in the field and I'm not there, the ravens will fly at the lambs, driving them away until the ewe chases the ravens off. They will keep using this strategy until they have driven the twin lambs so far apart the mother can't run from one to the other in time. Then they will peck out a lamb's eyes, and once blinded, the lambs are easy for them to kill and eat.

Although ravens can be murderous, they are also loving creatures. A couple will preen each other at night, even kiss with mingled beaks, and they will hold the feet of their mate in their own during the night. Ravens always make me think of Hugin (thought) and Munin (memory), Odin's two magical ravens who patrolled the world for him ever morning. He lived his life in fear that one day one or both of them might not return. Don't we all?

These days, the ingenuity of intelligence studies almost matches the intelligence of birds, of which we are seeing so much new evidence, not that human ingenuity hasn't excelled itself since the first words were carved into clay. It always makes me smile thinking of Charles Darwin in his elderly years talking his wife, Emma, into playing piano for a big pot of earthworms, to see if they reacted to classical music. I can only groan at the amount of research undertaken to prove that a Clark's nutcracker can keep track of the 30,000 seeds it stashes for winter and may use up to 7,500 caches. It only needs a third of these seeds, yet it doesn't take chances. More interestingly, like crows, if it sees other nutcrackers watching it, the bird will sneak back later and hide the cache somewhere else. This displays at least a rudimentary theory of self and mind. It also displays an ability for the tiny nutcrackers to invent stories involving deceit, theft, and concealment, as well as an astonishing amount of memorization.

Although birds might not be able to create the theory of relativity, their own thinking skills can be as advanced as their needs, and in various aspects of memory, they are likely superior to us. Other animals, from elephants to dogs, have also been known to have more than significant memory abilities. A German researcher claims one test subject, a collie, knows some three hundred words, and if faced with a request for an object she doesn't know, she will select that object from among objects she does recognize. For instance, if the dog knew the names of five among six objects in the room, such as ball, rock, etcetera, and the researcher called out the name of an unknown object, say, cushion, the dog would figure out what the cushion was through the process of elimination and bring it back. Another dog can pick out 1,022 objects by name, according to a study undertaken at Wofford College. The two researchers blithely admitted the dog, Chaser, could remember the names given to the objects better than they could.

Tuco's memory and wit are always fabulous, and I suspect that's why, when I tease him and call him a "dumb bird," he just cackles wisely.

In *Beautiful Minds: The Parallel Lives of Great Apes and Dolphins*, Maddalena Bearzi and Craig Stanford define intelligence as six things (which were once thought to be restricted to humans): tool use, understanding of language, self-awareness, the ability to imitate, behavioural flexibility, and an ability to demonstrate memory. This definitely makes Tuco intelligent, though his skills in certain of those areas are both weaker and stronger than those of other animals, including us.

Nevertheless, we continue to think of animals according to our values, not their values. That's why the behavioural psychologist Reduoan Bshary said: "Why should a leopard have to be smart? It's already perfect." Charles-Georges Leroy, the master of the hunt for Louis xv, insisted animals only learned what they needed to learn for their own good, and it was foolish to expect them to want to learn useless information (which appears to be a human specialty, especially mine).

For a hundred years, we embraced paleontologist Tilly Edinger's brilliant unified theory of brain evolution, which saw evolution as a direct progressive line from amoeba to human. Time has proved brain anatomy is even more complex than she originally noted. It's been clear for years that evolution occurred not only through gene transfers but also what's called convergent evolution, which can also include gene transfer, only from a different source. That's where non-related species all develop similar structures, such as feet, wings, eyes, and so on. Rather than our complex layered cortex, bird brains evolved a simpler yet still powerful brain structure. More is often considered an improvement by our species. It isn't. A bigger brain is not a better brain. Evolution, like this memoir, is not a linear process. It introduced me to both baby barn owls and scatter-guns. Evolution loops all over the place, and often simpler is better, though we also and always love the complexity of diversity— including the convergent evolution that gave us both the wings of nighthawks and bats fluttering in the dusky sky.

Meanwhile, neuroscientists and psychological anthropologists and archaeologists and rebel biophysicists are ripping down the walls with enthusiasm. These are exciting times. A new group of scientists, dryly calling themselves the Avian Brain Nomenclature Consortium, has rebelled against the traditional labelling of brain structures, recognizing elements of different brains, including bird brains, needed different names, because our historic nomenclature of that organ is outdated and glutted with the crud of biases built up over centuries. This new group is systematically renaming the parts of avian brains. Now, if we can only change the assumptions built into the phrase "bird-brained."

Whatever else, the next two decades of animal research are going to show revolutionary results on animal intelligence.

Convergent evolution created different forms of intelligence and skill sets. For instance, in many creatures the olfactory centres developed an enormous range, from non-existent to highly sensitive, whether in sharks or albatross. The black-footed albatross can pick up an odour from twenty miles away on the open sea. This is even better than Sharon, who seems able to smell bacon before I have even brought in the groceries from the truck. Smell is like a beautiful unconscious intelligence and has tremendous effects on our conscious minds. Since Kallmann syndrome deprived me of a sense of smell, I didn't even realize what smell was until the doctor asked me about it and I suddenly realized I couldn't smell. How strange that it took me twenty years to recognize this.

You always miss what you can't have, and the sudden recognition of that loss instantly made me sad, though I believe I was rewarded with an extraordinary number of taste buds, because I'm so sensitive to the six tastes (I follow the Asian identification of six tastes: sweetness, sourness, saltiness, bitterness, umami, and pungency). But even though I can recognize ingredients in dishes others can't, I know I am also missing out hugely on the supplementary joys of the rich odours of some foods, and that depresses me sometimes. Worse, I recently learned we are polluting lakes so extensively that some freshwater fish are also losing their sense of smell. Dolphins don't have one either, but like me, they can taste the world around them, only they taste the water instead of air.

And sometimes we just cannot figure it out. Parrots are supposed to have a poor sense of smell, yet, as I mentioned earlier, no matter how silent we are, Tuco will crackle with the most blood-curdling shrieks if he gets a whiff of his precious chicken roasting or eggs being scrambled downstairs. There's some other kind of intelligence going on there that we don't understand yet. Perhaps he can even discern the sounds of different varieties of flesh frying. But this is mere speculation.

Bird brains have larger portions of two mammalian structures, the claustrum and the amygdala. The latter is part of our emotional system, yet in birds it's used for information sorting. I sometimes wonder if that accounts for Tuco's acute sensibility to our emotional states. He might not have our logical abilities, but I'm betting his emotional intelligence is far superior to mine. This might be why parrots are especially susceptible to the bird equivalent of post-traumatic stress disorder, which is why those lonely parrots are locked away in rooms, screaming, and why they also take to the brutal masochism of feather plucking. Any pain becomes better than no feeling at all. Fortunately, Tuco is luckier than me in the PTSD department. He doesn't have it.

Birds have also been known to conquer so-called intelligence tests like those with labels such as "linguistic ability, spatial memory, social reasoning, personality, representation of self, tool manipulation, episodic memory, and vocal learning." According to Susan E. Orosz and G.A. Bradshaw in an article on avian neuroanatomy, they should be viewed as "comparable to those in primates." I wonder, Is that a measure of intelligence or just a not-very useful comparison?

These suspicions are why I'm so fond of those few stubborn scientists during the last hundred years who have gone outside the envelope to investigate the nature of intelligence itself and have found it in the unlikeliest places.

My favourite is the multi-talented and philanthropical Jagadish Chandra Bose, a world leader in radio wireless transmission more than a century ago, which he undertook two years earlier than Guglielmo Marconi, though Marconi received credit for the feat in the public mind. Nobel Prize winner Sir Nevill Mott claimed Bose had anticipated his own discoveries sixty years earlier. He's a national hero of science in India, though he is little known in the West.

He also went on to do some shocking research on plant reactions. He discovered that by connecting them to electrical magnification receptors, he could then project these electrical reactions onto a screen.

While everyone knows there are sensitive plants that react to touch, like the mimosa, which will fold up if touched, Bose went further and started testing reactions to stimuli of a number of plants, even carrots, and sure enough, he learned that, like a few of us, they became excited when irritated. He was the very first scientist I encountered who claimed plants were communicating, though he was careful not to make any loopy claims about this phenomenon and plant intelligence. However, he did demonstrate that minerals and metals also displayed similar responses and that plants, metals, crystals, sedimentary rocks, and animals were all capable of responding to their environments.

Bose, despite making no claims for vegetable or mineral intelligence, believed these experiments in the plant, animal, and mineral kingdoms displayed "a uniform and continuous march of law." I don't know if this concept is equivalent to the recently proven universal sea of energy that came out of the discovery of the notorious Higgs boson particle, or if maybe it presaged some of the current thinking on entropy being the godlike force behind life.

And once again, we are back into defining intelligence, going from such simple proposals as being "adaptively variable behaviour during the lifetime of the individual" to the increasingly refined and complex definitions uttered by the many researchers determined to definitively prove human superiority.

Darwin had much to say on this subject, notably in his *The Power of Movement in Plants,* in which he concludes: "It is hardly an exaggeration to say that the tip of the radicle thus endowed [with sensitivity] and having the power of directing the movements of the adjoining parts, acts like the brain of one of the lower animals; the brain being seated within the anterior end of the body, receiving impressions from the sense-organs, and directing the several movements."

Needless to say, Darwin's book and its amazingly impressive "root-brain" hypothesis of plant intelligence were castigated by one of the leading botanists of the day, Julius von Sachs, who abused "the Darwins for being amateurs who performed careless experiments and obtained misleading results." Once again, time has taken the side of the painstaking Charles Darwin (and his son) and not his virulent detractors. Darwin's speculation that intelligence could be found in two different locations on a living creature has now been verified in octopi, who think not only with their central brain but also with their arms, which have intelligence as well. I wonder how these two brains get along in one body. Impressively, it turns out. An octopus introduced to a jar with a screw-top lid can figure it out in less than eight minutes. Then there's the famous public aquarium story, where the zookeepers couldn't figure out how crabs were showing up dead and in pieces in their tank almost every day. They finally hooked up a camera and discovered the octopus had learned how to break out of its tank, climb up through the ceiling tiles, sneak along inside the ceiling, drop into the crab tank across the wide aisle, dine blissfully on crab, and then sneak back home, leaving no evidence of its travels.

The once-dreaded ugly-looking wolf eel is gradually turning into a good guy. It is only vicious when attacked or its lair is invaded. Forty years ago, a West Coast diver made friends with a wolf eel in Porlier Pass by Galiano Island. They often played elaborate games together. For various reasons, he couldn't return to the eel for forty years. When he did, the eel came out of its hole, recognized him, and resumed playing the same game they left off forty years earlier.

David Premack, the eminent primate specialist, once claimed if chickens knew grammar, they'd still have nothing interesting to say. He obviously hasn't met my feathery little thugs. Watching them in action, I wonder where he even got that idea. Even though I can't speak chicken, I find their flock communication and the politics of their behavioural habits too complex for me, and fascinating. Darwin had some choice words about our blind judgements of the intelligence of animals. "It is a significant fact, that the more the habits of any particular animal are studied by a naturalist, the more he attributes to reason, and the less to unlearnt instinct."

Clever Hans is often used as an example of fake animal intelligence. After it was realized the horse pulled off its mathematical calculations by sensing the reactions of those around him when it came to the right hoof-tapping number, everyone decided this proved the horse wasn't smart, yet no one seems to have even considered that a creature so sensitive to the behaviour of humans was probably more intelligent in certain ways than his testers. How fortunate it would be to have his emotional intelligence and skill in high-stakes poker games or a hard-fought debate?

Tuco has his own techniques. Intelligence is tricky to understand. When a joke is told in our house, Tuco is always the first to laugh, chiming in milliseconds before anyone else. Does he get the joke? Probably not. What he does is even smarter. It took me years to realize the greater part of his thinking is communal, emotional, not intellectual. He's a superior Clever Hans, deconstructing our conversations and conduct (even if Tuco is not in the same room, he's always following our vocal patterns).

For Tuco, the crucial factor in a joke is not the joke but the way it makes us behave. He measures the speaker's tone and recognizes it's a joke, not a drama or real narration of events. Then, if he is in the room, assessing the speaker's inflections and body language, he can anticipate the timing of the punchline faster than any person can, and that's why he always beats us to the laugh. The strength of his laugh will even vary according to the quality of the joke, perhaps because, though this is an extreme thought, he can gauge the joke's quality from the tone of the speaker. Right, he's far smarter than a joke.

He will also do the same with a dire story. If somebody, especially a child, is narrating some household disaster too enthusiastically, Tuco can usually detect the perfect moment to deliver a blood-chilling cry of doom—modelled, I'm sure, on the day Sharon met a giant dead goldfish mysteriously deposited on our doorstep by one of the dogs (probably gored by a heron). He converted her cry into a deeply melodramatic "Aiyyyyyiiiiiiiiii!!!!!" that can disarm any horror story that's being overtold. If it's a child narrating an accident or a household disaster, and Tuco gives his extended blood-curdling shriek, she will usually recognize her trauma was only a minor tempest and soon begin laughing along with us. Tuco doesn't unleash this cry if real mayhem is taking place, like a vase smashing to the floor. His tone changes then, and we receive his standard dramatic: "What's that!" Or he goes silent, knowing there will be trouble.

If Sharon and I quarrel loudly, he loves to participate, imitating both of us and shouting so many contradictory insults that we give up in confusion.

There is so much to learn from alternate intelligences, whether parrot or bonobo or carrot. Or termite and bee societies practising what's now known as swarm intelligence. When you look at the animal kingdom, you will also notice how many animals practise mutual aid. This was a theory that the gentle Prince Kropotkin, a Russian anarchist and scientist, proposed to counter the survival of the fittest mentality that appeared after Darwin's theory of evolution. Mutual aid is probably the dominant form of behaviour among more creatures than not. Schools of fish behave certain ways to confuse predators, as do flocks of birds. From my reading of the tiger hunter Jim Corbett in my childhood, I learned how he recognized that listening to its fellow jungle creatures was the best way to learn if the man-eating tiger was present or not, and if it was, in what direction it was moving or where it had stopped to rest or drink. He didn't track the tiger. He tracked the reactions of the living community who were mutually communicating the state of the forests, which meant they were also alerting the tiger to his presence. And Corbett was crazy enough, alone in the jungle, crawling along in the mud and rain, to want that tiger to come looking for him. He killed thirty-three man-eaters before refusing to kill any more and spent the remainder of his life working to preserve the remaining tigers of India.

Kropotkin pointed out more creatures practise mutual aid than enslavement or murder of their kin, except for *Homo sapiens*, who, when we aren't Othering the animal and plant world, are Othering each other in tribal slaughters and national wars. I had more than enough experience of this ugly behaviour in my childhood—all the times I was knocked down and kicked by the "friends" of my youth, the boot in my ribs and the split eyebrow forever torn by the ugly ring of my friend outside the Lougheed bowling alley what seems like so many centuries ago. Isn't that the way we behave? We get kicked and we get up again, and then we kick someone else. It took me until my mid-twenties to break out of that physical cycle, and sometime I still instinctively shout back, usually louder, when shouted at. My greatest regret in my life—I'm just a scattershot boy in a scattershot world.

Which brings us circling back to the crucial question: What the hell is intelligence? A field that's become a minefield, as animal activists insist on exaggerated claims for parrots—chimpanzees, foot-stomping iguanas, canary song-stealers—next to philosophers debating the qualities of cognitive thinking, while "hard" scientists make stunning advances in unravelling the cellular behaviour of the brain, and other "hard" scientists deny all intelligence that isn't human. These are exciting times in the field of intelligence, but we are still a long way from understanding it. We might never. Meanwhile, I only have to recall the cold black eye of that raven flying alongside a speeding truck, and I still remember the intelligence in its depth, a different intelligence, marvellous and inscrutable to me but still unable to calculate baloney mathematics.

This is where we encounter the field of what's known as heuristic thinking (intuitive judgements), which illustrates there are simple and clear rules why people can form wildly off-tilt decisions, judging situations inaccurately and with way too much confidence. There are biomechanical reasons why we can make dumb mistakes about even simple opinions, let alone complex scientific issues like understanding the intelligence of birds.

There's a similar term that's dangerously close to a tautology: the Dunning-Kruger effect—it insists incompetent people don't recognize they are incompetent because they are incompetent. This also applies to intelligent people with a blindness on a specific subject. The researchers' paper, "Unskilled and Unaware of It: How Difficulties in Recognizing One's Own Incompetence Lead to Inflated Self-Assessments," also won the ironic Ig Nobel Prize in psychology, an annual award for goofy papers, for demonstrating ignorant people are too ignorant to know they are ignorant. This concept was put better by Bertrand Russell: "One of the painful things about our time is that those who feel certainty are stupid, and those with any imagination and understanding are filled with doubt and indecision."

Perhaps the best thinker on heuristics is a real Nobel Prize winner, Daniel Kahneman. In his *Thinking, Fast and Slow*, he outlines two basic kinds of thinking we do. "System 1. Fast, instinctive and emotional; System 2 is slower, more deliberative, and more logical." Yes, we're back to the yin-yang hypothesis, only a more philosophical version of it. What's fascinating about Kahneman is that he illustrates that both kinds of thinking are prone to error and bias (scientist thinkers take note, and New Agers, too). Another outcome of his studies and tests is the realization that "people place too much confidence in human judgement." Logic isn't so logical after all.

One of the difficulties in sorting out simple problem solving is that although the original mistake might be pretty basic, the need to retain an opinion automatically involves increasingly complex and goofy justifications.

But intelligence is not about opinions; it's about seeing, collecting, understanding—watching the miracle and assimilating a theory of self and event. Intelligence is slippery to decipher. When two dozen prominent researchers were asked to define it, they gave two dozen, often different definitions.

What I often ask myself is if I'm supposed to be intelligent according to the tests I've taken, how come I often have to call out to Sharon in the kitchen: "Why am I in the storage room?"

We haven't even been talking. She's been busy cooking but calmly replies, "You're looking for fresh towels."

Now that's smart. Her physical intelligence, and her scary spying on me (unconsciously, I hope), makes my nerves start tingling, but she has a sense of place I can't even comprehend. It's the emotional intelligence that animals have. She knows everything that's going on at the moment, far more often than I do. She is "there," in the house, and I am lost in my head, infected with a serious case of what writers call novel-brain. So which one is intelligence?

I might be intelligent at certain limited skills, but generally, in the scheme of things, I'm a mess, always was a mess, emotionally damaged, and making idiotic mistakes over and over again, quarrelling with friends, executing bad financial decisions, and occasionally publicly making a fool of myself, a dangerous habit, especially when you're not afraid of public dangers and spectacularly full of self-hatred on far too many occasions. I've spent most of my life trying to forgive myself even for situations that weren't my fault, like being born with my syndrome or bullied. There is no such thing as the currently fashionable fantasy that we can find the "closure" people keep demanding. There's only forgetting and forgiving.

When I look at the foggy paths of this natural history of Othering, I cringe. It's embarrassing, dangerously egocentric, yet inspired by hope, unrelenting hope as I approach my imminent death. My interactions with birds often inspire my best idiocies and moments of love and communication and serenity. Just being there with them, whether they're chattering about my feet or staring into my eyes.

They've also got me into more than my share of trouble. Last year our peahen, Blanche, had four chicks, and I had an interested buyer for them. Peahens and their young bond impressively, and it's cute to watch them. They will ride on their mother's back or sleep tucked under her wings. If you make a noise, they will peek out from under her wing to see what's going on; then, once satisfied it's not news, they will slip back under cover again into the warm dark safety close to her body. Very beautiful. Very comforting to watch.

A good friend of mine was visiting when I received an order for the peachicks. Sean is a fine short story writer, and I've known him for forty years. In his youth, he spent a number of years in the back regions of England and Ireland and is familiar with the finer arts of poaching. I've always assumed Sean is smarter than I am. But give us a bottle of whiskey and what a pair of dummies we can both become. We've been getting into trouble together for four decades.

Come around midnight, he was well into his Jameson's, and my bottle of Scotch was showing major damage as well. Sharon decided she was done and announced she was off to bed. I looked at the clock and saw that it was midnight, so I said to Sean: "I'd say it's about time to catch the peachicks."

This puzzled him somewhat, as he was thinking more slowly by then.

"I got a buyer for the four peachicks, and the mother is roosting on the rafters above the deck. I've netted chicks with my big fishnet lots of times."

This immediately challenged Sean, who decided a net was boring and we should try the old Irish poaching technique of sneaking up under the mother and grabbing a chick by the feet and handing it down. This seemed all right to me, as long as he was the one exhibiting his "professional" prowess.

So I would hold the light on the peahen, and he would catch the chicks and pass them to me, and I'd put them in the box.

As we were heading out the door, we heard Sharon's lonely voice from the bedroom above: "Should you guys be doing this in your condition?"

Sean and I simultaneously replied: "Aw, what could happen?"

Fatal words, indeed. So out we went, with flashlight and box and ladder, which I'd already set up nearby. We slid the stepladder under the peahen, who was about eight feet above the deck.

As Sean climbed the ladder and I shone the light on him, Blanche, the white hen, turned her head and gave him the most baleful look. Yes, birds can give baleful looks. Sean reached up and snatched the first chick by the feet and handed it, squawking and flapping, to me.

As I gently put it in the box, Blanche whipped around and leaped onto Sean's bald head, grabbing him by the nose with her beak, which gave her a good grip as her claws skidded about on his skull, and she began boxing his ears with her powerful wings.

Sean managed to shake her off and retreated down the ladder. I think I would have died laughing if he hadn't been such a bloodied mess. We fled with the boxed chick into the mud room, stalked by the ferocious Blanche, or "Blanche the Bitch," as Sean soon took to calling her, while I chucked the chick back to her mother to distract her. I was afraid if we didn't throw it back, Sharon would probably get mugged by the peahen in the morning.

We slammed the mud room door and burst through the main door back into the house. "Sharon," I called out, "I think we need help." Sharon soon came hustling down the stairs and looked at us with horror as Sean tried to staunch all the bleeding with a towel. Then we discovered our first-aid kit was down to small bandages, and by the time Sharon was finished with Sean, his skull was patched up with a cockeyed network of about thirty little bandage strips, including one on his nose. Once we realized it was only scratches, we were hurting our stomachs laughing at the fate of our intrepid poacher.

With Sean so hilariously repaired, the three of us returned to the sun-room and our glasses of Irish and Scotch and Sharon's white wine, recounting where we had gone wrong in our battle with the peahen from hell.

Sean probably had the most lucid comment on the whole affair. "At least we still think like nineteen-year-olds." He left a few days later, resembling a sabre-scarred German duelist with a red nose. Fortunately, all the cuts and gashes healed.

I still had to catch and sell the birds. After that misadventure, Blanche had moved her chicks, spending the nights on the split rail fence beneath our second-floor bedroom, where they lurked under her wings. Once again, I waited until Sharon went to bed. Only this time, I decked myself out in my heaviest jean jacket and leather bee-handler gloves, a leather hat jammed down over my ear protectors. Then I put on my aviator sunglasses. I checked out my "look" in the mirror. I was a sight.

I snuck up easily behind Blanche and dropped the net, intending to push her aside and snatch the chicks out from under her. Only she noticed at the last second and leaped straight into the net while the chicks panicked and fled. She let out a ferocious screeching, flapping around in the netting, snapping at me as I attempted to release her. I finally got her out, but instead of fleeing, she just squatted on the ground, giving me the evil eye.

Suddenly, she lunged screeching into the air, landed on my hat, and attempted to work me over with the Sean treatment. Luckily, she could only catch the rim of the hat, so I was untouched, staggering around the field, wearing her flailing body like a headpiece. Sharon erupted out of our bedroom door and onto the deck above, screaming: "Brian! Brian! Something is attacking the peacocks!"

It was kind of awkward explaining to her what was happening in my position, especially since I was laughing so hard at this point that I couldn't shake Blanche off. But I finally knocked her to the ground, where she harrumphed and stalked off after her chicks.

Sharon was now exasperated by my incompetence. "Why don't you just catch them the way you used to? Throw some feed into the spare shed and shut the door on them when they're inside?" Strangely, I'd forgotten entirely about this, though we'd been doing it for years (but I should mention I'd also netted a number of the chicks over the years—only ones with less ferocious mothers). This is a classic symptom of the oddness of the human mind, how it works, where it goes, or more aptly, where it wants to go—ignoring the reality of the world and history once a fixed idea develops. It's another classic example of agnotology, or willfully not knowing what we actually know.

I trapped the chicks, painlessly, in the shed the next day and carted them off to their new owners, while Blanche moaned and called for her lost babies for a week or more, as any good mother would do. One of the areas where we match animals is mothering. So many mammals and birds are ferocious mothers, and even some reptiles and insects. I once watched a video of a rooster giving a hawk warning call, and the hens scattered. Then a terrified hen realized one of her chicks had been left behind, cowering in the middle of the chicken yard. The hen rushed back out and covered the chick, fluffing up her feathers as much as possible so that she would look big for a predator. It worked. The hawk left her alone. I can't think of a better way to demonstrate birds have a theory of self. It was clear the trembling hen recognized the danger to herself, yet she was willing to make the ultimate sacrifice for her chick.

Although I know thousands of researchers have worked on developing IQ tests and done their best to perfect them, they're still limited by our cultural conditioning. Our tests usually tell us as much about the intelligence of the test creators as they do about the test recipients. Interestingly, most depend on linguistic skills (a dangerous field of assumptions if there ever was one), except for that complex style of test involving spatial and physical intelligence given me by the psychiatrist after I started receiving hormone treatment. Is intelligence linguistic? No. Real intelligence uses the whole mind and body and hormones, not just logic and language.

As I noted earlier, according to Nagel in "What Is It Like to Be a Bat?," reducing an analysis of intelligence to common factors can create false questions and answers. This is very similar to Midgley's discussion of the aquarium windows, and why Nagel believes it's necessary to mix subjective logic with mechanical science. Them's fighting words, of course, but we have to keep remembering no materialist science can ever tell us what it's truly like inside there. We can only imagine it. And we do often, whether we're watching falcons circling a chicken or people conversing with parrots. We also imagine other minds when we are reading biographies and novels and histories. Nothing is ever black and white, or as Spinoza remarked: "No matter how thin you slice it, there will always be two sides."

Tuco has lots to say about intelligence, even when he's not talking about it, which is most of the time. You can see it in his awareness, his studying of the world around him. I love watching him when he's thinking. What do we know? What does he know? I'm baffled. Despite my copious research, all I can ever find are differences in modalities of communication, many better in some ways and others worse in other ways, as well as differences of degrees in the way we think and the forms in which we think. Thus, the greater part of me keeps returning to Tuco's deep driving question: "Whaddya know?"

I know that I agree with the American poet Wendell Berry in his book *Life Is a Miracle:* "We always know more than we can say. ... There is no reason to assume that the languages of science are less limited than other languages." And "I don't think lives can be explained. What we know about creatures and lives must be pictured or told or sung or danced." It's all stories. Stories within stories. Memory and inspiration and science, walking through the forest of time, hand in hand, up the mountain in the mist, looking for paradise. Dancing. Singing. Walking.

So many poets will tell you their poems arrive out of walking, paddling canoes, singing old songs, or talking old poems aloud. Intelligence is also movement. How much inspiration comes out of sitting at a desk with a pen, and how much comes out of rushing to the post office, or quarrelling with another scientist over some arcane point before the big picture suddenly explodes in the mind?

What do I know? Not much. I do know, though, like many of us, what I don't know. Intelligence shape-shifs like a snake, and inspiration is always a surprise. "Whaddya know?" Not much—not much, my bird, my love, as I watch you stretch your wings, laughing at my absurd, troubled, and too-dumb human universe.

Chapter 10

———◆———

THE OTHER BIRD

ANAKIN PUSHED OFF from my gauntlet with a whoop of wings and climbed rapidly. He didn't go far, alighting on a thirty-foot-high branch thirty yards down the path of our "hawk walk" at Pacific Northwest Raptors on Vancouver Island and waited, gazing back at us, anticipating his next reward. In many ways, though a Harris hawk in full form, he reminded me of an old horse at a trail-riding ranch. It knows when to gallop, when to saunter, which path to take. Only the horse does it with a kind of bored trained-seal approach. If you're a falcon, you let everyone know you are only doing this at your own pleasure, and if the person wearing the gauntlet doesn't meet your approval, then you might as well fly off and whack a robin or a rabbit in the nearby fields.

Humans can negotiate Othering, sometimes roughly in the heat of life, though an offered hand is always better. History is full of insane wars suddenly stopped, either from exhaustion or the mutual recognition that there was no need for a war at all. Defeat is not the only solution. Some creatures, like the hawk, will never be friends, but they will negotiate a truce if it suits them, like Tuco—even respect us and become companions if we fulfill their needs.

Anakin has a natural arrogance that reminds me of too many people I have known, snooty scholars in the academies, mothers who believe their child is the best child in the world, men who brag they know what women want.

Stacy is Anakin's handler for today. She draped the corpse of a poultry chick across my gauntlet, and I held my hand up toward Anakin, perched on his branch high in the leafless alder. He was half-dancing, bobbing, wings spread in anticipation. Then he saw the bird on the raised gauntlet and floated down like a ghost, hitting the gauntlet with a thud, demonstrating his power.

This reminds me of the teenagers sparring in a full-contact karate dojo where I once trained. Because I was the old guy, the big guy, about to win my brown belt, they were always pounding on me, even in so-called light-contact sparring, where you're supposed to merely touch your opponent. One tall, scrawny kid especially kept banging away at me with the cheeky insouciance of youth, like Anakin attacking the gauntlet.

After this gawky lad delivered a particularly hard smack with a kick against my thigh, I clasped the collar of his *karategi*, drew him close, and hard-whispered out of earshot of the sensei: "If you hit me like that again, I'm going to forget the karate and drive you so hard they'll be peeling you off the wall and picking your teeth out of your butt." His eyes widened as reality took over, and he nodded politely and never smacked me again while doing light contact. There are various methods for negotiating an end to Othering, but despite this moment, I don't recommend threats. They're only another manifestation of the slippery nature of Othering.

Pacific Northwest Raptors is a non-profit bird sanctuary that funds the rescue of injured raptors, educating the public about raptors, as well as allowing some species to breed for work—it exercises its best raptors in airports, landfills, mines, and factories where there's a need to discourage birds that could cause car accidents, bring down airplanes, or injure workers. It's impressive how the mere appearance of a big hawk will clear the air. At some land-fills, the operators would not be able to enter the worksites because of the assaults of the gulls, which can be violent and aggressive. Although Stacy tells me the centre generally sells no hawks (except to approved falconers for public protection), the income from its bird protection program provides the funds for themselves and other rescue centres. It has a number of enforcers, including pere-grine falcons, Harris hawks, owls, and bald eagles.

I was stunned on my first visit to the institution, several years earlier, when I saw the one-winged eagle in his large, open-aired enclosure. He strutted about his kingdom as if it were just that, his kingdom, and I was instantly fifteen years old again and the zoo officials were taking away my broken-winged eagle with their assur-ances: "We'll take care of him." Everything they did and said were lies, and then they murdered my eagle.

This eagle had been alive for decades past the day his wing hit the wire of a power pole and fried, and it had to be amputated. He reminded me of myself, injured yet defiant. After that, every time I returned, I'd sit with him for an hour or so, silent, and we'd gaze at each other until he grew bored and wandered off to another section of his enclosure.

He reputedly survived into his fifties, adding the forty years of his captivity to his earlier free years—an astonishing age for an eagle, far beyond the age of any eagle in the wild—until the day he had the unluck to be swarmed by a flock of rogue ravens and was killed before rescuers could arrive. That's the way the natural world works. I imagine he would have fought hard, screaming and lung-ing, an old one-winged soldier defending his food, until the ravens overwhelmed him. A tragedy for the centre after years of open-aired freedom in his huge enclosure. Perhaps the longest-lived eagle ever in captivity, dying in his den, fighting a devil flock of ravens. It was another shock to return to the sanctuary, shortly after, and face his empty run.

I thought of how my eagle trusted me and yet was so distant—that cold eye while he nestled in my arms. I instinctively knew he'd never rip my face off. Sometimes he even rested his head against my shoulder when I held him. He was telling me about our separate worlds, back then, but I was too young and lovestruck to pay attention.

Watching the eagle at the raptor centre made me recognize the wall between me and Tuco. Although we'd built a bridge between us, there were realms where he remained private, gaps our friendship could never cross. I can never truly pet him, mostly because of his fear of hands. I can scratch his neck, his chin, his wings with a pencil and his chest, beak, and forehead with a sideways finger. I often ruffle his feathers with a pencil, and he will curl into that, but it's only a tenuous link between different universes. Then again, he's always keen on French kissing and sticking his head inside my mouth.

Perhaps he's trying to figure out why my tongue is so much larger than his, though it's undoubtedly an affectionate gesture, even if I'm a little twisted up and nervous that he will regurgitate in my mouth, as mating parrots do.

Usually, we leave Tuco with a house sitter when we travel, though in the early days of our companionship I decided to take him for a trip to Hornby Island, since we'd be away for a week and we had the use of a friend's cabin. The first obstacle was transportation. Braking and starting, the lurching of my big Ford van with its standard shift would be uncomfortable for him, so I drilled a hole in one of the crossbars in the ceiling and put in a hook to hang his cage from. This, it developed, was more brilliant than I imagined. I hung his cage with the swinging perch facing forward, and he loved the swinging as the gears shifted or the truck stopped and started. We weren't five minutes down the road before he was babbling like a fool behind my shoulder, ecstatic as he watched the world swish by through the windows and offered a running commentary on everything he saw. I was soon glad this was not going to be a long drive.

We stopped in Qualicum Beach, a seaside town, for lunch, before we encountered the long ferry lineups to Hornby Island. When we parked in the middle of the summer town and its crowded sidewalk, Tuco was ecstatic. As we returned to the van less than an hour later, from a block away I could see a crowd gathered around the window on the sliding door of the van. I broke into a run, fearful.

Tuco was inside, cheering away to his audience: "Come in! It's a parrot! It's a parrot!" As if that weren't obvious. He was in full Tuco mode, saying hello to all the girls, wolf whistling, yelling, "Come in! Come in! It's party time!" I almost felt guilty for breaking up his little sidewalk shindig, but I was grateful I'd locked the doors, leaving the windows open only a little crack to create a draft with the screened windows on the other side of the van.

Tuco's flocking instincts had taken over, and all those people were apparently a good addition to his long list of friends. It occurred to me that parrots are not naturally inclined to Othering. Apart from predators, in their natural environment they tend toward inclusion of anything they become familiar with.

Parrots are also aggressive creatures, and Tuco always delights in anything that resembles conflict in the house, even if it's merely me shouting out to Sharon as I try to find the batteries in the storage closets far away in the laundry room. His Sharon-voice directions are invariably bad and comic, which confuses the issue more.

Science fiction space battles are his favourite. I think *Star Wars* is his apotheosis, and he joins in every science fiction fight on television, mimicking light sabers and laser guns and whatever else is exploding. Sometimes when we're alone in our room and he grows bored, he will start up a battle on his own, and it soon sounds like wwiii in the office, including the occasional death rattle and screech of terror. It's difficult to concentrate on my writing while Tuco is doing his best Han Solo laser gun fights, interspersed with machine-gun fire and bombs falling. He can launch the bombs, whistle them down to the ground, and then erupt into a variety of explosions at various distances, sometimes even overlapping his weapons fire so that it can sound more authentic than a war film.

Not only does he understand these conflicts involve deaths, he delights in the on-screen deaths. He's internalized the conflicts of the world, converting war and Othering into mere sport and gamesmanship, and maybe they are for some of us as well. This mental split is easily apparent with children, who will be enthralled by the goriest films yet become hysterical when one of them falls off a bicycle and does a face plant in the gravel. Like Tuco, they mostly recognize the difference between fantasy and the real horrors of the world.

Sometimes I swear he's taken lessons from the legendarily scary African grey, Coco, who once perched in the lobby of the Commodore Hotel in Beirut during the Lebanese civil war. It was claimed this bird could reproduce any kind of weapon fired in the city. Coco delighted in war. He lived for the war. Like kids and their fantasy movies, he'd Othered the real gore. The Commodore was where all the correspondents hid out when the street fighting grew too insane for even the toughest reporters. The owner had bribed the different factions so well there was a kind of invisible wall around the hotel and its residents. Coco's favourite trick was to notice a newcomer in the lobby and just when the reporter was sitting down with his drink, let loose with the whistle of an incoming artillery shell and enjoy watching the newbie drop to the floor in terror. It makes me think of Tuco and his evil pirate laugh when things go wrong downstairs. Othering for personal amusement is not just a human behaviour, as I've noted several times.

When you checked yourself into the hotel, the unflappable staff would ask if you preferred "artillery side or car bomb side?" The artillery shells usually fell around the back and the car bombs went off in the street. The car bomb side was more dangerous due to the loads of extra shrapnel. The old hands among the correspondents took rooms around the back on the third floor, figuring they could always jump into the pool if things went really crazy.

Gunmen were required to check their weapons at the reception desk. The equally unflappable bartenders reputedly kept their machine guns behind the bar, and when they ended their shift and went home at 2 AM, Mohammed and Younis told the late drinkers to pour their own and keep track. At checkout, the bar bills mysteriously became laundry or telephone receipts, much to the delight of journalists with expense accounts. What's also impressive about these stories is how conflict can break down barriers between different cultures. In the hotel, a reshuffling of sides and prejudices soon reformed into a new community. As war diaries and journals and novels tell time after time, Othering within a group disappears real quick when we are under fire. The hotel had become a village, and the Others were out there.

There's differing stories about the last gun battle. One version has it there was some kind of grim, silent standoff between Shiite gunmen and Druze militia when Coco suddenly decided he might as well start the fight, no doubt with an AK-47 and a few grenades. I prefer this one, because I know the parrot would have immediately sensed the antipathy between the two groups with his emotional intelligence, and goaded them into conflict. But for him, this was only a game. He was about to get a surprise. Reality.

The fight went on for two days, and the hotel was wrecked and looted. The last anyone saw of Coco was a Druze militiaman dragging him screaming out of his cage. It was a classic disaster. The parrot's Othering behaviour had made even him a victim. The parrot's owner has resigned himself to recognizing that Coco is dead, still remains a hostage, or has made a neurotic mess out of his new owner. The more likely alternative is that Coco's descent into that final Othering in the hotel led to his being barbequed on a spit.

I WAS ABOUT eight the year my father drove our family and my mother's younger brother, Geno, to Tijuana, which in the fifties was a slow drive from Canada. The freeways weren't what they are now. Tuco's sneaky defilings of my shirts remind me of our visit to the San Diego Zoo. At the gorilla cage, my father grew frustrated with the gorilla hidden in its enclosure and began beating on his chest and doing a near-perfect thumping Tarzan-style gorilla call. That woke the gorilla up. It came crashing across the enclosure so fast I thought it was going to go right through the iron bars. It hit them with a thundering crang and beat its own chest so hard we froze, terrified, at least until the gorilla scooped up a pile of gorilla shit and flung it at us, and we fled screeching to the much quieter reptile house, where Father, who had a phobia about snakes, walked around the corner and a tiny snake spit its toxic poison directly at the glass a foot from Father's eyes. There was also a two-headed snake in the reptile house. Father was a wreck by the time we got him out of the zoo, yet he talked about it for the rest of his life. Like Tuco, he always loved a good scare. Although I was only eight years old, this encounter with America, along with accompanying my father on his magical potato-peddling expeditions, led me to begin recognizing the immense diversity of the world. Looking back, I recognize how great a Virgil my father was, guiding me in his backward way during those early years in the comedy of my life.

Despite—or maybe because of—the pains in my bones, and the week-long headaches, and my loner tendencies, I felt even more a part of the animal kingdom, a strange and gimpy kid. Yes, I was beat up and raped several times in those abused early years, mostly because I crazily kept going to places where a young boy shouldn't go. *Yellowbird... Yellowbird... go down that hill to the unknown! Be a man!* Sometimes I think of myself as a kind of troubled but happy rescue dog. Although I went through nearly two decades of hell in those early years, I saw beauty and made friends, and I came to live in paradise on Salt Spring Island for twenty-five years in the home I dreamed into existence before I was yet seventeen and still hiding my tears from everyone. The woman in my dream fantasy years? Her name was Sharon. My wife. I dreamed her, though I didn't dream I would inherit two wonderful sons. It was decades before it all came together. Now it is winding up, and I find myself looking down the tunnel of death every day.

But there are a few things, before I go down that other road. And though I am what is called "a troubled man," the hope remains, and the knowledge that I escaped my outsider world enough to still celebrate the unlikely beauty and carnage of life and bond with the ecology of our world, whether in the jungles of Thailand, the casbah of Tangier, or the bright mountains of the Cascade Range, including Mount Baker, the volcano that shines across the water into my window. Hope is the driver of life, almost an invisible force, that push of energy, from stream to cell to the first shoots of spring. The driven passion of the mother to see her children advance in the world—whether she is the queen bee or a meerkat or Sharon with the children and the grandchildren. The naturalist Henry Beston once said: "Creation is still going on, the creative forces are as great and active today as they have ever been, and tomorrow's morning will be as heroic as any of the world."

Over the last 150 years, since Rimbaud's yawp *"Je est un autre,"* many poets have recognized that the road to becoming an artist lies in inhabiting the Otherness of everything, where the poem resides like a jewelled throne in a castle that is always fading into the foggy pathway of consciousness. Rimbaud loved his life best when he was outside of himself and his petty existence, when he inhabited another consciousness, a world consciousness. That's what attracted me when I was seventeen years old, and what changed my life. He gave me hope in his crazed poet's way that I could also inhale the Other and thus become whole, though the results have been a little dicey. Hope is both our greatest strength and our greatest weakness.

The first two accounts of Pandora are misogynist descriptions by Hesiod, though by the time of Aesop, and the version of the story I prefer, she was no longer regarded as the source of all evil but more an innocent victim of Prometheus's brave act of bringing fire to humans and annoying Zeus, who had a remarkably conflicted attitude toward humanity at various times. Zeus kept two jars by his side, one of "good things" and one of "evil things," and he would sprinkle a little of either onto the human race, depending on his mood. He gave a jar of these spirits to Pandora's husband, Epimetheus, who accepted it despite the warnings of his brother, Prometheus, about accepting gifts from gods. Pandora was then given the jar (which was turned into a box due to a medieval mistranslation by Erasmus) of good things, which, as long as she kept them in her jar, would help humankind. Her name actually means "all gifts"—and the inhabitants of the jar were the charities... trust... restraint... the graces. But when she released "the good things," they became too frightened of staying on an earth infested with the evil spirits Zeus had released from the other jar and fled to Olympus. Only hope got caught in the lid of the jar, and she is the last of the good things permanently enshrined in every human being. Hope is what will save us, if we are saved, because hope will drive us to find a solution. Hope and empathy are the shining lights of my history. Hope keeps us going, and empathy brings us together.

THE BORORO PEOPLE of Brazil can become parrots, announced the anthropologist Lucien Lévy-Bruhl, who also conjectured that "primitive" people live in a world that has no distinction between the natural and the supernatural. T.S. Eliot wrote several times about the Bororo, because of their sense of self. They have the remarkable ability to consider themselves their totem—a parrot yet also human. They do not see a problem with living in both worlds simultaneously. Nor is it a problem wearing a headdress of parrot feathers. Theirs is a vision we can no longer understand (our wall again). In their world, which binds people into relationships with natural and supernatural phenomena, it is possible to exchange abilities or powers, or at least share them, with the Other.

Similarly, the Khoisan of Africa can become lions, and this is not a metaphor but a reality in their minds. It's an ability, one usually reserved for healers and shamans. Solomon Islanders assume that when someone dies unnaturally, he or she has been killed by a "shark"—an evil shaman from another tribe. There appears to be several variations in their shark cults. Many villagers are said to believe they have a shark Other protecting them, and some are known as sharks themselves.

Some are parrots. Some are lions. Some are sharks. This is perhaps the ultimate way to deal with the Other. We may call the embracing of two opposing ideas mere doublethink, though there are also a few who joyfully accept this cognitive dissonance, and I can be one of them.

These tribal people know they are these creatures, yet they also know they are human. Only—usually when they return from their spirit shape—they are changed human beings. They have been through the crack of the world and now inhabit both sides.

After twenty-five years, I want to say I've felt I became Tuco on several occasions, though I suspect myself and wonder about those brief dreamy flashes of seeing the world through his eyes. I also have felt brief moments of becoming pigeon and eagle. Were these moments mere daylight dreaming or the root of what a real shaman would see and feel and pass down through generations, the way we pass our knowledge down?

One of Loren Eiseley's most haunting stories is told by a scientist who studied amphibians. The scientist became fascinated one night by a frog migration under the streetlights of his dead-end street that descended into the swamps beyond. On a whim, the scientist began hopping alongside the frogs; then became possessed by his hopping, became frog, and only just managed to break out of the "spell" before leaping into the black waters. He retreated to the safety of the last streetlight. At the end of the story, he reveals to Eiseley a webbed hand.

Edward Said became instantly famous when he published the previously noted *Orientalism* in 1978, the book that gored Western colonialism, notably the way our culture defines itself, continuously, against the Other it imagines. The Oriental. The Indian. The African. The savage cannibal. The Other is a figure "to be feared or to be controlled." Said claimed "every European was a racist, an imperialist, and almost totally ethnocentric." The only problem is that this also applies to, or has applied to, Hindu and Muslim Indians, to today's definitely un-Islamic jihadists busy Othering Western culture. The Han versus the Tibetans. Japan and most of the Far East in the beginnings of the last century. The near-continuous wars among some Indigenous peoples of what is now North America. New Guinea tribes. Othering is an evolutionary inheritance, and as I've noted earlier, it occurs often in various forms in the animal kingdom.

It's important to keep remembering that Othering will always be an evolutionary trait and is readily apparent in most creatures, at least in its most basic form. Sometimes its routes are territorial. Sometimes they are predatory. There are multiple varieties of Othering. Wolves will hunt down coyotes in their territory because they are competitors; the same goes for crows mobbing strange birds. The chairman of the board scans other, weaker corporations for take-overs. It can also be cultural. Just consider how many cultures are horrified by the music of neighbouring cultures. Othering is everywhere, and this is the issue. It isn't simple, so no solution will be simple, and combatting it will always have mixed results.

I once read an amusing account of an acorn woodpecker hen who tried to join another flock of male acorn woodpeckers. They drove her off, so she returned to her community and soon, accompanied by her brothers, attacked the rude group until they gave up and allowed her to stay with them. Acorn woodpeckers can behave very strangely, and this one reads like an Icelandic saga. The universality of Othering leads in many directions, whether it is within us or animals, whether it arises out of natural predatorial or territorial behaviour, whether it is kids taunting the fat boy, or the corporations of the tar sands pouring their poisons into the rivers and lakes so that they can extricate their toxic product faster and cheaper—it's all like that crow calmly stripping the guts out of a trapped, live starling.

Unfortunately, we have come to practise Othering with such finesse that it's now clear we must deal with it in our era if our species is to survive. Especially since we also practise our Othering against animals, the land, the ocean, and the air—the climate that supports our lives. Bluntly, we have to evolve beyond Othering, or go the way of the dodo. Some modes of Othering we will likely never beat, such as the predatorial instinct, which demands Othering for survival. The cougar's heart will never go out to the fawn when it is hungry, but it probably has a different attitude when sated. We know too little of this. Different forms of Othering, like physical abuse and bullying and callousness toward our environment—there's where the possibilities are, though we also have to remember some of the worst oppressions of political correctness can be misguided reactions against ugly behaviour. Abuse of children, and behaviour such as bullying, can occur without reason, yet they can also be learned. Nor is abuse common only to our species. A 2011 study of Nazca boobies illustrated not only that adults abused the nestlings of other birds but also that it was a learned behaviour, and the chicks most abused became the greatest abusers as adults.

A LITTLE MORE than a century ago, Hegel said: "Each consciousness pursues the death of the other." His masterful but complex master-slave-freedom argument uses the thesis, antithesis, synthesis—or the dialectic—to create a new form in which there is neither master nor slave but a companion. The synthesis. They merge. Or as the wonderful T-shirt says: *Todos Iguales—Todos Diferentes*. All equal, all different. Or as Aldo Leopold wrote in *A Sand County*

Almanac: "A thing is right when it tends to preserve the integrity, stability, and beauty of the biotic community. It is wrong when it tends otherwise."

George Orwell has pointed out how we need to create a special language to treat Others badly. In one of the finest, most simply argued essays ever written by anyone in any language, "Politics and the English Language," he points out how we manipulate language to create distance:

> Thus political language has to consist largely of euphemism, question-begging, and sheer cloudy vagueness. Defenseless villages are bombarded from the air, the inhabitants driven out into the countryside, the cattle machine-gunned, the huts set on fire with incendiary bullets: this is called pacification. Millions of peasants are robbed of their farms and sent trudging along the roads with no more than they can carry: this is called transfer of population or rectification of frontiers. People are imprisoned for years without trial, or shot in the back of the neck or sent to die of scurvy in Arctic lumber camps: this is called elimination of unreliable elements. Such phraseology is needed if one wants to name things without calling up mental pictures of them. Consider for instance some comfortable English professor defending Russian totalitarianism. He cannot say outright, "I believe in killing off your opponents when you can get good results by doing so." Probably, therefore, he will say something like this:
>
> "While freely conceding that the Soviet regime exhibits certain features which the humanitarian may be inclined to deplore, we must, I think, agree that a certain curtailment of the right to political opposition is an unavoidable concomitant of transitional periods, and that the rigors which the Russian people have been called upon to undergo have been amply justified in the sphere of concrete achievement."
>
> The inflated style itself is a kind of euphemism. A mass of Latin words falls upon the facts like soft snow, blurring the outline

and covering up all the details. The great enemy of clear language is insincerity. When there is a gap between one's real and one's declared aims, one turns as it were instinctively to long words and exhausted idioms, like a cuttlefish spurting out ink.

History has illustrated time after time that unfamiliarity is the cause of Othering—from bullying to ethnocide. There's that succinct line in the film *Withnail and I,* when the two famished actors are presented with a live rooster by a local farmer. "Let's kill it before we make friends." Othering and the failure of imaginative identification is the mother of cruelty; also, sometimes, it's also just a roast chicken.

Who hasn't been Othered by a husband or wife or lover or friend at some point in their lives? Where anything said is taken wrong as divorce approaches, where new beliefs about you take the place of the more loving ones. How cruel it can be, even when done without a shout or argument—the unfriending of friends and lovers. Watching your mate turn away from you, finding flaws where there used to be a search for the good even in the bad moments, the same with a beloved friend of decades. Incidents erupt. Perceived slights where there's been none. Then the companion is lost. This is the human condition we have to change. We need to retain our empathy, even with our friends who have turned away from us.

We are inclined to accumulate friends who are "like us." Evolution has burned into our brains the tribe, the family, the companion. These are the ones. Outside of that, well, that's where it becomes dangerous. The brain demands the familiar. That's possibly why the philosopher Emmanuel Levinas said: "The self is only possible through the recognition of the Other." If we take the Other into us, we can live with him or her or it. Levinas took a more interesting tack than most philosophers: "The Other precisely reveals himself in his alterity not in a shock negating the I, but as the primordial phenomenon of gentleness." Almost, but not quite, a paraphrase of Sarah Bernhardt's famous: "Without you I am nothing." This could be regarded as a little touchy-feely for today, as we witness the slaughters and rages erupting around the world. Yet empathy is the only solution—getting there is the problem. There is a South African term "*ubuntu*," which signifies a person becoming a person through relationships with other persons. Desmond Tutu said this of *ubuntu:* "You know when *ubuntu* is there, and it is obvious when it is absent. It has to do with what it means to be truly human, to know that you are bound up with others in the bundle of life."

The farfetched and delightful author, the late Farley Mowat, had his "click" when serving during the war in Europe. He came back, in an odd way, an anti-humanist. He loved his human friends, but he shifted to the side of what he called "the others," the animals. And he made sure to constantly point out that they would probably last longer than our lame-spirited, dangerous species.

We tend to insist on mechanical fixes rather than social solutions. People demand totality: "What's your solution? What's the cure?" As if there were a black-and-white point-by-point solution to complex issues. But perhaps the need for a defined cure is part of the problem. Black and white is too limited and too reductionist an approach. The answer is more behavioural. What's the solution? Hope. Which we all have. It drives us toward solutions. And empathy, which we need to learn a little more about. Empathy, or emotional intelligence, as it's sometimes called, should be a required subject in all schools, along with lessons in the history of that evolutionarily necessary but now-repellant behaviour, Othering, which needs to be regarded the way many of us now regard physical abuse and slavery. Every child should be taught to try imagining the way a bee thinks, dream how the bird flies, see the world the way her schoolteacher sees it, wonder how the worm knows its earth, make a new friend. Pen pals should be a requirement in schools. Innovations, and lots of them, are needed, both educational and in the corporate world, where it's going to be near-impossible to make inroads until the mythology of the invisible hand in monopoly capitalism is dismissed, along with the corporate globalization that has systematically crippled both low-income people around the world and the planet's climate. By 2016, half of the world's wealth will be controlled by only 1 percent of the world's population—talk about a world without empathy! Now that's Othering.

Imaginative education is already growing among various communities. For a while, empathy was almost a forgotten word, yet considering the many quotes in this story and the many philosophers who have examined our behaviour, it's obviously been an ongoing investigation that now appears to be surfacing dramatically.

Our history as a species is also the story of our doing the impossible: building pyramids, recognizing the rights of women in a growing number of nations, sailing off the end of the world, beating smallpox and rinderpest and near-exterminating polio, flying to the moon, suddenly shifting the paradigm and banning foot-binding, banning slavery and tracking down the remaining few who still enslave.

Our son Chris happened to be in Berlin the night the wall came down after almost fifty years of oppression. And just like that everyone was dancing in the streets. He said you could feel the joy in the air, the people smiling and laughing. A giant infectious spirit of delight instantly overwhelmed the city.

Many millions of people have died through the centuries and continue to die on a mass scale in this century, some for crazy religious solutions, others fighting for freedom, and too many just because they are different from their neighbours, but I can't think of many who were killed out of empathy.

Once, I unconsciously followed the traditional linear dream of history. I believed in progress and even the corporate world's insistence on growth, at least until I encountered that empty lot and the local politics of White Rock and found myself with Tuco on my shoulder, going through a sharp learning curve. Then a few years ago, I read the deeply pessimistic philosopher John Gray, who insists progress is a modern myth. It's close to being a joke. It might be a lovely goal, but it's not a reality. There has been no overall progress among our species in the crucial matters of suffering and happiness, in being able to feed and sleep. As for growth, it took millennia for some of us to recognize that the doctrine of unlimited growth is what environmentalist Edward Abbey called "the creed of the cancer cell." I prefer the old ways I was raised with: "Take what you need and leave the rest." This is now almost a dream, and I worry that despair has infected the young of the world and we have entered an age of looters.

Still . . . still . . . there's hope fluttering in its jar.

Empathy has constantly surfaced in cultures, faded, and then reappeared in other forms. A very few have come to worship the Other by making the Other the beloved. Notably, the Sufi people, but also the Sikhs, who worship a saint who gave water to his wounded enemies on the battlefield. The real Christianity of Jesus. The Koran insists we reach out to others. *Salamun Alaikum*—peace be upon you. I can't think of a better blessing.

And of course in Buddhism, Jainism, and Vedanta there are numerous variations on the idea of karma, how good deeds lead to more goodness. Buddha urged his followers to be sensitive to the suffering of all sentient beings. His first precept is to commit oneself to *ahimsa*, or non-harming. The Mahayana Buddhist bodhisattvas are generous individuals who vow to delay enlightenment until all beings are enlightened. I have several woodcuts and sculptures of Kwannon, that loveliest of bodhisattvas. In the *Metta Sutta,* Theravada monks and lay adherents vow to practice loving-kindness: "Even as a mother protects with her life her child, her only child, so with a boundless heart should one cherish all living beings." This line always reminds me of the brave hen protecting her chick from the hawk.

In a *New Republic* review of *Wired for Culture: Origins of the Human Social Mind,* a book by Mark Pagel, Adam Kirsch says,

Pagel argues that "cooperative altruism" can succeed if each of its participants and recipients share a gene for it. In this way, my death allows copies of my altruism gene to go on living in my neighbours' bodies. (For the same reason, he writes, amoebae are able to cooperate in the service of reproduction, even though only one of many cooperating individuals will actually get the chance to spread its altruistic genes.) That is why we have evolved to have warm feelings toward people we consider members of our group, yet are hostile to members of other groups: "humans seem to be equipped with emotions that encourage us to treat others in our societies as if they were 'honorary relatives.'" This is another wording for the evolutionary principle of mutual aid. Now all we have to do is learn to extend it beyond our community into all communities.

It might be that, as Kapuscinski suggests, Europe and its descendants ended up with a defiled vision of Eastern and Indigenous cultures because the early explorers were mostly rounders, losers, social rejects, and bandits, and so on. What normal person would sail off the end of the world? What normal person would look at a tribe of its own species and declare them animals deserving of enslavement and torture because their skin is a different colour. After decreeing Spaniards had "the right to enslave Indians at their will," Cardinal Garcia Loaisa, who later went on to become a head of the Spanish Inquisition, was confronted by the protests of a missionary who advocated Indian rights at the time. The cardinal dismissed the missionary's appeal by announcing "the Indians were no more than parrots."

If this is the way we treat each other, how are we going to learn to live with the animal kingdom? How are we going to live with our environment and respect its needs?

Schopenhauer said: "The assumption that animals are without rights and the illusion that our treatment of them has no moral

significance is a positively outrageous example of Western cru-
dity and barbarity. Universal compassion is the only guarantee of
morality." He also writes: "Compassion for animals is intimately
associated with goodness of character, and it may be confidently
asserted that he who is cruel to animals cannot be a good man."

The American naturalist Henry Beston, in *The Outermost House*,
expanded more on this issue:

> We need another and a wiser and perhaps a more mystical concept
> of animals. Remote from universal nature, and living by compli-
> cated artifice, man in civilization surveys the creatures through
> the glass of his knowledge and sees thereby a feather magnified
> and the whole image in distortion. We patronize them for their
> incompleteness, for their tragic fate of having taken form so far
> below ourselves. And therein we err, and greatly err. For the ani-
> mal shall not be measured by man. In a world older and more
> complete than ours they move finished and complete, gifted with
> extensions of the senses we have lost or never attained, living by
> the voices we shall never hear. They are not brethren, they are not
> underlings, they are other nations, caught with ourselves in the
> net of life and time, fellow prisoners of the splendor and travail of
> the earth.

IT WAS THE wild years, my most troubled time, around 1970. I
was twenty and going through the turmoil of my introduction to
high-powered testosterone injections, lonely and living inside my
head, in the shadow land between male and female, inhaling the
hallucinogens of the era, the weird spirit land of peyote, the harder
edge of its twisted brother, mescaline, and LSD, the king of them
all, especially when it was pure. I would pack up my Trapper Nel-
son canvas bag, my cast-iron frying pan, rice, mixed bannock flour,
and a pile of books, and then hide out in mountain caves or deep
cedar forests, tiny among the mossy giants, or along the shores of

Long Beach on Vancouver Island and, a few years later, the rogue beaches of Rennell Sound in what was then called the Queen Charlotte Islands, now Haida Gwaii.

I loved being alone in an elemental world—a wild child at home in a wilderness, as we all are. Instinctively, I wanted to be in a world where every one of us, from beetle to giant spruce, is just another insect in the web. Scared of bears yet determined to share that wilderness, even after I witnessed a giant sow grizzly run over an outhouse in the dark of the alpine meadows at a base campsite near the glaciers below Diamond Head in the Coast Range, or after a prowling grizzly caught its paw in the long anchor line of my tent in the North, ripping the tent right off me as it ran back into the bush, probably as frightened as I was. We were two strangers passing in the night. Now, remembering the moment, it is funny. At the time, it was terrifying.

Long Beach, and its satellite sandy beaches in the late sixties and early seventies covered dozens of miles of deserted shoreline. At that time, the local tribe had moved back from the brutal weather of the stormy waters, though they would soon return to the shoreline. On the West Coast, the shore tribes are one with the water, their homes facing it, the backs of their longhouses shut to the forest, which was sometimes an Other to them. I also could not live long where I was unable to glance at the ocean. I'm a child of my habitat, born to live within the realm of the arbutus and the wild rhododendrons, between glaciered mountains and the blue surface of the Salish Sea. I was born for water.

It was considered rude then to make your beach camp within sight of another camp. I'd build driftwood log shelters against the violent Pacific storms, gather a week's supply of firewood, sometimes drop acid, and spend the days reading and walking the beach, mesmerized by the acid-illuminated patterns in the grey sand. Alone, determinedly alone, and looking at the world with my outsider eyes.

There was a creek above the beach—with red water due to the cedar soil, yet delicious in its red way in the days before people invaded every creek and river and infected them with beaver fever, or *giardiasis*, as it's technically called, and it still shocks me that during my lifetime, all the pristine creeks and rivers of my youth have become contaminated and made dangerous by our actions.

I was walking back down the narrow, brush-invaded trail with my full water jug, when something fluttered against my chest. I instinctively slapped it away, and it squirmed black and spastic on the trail. A crow. I'd obviously broken something. It could only gasp and squirm and spasm. I was appalled by what I'd done, and I watched with terror as it convulsed, until I couldn't take any more. I grabbed the bird and swung it against a tree to put it out of its misery, but it didn't die, so I slapped it against the cedar again, the crack ringing through the forest. It was still alive. I went crazy, hitting it again and again, until it was finally dead, and I was ill with the horror. Then I looked up and perched all around me were crows, some only a few feet away. I had no idea how they got there. They were silent, staring at me, and there I was, stoned, a troubled kid going through the late puberty of an injected sexuality, the horror frozen on my face. I could actually feel my skin without touching myself.

The crows remained soundless, solemn. I was being totally Othered.

I picked up my water jug and returned, forlorn, down the trail.

This incident happened almost a half century ago, yet it still sticks in my brain. It's another story I keep telling myself, one in which I was helpless, a victim, though my victimhood caused me to murder an already injured bird.

One of the glories of fiction is that you can move back and forth between reality and fiction. Like most writers, I often use real incidents in my stories, and it's amazing watching how fast they become fiction. Writing non-fiction, however, especially a personal history, is filled with the temptations to change, to make the story a little better. I've resisted that temptation, as farfetched as some of the tales in this memoir may be, though I'm often ransacking my memory, constantly rewriting stories until I can get them right. It's difficult. "Is that the way it happened? How's my memory today?"

In the short story where I used the sad accident with the crow, however, I let loose and turned the man into a predatory crow-monster, strangely welcomed by a woman, in a surrealistic horror story, and I recognize now I was punishing myself while writing that story, Othering myself again into the awful. Too many of the weak and injured want to be punished out of self-hatred, and that's why we admire those who live above their hardships.

In the whirl of stories that comprises every life, beliefs and events and relationships cling to us, so the stories keep returning, sometimes remoulded in the dangerous cauldron of memory, and we become creatures imagining ourselves into existence every morning.

I have no short-term memory—it's all poetry brain. I can remember details of flowers seen forty years ago and whole passages from books I read when I was twenty, but the car keys are another matter.

Fact-checking a memory is daunting. I've already discovered science misinterpretations in a few places to my horror. Now I wonder if I would ever be able to find that red creek again. Then I started trying to verify some of my childhood stories. A few have no witnesses, and when you're a hopeless truth seeker, that can be scary. I can't remember the name of the boy beside me who was slapped with the salt-and-pepper shot. Was that the barn with the owls? Or were the owls and the cranky farmer a half mile farther down the valley? Hell, I can't even find anyone who actually was spanked with a scatter-gun to affirm that's what it felt like, but this is all part of that scattershot world where pain and laughter and beauty walk hand in hand into the confused ocean of life, even if every morning is injected with agony, and I often lie in bed, soaking up the pain of my bones, and think: "Today? No, not yet—one more day." There will always be one more day, until there isn't, and that will be that. Get up and go to work. *Be a man. Get up and go get your books.* And thus the decades pass as I limp out of endless beds into delight.

Troubled by the crippled crow incident, I found my way back to my lean-to shelter, stoked my fire, and cooked my dinner. I had only a few days left in my retreat, and the food was running out. The next morning, I pulled aside the beach towel I used as a door and noticed a single set of footprints in the damp sand outside the door. They looked like crow footprints—one set of prints—as if the bird had flown in, stood facing the towel-door, and then flown away. I grew so paranoid that I thought he was putting a spell on me. I had met my crow spirit-guide, and he wasn't happy.

Later, on the path again, for more water, I saw the crows in the branches, in the trees, their eyes peeking out from the evergreen salal bushes. It was creepy, though they were motionless. Coming back from the spring with my water, I stopped by the corpse of the dead crow where I had left it, half-hidden under the brush. The flies were already laying their eggs, like tiny grains of rice. I couldn't decide whether to take the crow to the beach and bury it in the sand, or leave it to decompose where it fell. Suddenly, I was attacked, crows flying at me from everywhere, pecking.

I made a snap decision and grabbed the dead crow by the foot, shaking the fly eggs off. With the flock in pursuit I fled with the crow and my water jug, down the trail to the open beach, where they circled or perched on logs, though none dared attack me in the open air now. I used a piece of a driftwood board as a shovel to dig a deep hole, laid the crow in the grave, and covered it with sand. I didn't think this was going to earn me much crow forgiveness, but I thought it was worth a try. I needed to make a gesture of respect, and I couldn't bear the flies on the corpse. In my deranged state, I wasn't thinking clearly. Then I continued on down the beach the hundred yards to my shelter, the crows following but still not attacking.

Back at camp, I decided to calm myself with a meal. I was now down to one meal a day. I'd buried a dozen eggs in the sand near my lean-to, and there were four left, along with a can of beans. While opening the beans, I considered the crow. It was obvious I'd struck down a crow defending her nest, and her extended family was out for revenge. There might be starving chicks or cooling eggs concealed in the salal. I was definitely being Othered by the crows. Then I dug my own eggs. It was always a delight to sweep away the sand and see the egg appear, like treasure hunting. Only when I picked up the first egg it was light. Empty. There was a hole in the other side. It was as if the egg was sucked out. I found another egg—the same— the final two were just broken shells in sticky sand. When had they even done this? At dawn? While I was on the trail or burying their friend? I looked around and saw I was circled by crows perched on the driftwood and walking on the sand, as if waiting for a reaction from me. I felt I deserved what I got, so I didn't react. I finished my beans and cleaned out my cast-iron frying pan with sand and sea- water and then napped against my lean-to in the fresh, salty breeze, dreaming of dead birds and a confused, lonely life.

When I woke up, I looked down between my stretched-out legs. A crow sat, snuggled into the sand between my bare feet, gazing at me. I didn't move. Nor did the crow. Finally it stood up, walked sideways around my lean-to, and disappeared.

I wanted to stay another day, but all I had to eat were an orange and a bag of unshelled sunflower seeds in my canvas sack. I decided I would fast. I was also out of acid, coming down, and it struck me that the acid and all the rest of that junk weren't doing me any good anymore. I'd needed their exploratory powers to self-medicate at first, but I was near done. My days of psychic experimentation were winding away that summer, and it made me feel good. I went for a long walk and returned to the shelter tired and hungry.

When I woke in the morning, I realized it had rained. I didn't see the sunflower seed bag. Had I gone out to eat them under the stars before the rain clouds came? Beyond the towel-door there was a large pile of shelled sunflower seeds, neatly stacked into a pyramid in the sand but no footprints, man or crow, in the rain-dappled sand around them. And no sign of the bag. I decided it was time to leave. The crows were winning.

As I was packing my few bits of gear and books into my canvas backpack, I noticed the large mandarin orange in the front compartment. I'd forgotten it. Taking the orange, I went back outside and peeled it, leaning against the driftwood. I'd eaten almost all the bright slices, slowly, lovingly, before the crow appeared again and strode up, unafraid, and sat down between my feet, watching me eat the orange. There were two slices left, and I couldn't help but smile as I divided it and tossed the crow its share. He didn't move, except to glance at the slice in the sand and then at me, no doubt annoyed that I'd dirtied his share. Finally, he picked it up and hopped onto a log and walked behind the shanty, the same way as yesterday. And when I got up to check, he was gone again. He probably walked along the log into the salal and was even now washing his slice in the stream up the trail.

I like to think of him as my magic crow, even if all the magic was in my mind, and even if he wasn't a he. But isn't that a glorious magic also? Then I got a paranoid jolt and thought that this was all a big acid flash. No. It wasn't. For a moment in time we were two creatures meeting in a stunning landscape, unconsciously united in the strangeness of life.

I hauled my now-much-lighter pack onto my shoulders and took the final walk up the creek trail and beyond, where I would begin my long hitchhike on the highway to the ferries and Vancouver. I could see shadows, half-hidden shapes in the thick brush lining the trail. The crows were there, but this time they didn't attack. They knew I was going, I suppose, but crows are such stubborn defenders of their nests I was surprised they didn't give me another beating. I couldn't fool myself into believing I was forgiven, and I assumed the weird crow between my feet was just that, a weird crow. I had no idea what the crows were thinking, still don't, never will. It would be fun to believe for a moment we dropped the borders and accepted each other's world. Or even that my weird crow was some kind of spirit crow, rather than just a clever beggar who cadged the last of my orange out of me.

Whether I'm like him, whether he is sympathetic to my dreams, or whether he is the bird king that stands on the stump and lectures the flock in the field, whether he thinks I'm the asshole who killed his friend, or whether I'm just another lost traveller in a mysterious world where the meaning of meaning is without meaning, we're all in this together, and I can't help smiling. I loved how he betrayed nothing, his cool, easy stare watching me, maybe trying to figure out whether I was capable of crow thought or whether I would make a great meal if I died in front of him. He was definitely his own bird, bird-like in his bird-like way, watching me with his bird nature, one I'm not capable of understanding, though I believe in the trying.

In all my journeys I've been lucky enough to find those moments with creatures and friends and landscapes where I lose myself, become the Other, becoming crow, and the experience is raw life itself. Aristotle said: "In all things of nature there is something of the marvellous." Poetry, wilderness, chopping firewood, our relic history, and birds, especially Tuco, have all led me up many pathways for more than half a century, though so much remains unknowable, so Other, when walking through this forest of miracles on a foggy mountain trail.

Chapter 11

TIME'S ARROW

D ESPITE MY SUSPICIONS about some of our compulsive birdwatchers, encountering a new bird or any other kind of animal (mammal, reptile, or insect) is always a thrill, even after
sixty-five years of riding time's arrow.

Sometimes it's just a glimpse—a surprise. Walking through the
dry jungle of Coba in Quintana Roo, Mexico, I suddenly heard a
loud croaking and breaking of branches above me and to my right
and found myself within twenty feet of an exhausted sandhill crane,
wondering what this giant was doing here, far from his winter quarters in Cuba. No doubt he was wondering the same, gathering his
breath from whatever had driven him into this thicket, and I was
so grateful I could only bow awkwardly. The crane shook itself erect
out of the twigs it had crashed through and slowly clambered up a
sturdy branch to a take-off point but never left. It chose to contemplate me, and I was grateful he stayed. Yet I didn't want to disturb a
distressed, lost bird, so I backed diplomatically out of sight.

Does this make me an inept birdwatcher? I'm more of a bird
empath. And I've also learned looking for birds and other wildlife
can get you into more trouble than you ever imagined, as I discovered in Thailand several years later.

Khao Sok is perhaps the last remaining tract of the magnificent wilderness that once ruled southern Thailand, the core park in a four-part reserve that surrounds it. A friend, Thom, was setting up a new ecological tour of Khao Sok and invited us along for company. This was a journey I couldn't miss. Here, the giant honeybee and the Sumatran rhino still roam free. Two years earlier, a tiger had been spotted leaping up into a tree and snatching a monkey before disappearing into the jungle. Thom noted that the park had an amazing population of hornbills and kingfishers, as well as monkeys in the wild. Here, I would get to wade through elephant mudholes and ascend trails pocketed with cobra dens. It was a stunning place. I was also promised 180 species of birds, including the rare blue-rumped parrot.

Then there's rafflesia. The largest flower in existence. More than three feet around when it erupts mysteriously on a vine from nowhere. The greatest flower in the world, it can weigh as much as eighty pounds.

Khao Sok had its beginning in the early 1970s, when a group of university students was protesting in Bangkok, not an uncommon event then, but the military flew out of control, and helicopters sprayed the students with deadly fusillades. Hundreds, maybe thousands, were killed. Nobody knows. The few survivors, about 170, fled for the southern jungles and developed a hideout at Namtaloo Cave, protected by a sniper's bunker, trip-wire jungle traps, far too many cobra holes, and an intricate warning system. Like the bandits of old, they also kept scary hives of giant Asian bees around their camp to discourage the nosey. Since they were afraid of the army and the army was afraid of them, there was only one fatal encounter—a student was killed when he was surprised by a patrol, panicked, and fired on the soldiers. The little band learned to trade with local villagers, and even the army bases, where more than a few soldiers supported them. They were intelligent, well-armed, mostly polite, and organized. They built their farm plots and a rice mill under the protective canopy of the banyans and magnolias. Since they feared attracting the army's attention, they hardly hunted, leaving most wildlife untouched. Not wanting any roads or incursions that might bring the army into their territory, they scared off loggers and poachers. This was during the era of the great gutting of Thailand's forests. When an amnesty was finally declared (after all, these were the daughters and sons of the wealthy), the students emerged from the jungle, and the new, liberal government, in an astonishing moment of wisdom, declared Khao Sok a national park.

Then the government lost all of its wisdom and flooded a vast section of the park, creating electric power for the growing tourist traps to the south, destroying fifty-five varieties of fish and isolating many of the indigenous species on karst mountaintops that became islands. The biggest animal rescue operation in the world until that date was carried out, as many species, such as monkeys and gibbons, will not swim. Some are still trapped, interbreeding hideously on the smaller islands. The carnage was so great that the man leading the rescue operation committed suicide to protest the disaster. The flooding also left the park accessible to poachers in boats, who began hunting the rarest creatures toward extinction. Villagers who'd originally lived in the park were allowed to continue their traditional fishing, which soon expanded to include guns and traps.

Occasionally an enterprising ranger will discover that under a thin layer of ice a crate load of "fish" strongly resembles dead endangered leopards or macaques, but these discoveries are rare—bribery and graft remain the rules at the park, and the tourist appetite in the southern fleshpots for exotic jungle meat is endless. This is how the world preserves itself in many continents.

It is also where we see time's arrow piercing the heart of an environment. Once a great jungle, now an island sanctuary being crushed by human demands, this park is entropy alive in our eyes, rich life becoming sand.

This topic can be complex, which is why I've been saving it, yet entropy is also exquisitely simple and utterly necessary to life on earth and our story, all of our stories....

One of the most marvellous features of the natural universe is time's invisible arrow, the phrase I've mentioned several times now, the driving concept of the second law of thermodynamics. It states that energy flows to an area of less energy or greater disorder—from the hot to the cold—but is never lost in a closed system.

This law has metamorphosed into numerous definitions over the years, leaping from physics into a shorthand term in information theory, sociology, psychology, mathematics, economics, ecology, and more. It's a unit of measure, but it's also a law of nature, like gravity or electromagnetism.

Time's arrow is the flow we intrinsically recognize and both unconsciously celebrate and mourn. It's the dance toward death. Yet, fortunately, our planet is also the child of very special accidents of time and space. Even as entropy envelops the earth, and its great order flows toward the final disorder of sand and stardust, our sun, undergoing its own entropy, throws more energy at the planet, simultaneously recharging the planet's entropy. Thus, time's arrow, on earth, is a godlike energy movement that flows into nothing while simultaneously rebuilding itself. Like the Hindu god Shiva, it's a creator and destroyer, builder of diversity and demolisher of lives.

Not resting on his laurels after "What Is It Like to Be a Bat?" Thomas Nagel published a book, *Mind and Cosmos*, in 2012, and was heartily reviled, mostly because he suggests there is a natural teleology (a purpose), which, according to Michael Chorost, means "that the universe has an internal logic that inevitably drives matter from nonliving to living, from simple to complex, from chemistry to consciousness, from instinctual to intellectual." An almost perfect description of natural selection and the reversing of entropy triggered by sunlight yet also with a determinist snap to it.

Unfortunately, other scientists accused him of embracing the intelligent design of religious fundamentalists, although Nagel also rules out a god as a creator, just as he suspects natural selection is not the sole producer of life as we know it. He considers his concept another natural law. A lot of this is suspect, but it is interesting thinking. For instance, it could imply entropy behaves like a force, as natural selection does in its own stumbling way, and together they determine the paths of life, not intelligently but mechanically.

Immediately, in my own fuzzy way, I began to wonder if his teleological law was merely another name for entropy. Couldn't entropy be the end purpose? Why can't a law of physics have an internal logic? Others do. Is entropy another way of describing Spinoza's personal relationship with God—his god being an interdependent living organism in which we are all interconnected, a living, moving energy? Time's arrow flowing permanently through us? The dance of Shiva.

What if entropy itself is not only a natural measurement of energy flowing but also a natural force that affects all things, such as consciousness, or that the continual discharges of energy from the sun feed the drive toward ecological diversity? People instinctively want to believe in a hidden energy, some godlike process, and it has been called many things, Henri Bergson talks of the *élan vital*, the creative energy that spurred evolution. The Chinese call it *Chi*. The Ether. The Quintessence. Psychoanalyst Wilhelm Reich's wacky "orgone." Schopenhauer's "will to live." The *ashaka* of Hinduism. After all, we now know that "the universal sea of energy" was a by-product of the discovery of the long-fabled Higgs boson particle.

Tribal cultures also have a tendency to recognize the underglimmer, the *delerium tremendium*, as it's been called, of the planet. Ralph Waldo Emerson thought of it as the "undersong," what he defined as "the emotional undercurrent which carries us along through the life of the inner world." "May the Force be with you," as Obi-Wan Kenobi would say, if you want to be amusing about all this theorizing.

This concept, though extravagantly speculative, allows science to find order in the disorder. I have always celebrated disorder as a natural fact of life. And it was only when I discovered entropy that I realized how disordered life truly is and always will be. It is disorder becoming more disorder. Disorder is my transcendence, the recognition that this second law of thermodynamics decrees energy will always flow toward a greater disorder, even if that disorder can recombine in moments of unfathomable complexity due to the free energy coming in from the sun, which is what really causes the fabulous, delicate diversity of our planet that we are busily destroying with our technology and lifestyles. Time's arrow travels inevitably toward the dispersion of energy, yet the energy from the sun creates those millions of little arrowheads on the shaft, flowing toward the point before losing their charge and then merging into disorder. Life dancing in an invisible stream of particles. It's a marvellous system yet eventually fatal, as we have all witnessed.

On our first day of the journey to Khao Sok, we left the charming seaside village of Krabi at dawn and drove for several hours until we reached the extended finger of the lake and the long-tail boat hired to take us deep into the park. My friend Thom, whom I'd met almost four decades earlier, when he was a guiding light among environmentalists, nicknamed Huckleberry, during the first big ecological campaign in the Queen Charlotte Islands before they became Haida Gwaii, was now devoting his attention to environmental campaigns in Thailand, organizing eco-tours to supplement his income and raise consciousness. Along with Thom and us, there was an intrepid Swiss couple; a young Canadian traveller; Thom's chief guide, Choi; and a few Thai helpers Thom was training to act as guides.

The long-tail has a tall prow traditionally festooned with protective ribbons and is powered by a noisy car engine innovatively mounted on a fulcrum leading to a ten-foot shaft, with a tiny prop on the end. This shaft can also be used as oar and rudder, hence the name long-tail. It allows the boat to shift instantly from high-speed deepwater journeys to jungle creek touring. The motor is so noisy all the drivers are nearly deaf.

Our intent was to spend a night in one of the park's three fabled raft houses—primitive floating bamboo hotels that accept a limited number of visitors. Then we'd take the long-tail for some night viewing of animals. The next day, we'd idle through the jungle fjords, wild viewing and admiring the spectacular karst geology, travelling to the trailhead leading to the Namtaloo Cave, where the Swiss couple and Choi would camp out for the night, before exploring the cave with its blind fish, frogs, cave crickets, and enormous spiders, while Sharon and I returned with Thom to leave the park. I had those vague dreams of seeing a few rare hornbills and especially a rafflesia flower, and maybe even that rare blue-rumped parrot.

We jammed our gear into the long-tail and followed the karst limestones in the grey afternoon, delighted by the monkeys and ancient palms on the cliffs. Tall spires of islands erupted out of the misty waters like ancient melted castles, ornamented with mysterious gibbons shuffling under the leaves.

Around a bend, we encountered one of the floating fishing villages, a ramshackle bamboo construction of brutal poverty and cheerful faces. Tying up, we clambered onto the rickety platforms housing miniature aquafarms strung with nets, where ancient-eyed carp glared malevolently between the bamboo paths. It was a combination of float home, fishing camp, and grocery store, open to the elements yet deliriously exotic in a *Huckleberry Finn* way. We bought some garlic and fish from a woman who spoke no English but could count in several languages. After much laughter and sign language and the confused transfer of bills and some coins that nearly dropped through the bamboo floor into the lake, we sorted out the requirements for tonight's dinner, while our Thai companions remained in the boat, enjoying the theatre, and I wondered how many carp over the years had swallowed shiny golden coins.

That's when I realized, here I was, in the heart of time's arrow, floating amid beauty yet already knowing where this beauty was going, that this park, at this time, is slowly becoming a fake wilderness—a pretty jungle gradually being stripped of its wildlife.

Speeding down the central lake and up an inlet, we arrived at the Krai Son raft house, an oasis of beauty and silence in the jungle. The raft house consisted of a central building joined by a surrealistic twig walkway strung with Christmas lights for guidance in the dark, which led to a row of several tiny floating huts. Another twig walkway led to shore, where the cement toilets sat like ugly toadstools on the muddy hillside. A third floating ramp led to a few parked long-tails and a bigger toadstool that was a cement building used for meetings, perched on the peninsula's end, surrounded by a few glorious red flowers.

I had to be careful, since I'm six feet tall and weigh nearly 220 pounds, and I could feel the rotting branches of the walkway crack if I stepped too hard. Sharon and I took one of the tiny bamboo raft houses, barely five feet at the peak, its entrance perhaps three feet high. It also had a back door out to the water, where you could leap off the slippery, water-slimy deck for a swim when the air grew hot and muggy. The lake water was limpid and soft, almost silky. Our little hut barely slept the two of us, and since it already had a lean, I took the high end, righting it. The hut was very romantic. I noticed the floor of our deck had a few fresh bamboo leaves. Life sprouting between our lewd naked bodies.

This was when Thom called us outside our room and informed us the staff had spotted a king cobra swimming to the raft house, and they'd spent the last day searching for it to no avail. He also said they were worried because they had important guests arriving, and the last thing they needed was a king cobra arising out of the reeds of the raft house. I told him they needed a mongoose or a peacock to deal with the problem. We laughed and left ourselves to our fate.

At dinner, we grouped around a table, excited and joking, planning our night expedition along the shoreline to spot wildlife, while a pair of uniformed park wardens sat on the mat floor, drinking Mekhong whiskey and scooping down their dinner. On the open deck, about twenty young Thai were singing hauntingly beautiful traditional ballads, and I realized I had a near-permanent smile on my face. On the floor beside them, a cluster of grumpy-looking older men and women played a card game involving a lot of money. Piles of Thai bahts littered the rug while they chugged an expensive bottle of brandy. I studied the game, trying to understand its rules, but they glared suspiciously at me, so I thought I was being rude and turned apologetically away, only to be enthusiastically invited by the rangers to have a drink and inspect their rifles, which I'd noticed earlier. I refused the drink politely but admired their guns. They resembled leftover Lee-Enfield's from wwi, only with enlarged cartridge cases. These guns can be uncannily accurate in the hands of a trained sniper, and an amateur could miss a barn, so they're a little iffy. The happy rangers made lots of tough-guy gestures and American movie star combat feints as they demonstrated how they fight dangerous poachers. I laughed agreeably along with them but didn't believe a word.

Later, back at our table, I noticed the raft house manager talking to the wardens; he nodded discreetly toward the gamblers. Then he came over to the table and began to apologize profusely to Thom, whom he'd known for several years. Thom said there was nothing to apologize about. We all had our rooms. Everything was fine. The man kept apologizing, even as he backed away, which we thought mysterious and amusing. Thai politeness can be a delightful puzzle. When I looked back, I noticed the rangers had vanished, taking their whiskey with them. Only their plates of food remained on the floor, half-eaten.

Our meal arrived and all was forgotten as plates of delicious Thai cooking hit the table. Potatoes and cauliflower in a milky green curry. The fish we'd bought earlier were deep-fried whole and cross-hatched, sprinkled with ginger and razor-sliced green onions. Fragrant rice. We sat back, sipping our beers after dinner, chatting, when Sharon returned from touring the tiny garden beside the cement building. "What's this?" she asked, leading me away from the table to behind the floating cookshack, where two long-tails were moored, improbably stacked almost eight feet high with black boxes and electrical equipment. I studied the black boxes for a second, unbelieving. "They're speakers."

"Oh no," Thom said, suddenly standing behind us. "Oh no."

"Does this mean what I think it means?" I asked.

"Now I know why he was apologizing. We're going to get a karaoke night."

The rest of the night was a hallucinatory dream of exquisite beauty and nightmare, the rickety raft house illuminated by Christmas lights, the banging, driving rhythms from the cement compound onshore echoing across the deep jungle. We fled the camp to spot wildlife, but the rain howled and poured, and our boatman, like most long-tail drivers had two speeds, full roar or stopped. The Thais are a wonderful proud, stubborn people with many principles. Anger is a dark taboo. They regard it as impolite to show annoyance, even if you are annoying them. So we suffered as he roared at high speed up to the shoreline and blasted it with hot lights. This was not our idea of communing with the local wildlife. Complaining was a terrible mistake because that accidentally belittled his guiding skills. The angrier we made him the more he smiled, and the harder he cranked the motor, until we finally asked to return home because we felt like abusers of the park—frustrated by our crazy boat booming along the shore at high speed in the darkness, scaring away any wildlife. There would be no hornbills or tigers flashed in the forest this night, thankfully.

As we later discovered, the elder celebrants were all senior officials who ran the parks branch, accompanied by their junior staff. That's why they could drink hard liquor and gamble, both illegal in a park, so imperiously at the raft house. They ran the place. That's why the wardens disappeared with their whiskey. They feared for their jobs.

ENTROPY ALSO LED to the stardust that gave birth to us and to what we will become again. Did entropy and natural selection make me? Yes. The beautiful yet molested Khao Sok? Yes. The birds that have surrounded my life? Did time's arrow make an African grey parrot I named Tuco and make me live with him for this past twenty-five years? Yes. As individuals we might fight the terrible silence, that is the death of each of us. Our molecules are constantly reforming and forming through entropy and a dash of energy from the sun—creating more fabulous descendants, while we follow time's arrow to our deaths.

We are all flowing down a mysterious river where, in the eddies and the deep pools, new kinds of amphibians slide through the reeds, or a few new fishlike creatures become the giant sturgeons of the deep river over the millennia. Birdsongs are created by the thousands, adding to the flow, even while some of us fade away. It's built into our consciousness, another reason why we recognize and reach for the flow, "the zone," where energy transfers and we suddenly skate like the wind, or sing the poem that enthralls our bones, or feel the right gear click into the right notch.

It's a one-way journey into quietude, yet for the planet, it's the joyful, constant rebuilding of wild lives by a sun, combined with the law that will inevitably lead to sand and silence. This is the mystery, the ebullient scattershot of life dancing.

THERE IS A theory of emergence that might apply here. It states that an independent organism, multiplying, will eventually overcome randomness and develop patterns and behaviours without guidance. Or as Berkeley psychologist David Krech noted: "There is no phenomena, however complex, which when examined carefully will not turn out to be even more complex."

Almost everyone intrinsically admires diversity—the richness of life—and it is commonly thought the destruction of diversity is an unnatural thing. It would be the same as destroying the sunlight, and this is what we are facing today. It's as if our cells are telling us what's going on in the background. Are we attempting to deny entropy—the love child of thermodynamics?

Myself, I like to think there's something to be said for simplicity, and I often joke we are going through the devolution mysteries: we began as perfect one-celled creatures and have gradually grown so complex that we're destroying our own environment until we return to that single cell again.

It has to be remembered that evolution goes in every direction.

AS THE KHAO Sok party got drunker and louder, and our ears hurt with the shattering decibels roaring out of the speakers, we asked the partiers several times to diminish the noise, which they would do, for at least five minutes. Even our main guide, Choi, stood aside shyly, uncomfortably trapped between us angry *farangs* (foreigners) and the wealthy park bureaucrats. He was a handsome man in perfect physical condition, a former commando who was once trapped behind Cambodian lines, and some nasty rumours about starvation and survival followed those poor men when they returned. I never asked him about them because I assumed it was either some twisted Cambodian gossip or the fantasy of an infatuated tourist who liked her Thai men hot and scary.

When I finally cornered one of the young park minions belting out Madonna at ear-splitting decibels, I asked him: "Why, why would you do this? Come here to the wildest, quietest part of all Thailand, the place you are supposed to be protecting, in order to make so much noise?"

He looked blankly at me, as if he couldn't understand my problem. "Why, of course! Because it is the wildest, most rare, quiet jungle. So we could make our impact!"

These are the protectors of the dream, and my heart fell at these words. All I could see was time's arrow.

By 2 AM, I could stand it no more. I stomped up to the cement room on the shore again, the broken twigs of the bridge crunching beneath my feet. The last drunken dregs of the party were rolling in spilled noodles and whiskey bottles, happy as clams and delighted to see me, trying to feed me, offering me whiskey. Then they realized how angry I was, and the party went silent. I denounced them all, a foreigner explaining what their wilderness meant, and they nodded politely, while I noticed our ex-military guide standing outside the door, holding his machete, and it was clear he'd decided he would have come to my aid if they attacked me, whether he liked it or not, in that great loyal way you will find among many Thai men like him.

The room was crawling with giant, golden cockroaches; one slipped inside my shoe. It was nearly two inches long, and I had to take my shoe off and shake it out while continuing my harangue. Fortunately, the elder heavies had gone to bed earlier in a drunken stupor, and only their gentle young staff remained, respectfully listening. Then a cockroach fell from the ceiling onto my head and down my shirt, and I had to rip my shirt off to get it out. Nobody laughed, as if this were a commonplace occurrence. When I was finished and putting my shirt back on, exhausted by my anger, a young man politely said, "We will turn the music off in five minutes. Thank you." Then he smiled.

I couldn't help but smile back, knowing I was a fool and an intruder as I strode down the rickety walkway now rendered dangerous by my many branch-breaking trips. They kept their word this time, and soon, the calm, eerie, soundscape of the jungle settled over the raft house. It was shortly before dawn.

I rose a few hours later. They were smiling once more, only wistfully now, as they clambered, hungover, into their long-tails. Some of the elders glared threateningly at me when I took their picture so that they could be identified when I complained later, a complaint I'm sure was almost flamboyantly filed in the oblivion folder of a Bangkok newspaper. The long-tails started up and all were soon motoring along the shoreline. Then I went up to the ghastly cement toilets, where I amused myself watching the geckos and frogs keeping the insect life down while I dealt with a sudden attack of diarrhea. Distantly, there was the sound of automatic weapons as the departing guardians of the park shot a few monkeys out of the trees and probably some of the rare hornbills, and who knows what else, while on their way home—jungle meat souvenirs from their karaoke night at Khao Sok. And I contemplated the day's approaching long journey to Namtaloo Cave, the pale cave crickets, the giant frogs, the rafflesia?—an outsider and ashamed once again at my rudeness last night, even though it was also clear this park was doomed if these were the people running it. How can we ever save the planet from climate change and extinction when even our park keepers are encouraging our return to sand and silence?

If our fabulous ever-changing entropy is the god of creation—the whirl of the leaves in the stream like a book of stories inside stories, the striving to reproduce, to make more (Oh, don't we love our children), until no more can be made in the great beaker of the earth, and it all comes tumbling apart, and the entropic drive dusts itself off as it renews its inexorable push toward disorder throughout the universe—I guess I can live with that, I decide with some irony. I have to. We all do.

As long as the sun's energy lasts, there will be life. It's the noise of creation, this stirring out of rocks and elements into enzymes, into the orchid and the liver fluke and the elephant. It's the natural world's cry against the silence where we all go, until the cells break down and begin their journey again on this forever river of new forms. That silence is the death of the individual in the roar of creation. I can feel the thrum of its approach in my crippled bones. I have a few years ahead of me, but time's crazy arrow, creator, and destroyer, with its mighty hammer, has been stalking me for years.

THE EVIL TALENT of Tuco is that he takes pleasure in teasing people. Like all of us, he demands amusement, inventing stories as he goes, usually with us as characters in them. I've learned a lot from watching him constantly constructing and deconstructing the world to make his stories, how it's such a universal impulse yet so very different in its demands. We tell our stories to make sense of the world. He tells his stories to drive away the silence. As I've noted earlier, he's a flocking bird, and he needs lots of noise to feel alive, like the Khao Sok partiers in the raft house.

We were away from our home in White Rock one night, but our long-time friends Lesley and John were driving in from Alberta and would arrive while we were out. So we left the lights on and the key in a place for them to find. Upon arriving, they let themselves in, took their luggage to their room, and went to bed. They were in bed only a few minutes when they heard someone banging the knocker on the front door.

Lesley got up and went to the door, but there was no one there. Back in bed again, she soon heard another knock. Again, no one there, but as she was returning to her room, Tuco accidentally gave away the show by knocking before she reached her room.

Alone in the silence of the night in his room with the light accidentally left on, he had decided to amuse himself. And since Lesley and John hadn't knocked but quietly let themselves in, he must have decided to punish them for not knocking. Was he demonstrating the proper protocol to strangers? He only started knocking after this incident, and wouldn't do it often. It's a story that only the mind of a parrot can understand.

If you think about it, all the forms of beauty, whether in sound or animal or landscape or dance or painting or these stories—all of them take us outside of ourselves, away from self-awareness and the knowledge of our fate. It's like a reprieve from life while being in the heart of life itself. That cognitive dissonance again. Perhaps our art is what takes us closest to Tuco and the animals of the world. Their ability to pay attention. When we are in the music, when we reach that peak for that brief moment; then we are finally the Other.

Imaginative identification crosses the border into possession, and that's the beauty in any art we chase. And those moments when Tuco and I make our noise together, when we forget all else but our extraordinary conversations; then we are both inside the Other. When Tuco knocks, he is truly the knocker. He inhabits it.

Perhaps this is why I have always loved chopping firewood or being inside the poem as I'm composing it, lost to all else but the chopping or the poem. I am in the rhythm. The zone. I am time's arrow. I am unconscious. I am the will to dance. *"Je est an autre."*

This is what happened to the naturalist J.A. Baker in his small, elegant book *The Peregrine*. He became the falcon at several points, unconsciously—paying attention so hard he became invisible. I've felt the same many times over the years. Sometimes I am a parrot, asking Tuco's important question: "What's that?" Sometimes I am a story. Sometimes I am this story, and that's why I have to write it.

The anthropologist Bronislaw Malinowski says in *Magic, Science and Religion:* "To judge something, you have to be there." Tuco doesn't have to be there. He is there, and that's why he has a real passion for events, the arrow flying. The better a disaster the more he enjoys it, at least as long as it's not happening to him.

One of his finest moments came when our older boy, Chris, was still living at our home in White Rock, before we moved to the farm on Salt Spring Island. He was studying at university, and being a typical nineteen-year-old, he was happily multi-tasking, writing an essay on my computer in my office while cooking french fries in a shallow frying pan in the kitchen. Not surprisingly, the chips caught fire. The fire soon began to run up the wall behind the stove. He smelled the smoke, rushed out, and proceeded to do every possible wrong thing with spectacular finesse. He grabbed a towel and carried the flaming, splattering frying pan across the newly refinished fir floor to the other side of the room and heaved it into the sink, where the flames continued up that wall. Now he had two walls on fire, so he turned on the water, which splashed the burning oil everywhere. Panic can be a fabulously interesting response, and it's not confined to people. Somehow, he remained relatively unscathed in this mess, and after flinging a pot of water at the stove, as if to make sure he'd destroyed that too, he finally got his act together and used a towel to snuff out the flames that hadn't got a solid grip on the wall yet, while in my office, Tuco was cheering on all the running and splashing and clanging of pots and the smoke pouring around the house.

This was the moment I walked through the door, saw the smoke, and heard the crashing. I checked to see Tuco was safe so far, and then I entered the kitchen. It was a mess, and Chris was standing there, a little abject, practically in tears at all the damage his panic had caused. That's when he told me he'd called the fire department, too. *Oh no,* I thought, *not the fire department*—knowing how much damage firefighters could do to a building while ensuring that a fire is out. Also, since I was the former hell-raising alderman for the city of White Rock, I guessed this opportunity would bring every firefighter down to check out the house of the crazed revolutionary who'd been on town council.

I began opening doors and windows, releasing the smoke. Then I helped Chris clean up while Tuco cackled in the office. The floor was particularly galling. Someone had put ugly linoleum tiles over it before Sharon bought the house, and Sharon and I had spent close to five years peeling it off one square at a time, along with the impossible tar that glued the linoleum to the wood floor beneath. Our goal was a square foot a night. It was that bad. We'd only finally accomplished this job and refinished the lovely fir floor that had been beneath. Now it was spattered with burn marks and water that would no doubt stain the burnt wood. It was shot.

We were contemplating the watery, burnt kitchen and the poor budgie, Blue, who'd protected himself from the smoke by sticking his head under his bell, when several burly firemen came charging into the house through the open front door. Firemen are very big these days, with all their gear, their air tanks, their coats, the entire regalia, and this was too much for Tuco, who had already been enjoying our antics in the kitchen. "Over here!" he called out. "In here! Come here." And before I knew it, there were at least half-a dozen, wide firemen in their bright coats and hats, a few with axes in gloved hands, cramped into my small office with Tuco.

"Hi, boys," he said.

"Where's the fire?" someone asked embarrassedly. I hoped he wasn't asking the parrot. The room was so packed I couldn't even get into my office.

"Not in there!" I called from outside the door. There was an amusing moment of silence and I couldn't resist it. "The fire was in the kitchen. That's the parrot."

They sheepishly shuffled out of the office, while Tuco called after them: "Byyye...." And then. "Come here! It's party time!" These many years later, it's hard to remember all that he said, but I think he even copied them: "Where's the fire?" He has a real skill at recognizing words that work. I shut his door so that he wouldn't confuse the issue any further.

One is the all. All in the one. Everything echoing. These are the memory circles, the Gordian knot of the brain—only if you cut this knot, you just get a bunch of loose ends. How do we see Midgley's whole aquarium? How do we tell a story? A story of ourselves or a story of a bird, of many birds and how these many birds meet our many selves in the biosphere. A story with so many voices conflicting, a babel of stories, one shouting over another, one whispering his truth to stones, one carving her story on a stone. That's a life, and this life has been like that, all the circles of pain and abuse and guffaws and beauty, never finding an answer except in the stories themselves.

Once I saw a nature documentary that suddenly focussed on a small white spider in the forest. The spider was scampering along until it noticed a bug perched on a leaf across a tiny clearing. The spider stealthily backed up, walked around a tree, and came up behind the leaf. It climbed the leaf until it suddenly leaped over it and onto the bug.

Amazed, I realized I had just witnessed a spider telling itself a story. It was a white spider quest. It saw the prey. It made a plan. It executed that plan and snuck up behind the prey. It was a story told with a pure and tragic simplicity. And it made me wonder if I was nothing more than a little white spider in the scary forest of life, telling myself stories.

This story has called for stories within stories, a sea of stories among stories, and all of these stories within a larger story. The Other comes in too many forms to simply grasp. Knowledge needs to find its own route like water, and we have to each find our own way to defeat the Othering, break out of the paradigm of false assumptions about evolution, of progress, of our history. A tough, possibly impossible task on a misty mountaintop.

The legendary second-to-last paragraph in *On the Origin of Species* states:

> When I view all beings not as special creations, but as the lineal descendants of some few beings which lived long before the first bed of the Cambrian system was deposited, they seem to me to become ennobled. Judging from the past, we may safely infer that not one living species will transmit its unaltered likeness to a distinct futurity. And of the species now living very few will transmit progeny of any kind to a far distant futurity; for the manner in which all organic beings are grouped, shows that the greater number of species in each genus, and all the species in many genera, have left no descendants, but have become utterly extinct.

That's the nature of our fight for survival. The now-famous line from *Jurassic Park* applies with a vengeance: "Life finds a way." And Spinoza put this in perspective. "All things excellent are as difficult as they are rare." I guess I learned this from my earliest memories.

My first bird death was one of my father's beautiful tumblers. I was smaller than memory then, but I still remember. I saw the bird land on the road in front of the house just as the car came down the hill. There was an explosion of feathers and that was beauty, gone in a casual instance, those awful feathers floating down.

This was the house of my first remembered lessons in fate. My parents had moved from the city centre. I was in the forest behind our home. This is hard to imagine now, because I was all alone out there, barely five years old, amusing myself on a rope swing. Those were the days when children could still wander in the woods.

I fell off the swing, and sitting on the ground, I watched the board knotted into the hemp rope slowly return. I lowered my head and let it go right past me. But I was too young to understand pendulums, so when I sat erect again, the board returned and cracked the back of my head. Stunned, I knew there was blood running down my back, so I ran home and knocked on the kitchen door, which, strangely, was locked. My mom was mopping the floor and yelled something like: "Go around to the front door. I'm washing the floor." So I did. I knocked on the front door. Who knows why I knocked so timidly. Knock, knock. Perhaps it was because I was so stunned. My exasperated mom flung open the door this time, and I think she started shrieking right away, aghast at seeing me so silent and bloody. Sixty years later, she still feels guilty about making me go around to the front door. She took me to my first emergency visit at a hospital.

Fortunately, it wasn't a serious wound, but we often talk about that incident, and our memories are fading, so we've lost a little of the story over the years. I was always annoying her when I was a child, or scaring her, like the time I fell on the hot stove and burned that target into my belly.

I don't think my kind was ever designed to live. In the Greek universe, and many other ancient societies, I would have been left on a mountain after birth. That's why, when I contemplate Tuco, I realize I never truly belonged to the world the way he does, and perhaps that's why I came to love with an almost excessive emotion the beauty of our life on an earth so extreme. What a treasure we have all been given. Even pain can be a gift. It made me pay attention.

There are so many birds in this history of my many selves. The eagle in my arms, proud and staring into my eyes, inches from my face. I'm glad I never thought to taint him with a name. He stayed wild, unlike Blue, the budgie who tried to save himself from the fire by sticking his head up into his bell and then slowly died after suffering from the after-effects of the fire and smoke which fortunately had not gone in Tuco's direction.

The soft-singing canary of my childhood, Yellowbird, who strangled itself in its cage; Zero, who quit singing when he met his female nemesis. My first chickens, me groping for a warm egg underneath a hen as it clucked nervously; their ripped-apart bodies after my friend's dog killed them in the night. The boy with blue hair and the fist out of nowhere. Dozens of naked boys turning and staring silently at me in the school shower. My pigeons, the rollers and tumblers, pouters and kings, barred homers—memory returns them to me often. Standing in my coop again with my arms outstretched, inviting the birds until I am floating in a rain of feathers and bird shit and fluttering dreams, close to the way I dreamed fifty years later.

The dance of a hundred rescued hummingbirds erupting out of my palm, one by one, over the decades—their trembling, defiant need to be alive and free. My disco dancing nights with Tuco, how for a moment, the dance and the song became everything and we forgot we were man and bird. We were dancers who gave all away for Shiva's dance.

Get up and go back and get your books. History is now. With age and poor health catching up to me, I find the "now" my most beautiful era, since the future is short and I've walked past the bullies of my childhood, though not past the crumbling bones and their electric stabs of pain in the mornings of my life. I've been lucky to have good guides. My father hauling me up and insisting I walk through the fire. Tuco always flying ahead, a grey-feathered crazy Beatrice fluttering up the foggy mountain. I've almost travelled my little comedy all the way from the inferno to the paradise of silence and stardust.

I no longer laugh at the dinosaurs. All brawn and no brains—when I was a child that's why we thought they went extinct. The evidence today suggests our chance of lasting as long as dinosaurs is close to nil. Although we do have that amazing ability to change the paradigm, dig ourselves out of the holes we've dug ourselves into with our nearly unnatural knack for changing the future when it looks most dire.

The general conclusion among climate scientists and a few philosophers is that there will be an "event" in the next fifty years. In the whirlwind of climate change, dangerous epidemics arising out of factory farms, and the too-tightly knit economics of globalism, something will break our chain of history. It's not hard to imagine how fast our intricate, globalized lifestyle can collapse. Also, we've overflowed our ecological niche and skimmed the easily attainable major minerals and metals from the biosphere. As several philosopher-writers, like Ronald Wright and Margaret Atwood have noted, if there's a collapse it will be nearly impossible to rebuild another economy as powerful and intricate, just as happened with the Khmer civilization, whose capital, Angkor, the world's biggest pre-industrial city, collapsed, probably due to ecological changes. The same with the Mayan empire.

The oil will be too deep, the metals already dug out of the ground. There might be a road warrior era of post-industrial tribes salvaging the wreckage before we return to what we were before the invention of the farm and writing, a bunch of hairy creatures with sticks, painting the walls and carving flutes out of thigh bones of cranes, singing and dancing around the fires in the caves of the world. Millions dead, the climate careening back into its socket.

Despite the doom that's in the air today, if the worst does happen, the odds are good a few of our grandchildren will find life back in those caves again, where we caused the least harm as a species, while the night birds sing raucous in the jungles, creating new species, everything from liver fluke to crocodile. And some woman will stand up beside the fire and tell a story about time's arrow, without even having a clue what time's arrow is, yet understanding it in her gut.

Since we are story creatures, that's what will survive in us, the stories. "Come in. Come in. It's party time!" I will be dead in a few years. And eventually my family and friends with follow, each of us leaping into silence as we make our final bow to the powers of entropy recycling us once more. Yet I don't have any doubt the party will keep starting over and over again.

We are such wonderful dodgers of the dooms we make. I remember the peak oil panic, the population bomb, and the threat of nuclear cold war. Despite those predictions, we survived. We dance on our own graves, a little bit Shiva ourselves. We have a knack for creative destruction. Hope still compels us toward creating a future that works, like my dream of the defeat of Othering through education and the outstretched hands of empathy. That's a fantasy. But it's a good fantasy, and it has a chance of becoming a reality. The simple truth is that we need cultural solutions to complement scientific and technological solutions. And we will always need hope. It's Tuco looking down the road and inviting everyone in. Occasionally the crowd does arrive, and the world changes. Then it actually is party time again.

Ice ages. Fire ages? Disease? Nuclear wars? What will get us? Who knows? If the worst happens, I'm still placing my bets on our remnant descendants, the beautiful survivors, inhaling the gift of the sun's energy and song-dancing their anthems of triumph and defeat, while the new birds sing all around the caves where we'd retreated for shelter, and the mystic world rebuilds itself.

Epilogue

I WAS TEACHING AT a university in Vancouver and returned to my room shortly after dinner so that I could phone Sharon and engage Tuco in one of our clucking, lip-smacking chuckling, beak-tapping conversations. Every once in a while, he'd give me a hello, but he'd long since trained me to converse in his language on the phone. Then I got distracted by some thoughts about this memoir. I was just beginning the third draft and forgot to call, lost in the computer screen, until the phone rang.

It was Sharon. There was a long pause before she spoke. "I have some bad news."

"Bad news? What happened?"

"Tuco died."

"Tuco died? How could he die?"

"I don't know. I think he had a heart attack."

"A heart attack? He's too young to have a heart attack!"

"He was good in the morning, but when I stopped to talk to him at lunch he was very quiet and maybe grumpy, and I thought he should come downstairs for company. So I went downstairs and got his other cage ready. But when I came back in the house from the garden at dinner time, I didn't hear him upstairs. So I called up. 'Tuco? What are you doing? Why are you so quiet? Are you dead?'

I was just teasing him like usual, but I didn't hear anything. So I went up the stairs and found him dead in the bottom of his cage, like he fell off his perch."

And that was it, the stunning news, a surprise from nowhere, the way death arrives at our door. Oh death! "The mother of beauty," as Wallace Stevens once said. She made me so many promises over the years, put me on the suicide express and then took me off it, made me live my life against her promise of a death by forty, waiting still, twenty-five years later. Then she slipped in through the back door and took Tuco instead of me. We'd always joked about how we'd have to leave him to Roben in our will.

Sharon photographed him at the bottom of the cage so that I could see how he died and then lifted him up, wrapped him in a favourite scarf of hers, and put him in the freezer, since I couldn't return home for another week. Oh, the freezer! After all those freezer and parrot jokes. How our fate burns us.

She took him out the night before I returned and found him a beautiful wooden jewellery box. He fit perfectly in it. She cleaned off my oak desk and put a vase of roses and a vase of scarlet daylilies on either side of the box.

I played some of the music we had shared over the years, dancing together, dancing. Oh, we danced so much in our time. I poured a glass of Scotch and then removed his covered body from the box, put it on the desk, and slowly unwrapped the silk scarf until his head was revealed. He was so tiny, so frail, so dead, a little blood around his upper beak. My friend. My master and mentor and my child. My spirit bird. My Beatrice. He was also his own bird. He thought he was a giant, yet he was small and frail and dead at thirty-one, only a little older than the legendary Alex when he died.

I held him in my hands. The touch was familiar yet distant, and then, Oh, horror, he started to bleed profusely through the nostrils on his upper beak. He'd thawed out. I was sure he'd died of a brain aneurism from the small amount of blood already in his nostrils.

The freezing had ruptured it further. I kept wiping up the blood. Another tissue. For a few minutes, it seemed endless, and his face grew red with blood behind the feathers. Tuco, in front of my eyes, was becoming not-Tuco. Cellular life was making its demands, and those demands are always final. I wrapped him in the scarf and put him back in the box. I had a last glass of Scotch.

We buried him under the willow tree with all the other lost heroes of our farm. I put one of my small hand-fired celadon drinking cups next to the box. We covered him with dirt and planted his cement-based perch above him, where the applewood perch will rot away, like the rest of the living world.

Sharon and I sat on the stone bench by the willow overhanging the pond in the large pasture. After a while, Sharon left quietly, letting my hand go, but I stayed on the bench under the willow… and wept… and weep even now, writing these words.

I don't cry just for Tuco, I cry for the scattershot world we lived through. My small god-bird, he taught me how to think parrot a little. I didn't fully understand how much I was an outsider, an outlier, until I met him. He taught me how to understand the thinking of the Other, how our world is becoming an Other, and how to respect the Other. Like that rock salt from the scatter-gun of my childhood, we evaporate. We are gone—the leftovers of an interstellar explosion. All this rich life come out of that dust, and all this rich life will return to that dust. This is not a possibility—it's an inevitability. The only question is when.

"Knock, knock!" And then nothing is there. The answer never arrives. It's a scattershot world.

I weep for the ending I cannot know until I meet it, and I weep for what our species has failed to learn as it rides its increasingly faster freight train to oblivion.

"Whaddya know?" Not much. I know only the reality out there. I still talk parrot when the door is closed and I am alone, and I often hold imaginary conversations with Tuco. I know I am still becoming

Tuco, though I never will travel far enough, of course. I'm trapped here, reading about the fate of the birds around the world, the constant wars between the Us and the Other on every continent, the climate shaking its rough dust of fate upon the earth, and I'm still talking with a dead parrot, *Je est un autre,* talking to myself with a parrot's voice—knowing what's yet to come for me.

"What's that?"

"That's silence, Tuco."

APOLOGY

————

I KNEW I WAS going to write about Tuco one day. I didn't know it was going to take me back down the rabbit hole of my childhood.

Like Flannery O'Connor, "I write because I don't know what I think until I read what I say."

My books begin with images, stray thoughts; they daydream themselves into existence out of some strange urge to adventure into an unknown and sometimes scary territory. It has to be scary, because otherwise, it's not new country, and if there's no adventure, there's no new story. Why use up all that paper unless you are going to go "Further," as the famous sign said on the *Electric Kool-Aid Acid Test* bus of Ken Kesey and the Merry Pranksters in the sixties?

I explained in the foreword that I thought I had dealt with my childhood in *Uproar's Your Only Music*, the first of this trilogy. I only gradually realized that there were other stories buried within it. I am returning to this subject here, because I think it important to mention due to this new journey into my life with birds, and because *Uproar* is now out of print, and copyright issues could make it difficult to reissue in its original format.

Still, this has left me in the wonderful and weird, almost unique, position of having written a three-headed memoir, each book branching out from the same origin stories and then travelling in different directions. *Uproar* is the story of my childhood tentacling into the years beyond my twenties, but only slightly. *Trauma Farm* follows my childhood into the years after I reached forty, and at our farm, and *Tuco* explores my life with birds until old age and today, and what I learned from him/them and the bullying of my childhood.

If I am blessed with enough time, despite my crumbling health, to bring back *Uproar*, its final edition will be different and will include more of my street life as a wild child. Stories are strange kingdoms—like life, constantly evolving. Some of us lock into an early and often limited version of the "truth" and fossilize. Others have to keep following those foggy paths. I enjoy the craziness of the wander, even though my "rewriting" of my childhood might irritate some readers, and I apologize for that. After more than sixty-five years, I still have no idea what my life means—or even if it means, which I doubt—but I remain willing to learn the story, and remember more of it.

This final volume of the trilogy has been a hell of a ride. Until a few months ago, I didn't even recognize I was channelling, in my eccentric wounded peasant way, the elegant *Divine Comedy* of Dante. But there it is—paradise—only paradise in my world is the magic of entropy, the dust and the whisper of energy that throbs through us, and I'm bemused that I would eventually come to grow comfortable with the second law of thermodynamics, its implications, and its philosophical possibilities. I'm very aware of how cheeky some of these speculations are. But in the end, that's what they are—speculations inspired by the devilish spirit of Tuco.

I had no idea that *Tuco* would evolve into a meditation on life itself and on human behaviour, but this is the story that wrote me (with much help from Tuco), and I ask the reader's forgiveness for my wanderings through the fog of my life. The story told me, and for that I can make no apologies.

ACKNOWLEDGEMENTS

THERE IS MANY a "thank-you" called for in the creation of this memoir. I can't name them all, but there are some people I don't want to miss. First, I need to thank Tuco for inspiring the story of us, and I need to thank Sharon Doobenen even more for surviving five years of me intensely reliving my past and some of the torments that caused us, as well as for her quick reaction in snapping the cover photo of Tuco, just as he was about to attempt a Tuco more than two decades ago.

I want to thank all the members of our family who were friends of Tuco (Chris, Roben, Nancy, Kylie, Jenna, Ajra, and Aubrey), especially Roben, who had a deep empathy with Tuco.

Bringing this book to completion was an enormous task that none of us expected, so I want to thank all the wonderful gang at Greystone Books, notably Nancy Flight for flying with me even when neither of us knew where we were flying. We went through a lot of bad weather together, and I have never worked so closely with or trusted an editor so much. Even when she flew astray, I always knew why. Also, credit should go to Rob Sanders, Shirarose Wilensky, Nayeli Jimenez, Stefania Alexandru, Jennifer Croll— all of you (including any I may have missed here). I also wish to thank champion bird man Robert Butler for his pages of notes on my birds—some of which were hilarious and took a real strip out of me, which I usually deserved. Hans van de Sande and Lawrence Dill fact-checked my shifting comments on the slippery subject of entropy. I also need to thank, for their companionship and the advice they didn't always know they were giving: Wayne Grady, Margaret Atwood, Robert and Birgit Bateman, and Graeme Gibson for his kind words (as always). I also want to thank my anonymous friend at the anonymous parrot sanctuary, who filled me in on the somewhat secretive world of parrot rescue, as well as Wendy at World Parrot Refuge and Stacy at the Raptor Centre. Graeme Gibson Jr. and Sumiko Onishi at the Pelee Island Bird Observatory must be thanked for allowing us to watch them at their fine work for migrating birds. And, of course, I thank the B.C. Arts Council and the Canada Council for their financial support during my troubled journey.

BIBLIOGRAPHY

ALTHOUGH MANY YEARS of reading and experience went into *Tuco*, the books listed below were specifically chosen for research. A number proved irrelevant. Some I disagreed with wildly. *King Solomon's Ring* long ago inspired much of my initial thinking about relationships with animals. The reputation of its author, Konrad Lorenz, the man who once was a Nobel Prize–winning god of ethology, unfortunately, has slid since it was discovered he was a little more involved with the Nazis than he previously admitted. Marc Hauser's *Wild Minds* gave me numerous ideas, even though since writing it he's been involved in a controversy over the verification of a few of the many hundreds of studies in his labs. This is the nature of the world and, in many ways, the subject of this memoir. It's full of scattershot surprises, as both Kapuscinski and Kundera discovered in their lives. Other books, such as *Parrot Culture*, have been extremely useful. Despite being a dry read, it's an impressive collection of historical facts about our relations with parrots, though mostly from a European perspective. It was an essential source for many of the facts in chapter 6.

Since this is a memoir, I did not want to clutter it up with footnotes for all the quotations, a majority of which are derived from the books in this bibliography. The others came from previous reading or the Internet. On a whim, I started checking the quotes on the Internet, and to my shock, even some of the quotes from the most obscure books showed up. All except a very few can be found there. During the few years of *Tuco*'s creation, so much has gone online. Being a book lover, I found this a little depressing, but if the reader wants to read further or source any of the quotes, they can be easily searched for on the Internet, which also provided me with a filing cabinet drawer filled with useful and interesting scientific studies to quote for *Tuco*.

Abram, David. *Becoming Animal: An Earthly Cosmology.* New York: Vintage Books, 2010.

Beresford-Kroeger, Diana. *The Global Forest: Forty Ways Trees Can Save Us.* New York: Viking Penguin, 2010.

Birkhead, Tim. *Bird Sense: What It's Like to Be a Bird.* London: Bloomsbury Publishing, 2012.

———. *The Wisdom of Birds: An Illustrated History of Ornithology.* London: Bloomsbury Publishing, 2008.

Boyd, Brian. *On the Origin of Stories: Evolution, Cognition, and Fiction.* Cambridge, MA: Belknap Press, 2010.

Boehrer, Bruce Thomas. *Parrot Culture: Our 2,500-Year-Long Fascination with the World's Most Talkative Bird.* Philadelphia: University of Pennsylvania Press, 2004.

Burger, Joanna. *The Parrot Who Owns Me: The Story of a Relationship.* New York: Random House, 2002.

Eiseley, Loren. *The Night Country.* New York: Charles Scribner's Sons, 1971.

Geary, James. *I Is an Other: The Secret Life of Metaphor and How It Shapes the Way We See the World.* New York: HarperCollins, 2011.

Gibson, Graeme. *The Bedside Book of Birds: An Avian Miscellany.* Toronto: Doubleday Canada, 2005.

Bibliography

Grady, Wayne. *The Bone Museum: Travels in the Lost Worlds of Dinosaurs and Birds*. New York: Four Walls Eight Windows, 2001.

———. *Bringing Back the Dodo: Lessons in Natural and Unnatural History*. Toronto: McClelland & Stewart, 2007.

Hauser, Marc D. *Wild Minds: What Animals Really Think*. New York: Henry Holt and Company, 2000.

Heinrich, Bernd. *Mind of the Raven: Investigations and Adventures with Wolf-Birds*. New York: Cliff Street Books, 1999.

Herzog, Hal. *Some We Love, Some We Hate, Some We Eat: Why It's So Hard to Think Straight About Animals*. New York: HarperCollins, 2010.

Jaynes, Julian. *The Origin of Consciousness in the Breakdown of the Bicameral Mind*. New York: Mariner Books, 1990.

Kapuscinski, Ryszard. *The Other*. Translated by Antonia Lloyd-Jones. London: Verso, 2008.

Kolbert, Elizabeth. *The Sixth Extinction: An Unnatural History*. New York: Henry Holt and Company, 2014.

Laland, Kevin N. and Bennett G. Galef, eds. *The Question of Animal Culture*. Cambridge, MA: Harvard University Press, 2009.

Linden, Eugene. *The Parrot's Lament: And Other True Tales of Animal Intrigue, Intelligence, and Ingenuity*. New York: Dutton, 1999.

Lorenz, Konrad. *King Solomon's Ring: New Light on Animal Ways*. New York: Thomas Y. Crowell Company, 1961.

Morell, Virginia. *Animal Wise: The Thoughts and Emotions of Our Fellow Creatures*. New York: Random House, 2013.

Page, George. *Inside the Animal Mind: A Groundbreaking Exploration of Animal Intelligence*. New York: Doubleday, 1999.

Pepperberg, Irene M. *Alex & Me: How a Scientist and a Parrot Uncovered a Hidden World of Animal Intelligence—and Formed a Deep Bond in the Process*. New York: HarperCollins, 2008.

Pinker, Steven. *The Language Instinct: How the Mind Creates Language.* New York: Harper Perennial, 2007.

Ramachandran, V.S. *A Brief Tour of Human Consciousness: From Impostor Poodles to Purple Numbers.* New York: Pearson Education, 2004.

Rothenberg, David. *Survival of the Beautiful: Art, Science, and Evolution.* New York: Bloomsbury Press, 2011.

———. *Why Birds Sing: A Journey into the Mystery of Birdsong.* Philadelphia: Basic Books, 2005.

Savage, Candace. *Crows: Encounters with the Wise Guys of the Avian World.* Vancouver: Greystone Books, 2005.

———. *Curious by Nature: One Woman's Exploration of the Natural World.* Vancouver: Greystone Books, 2005.

Shepard, Paul. *Thinking Animals: Animals and the Development of Human Intelligence.* Athens, GA: University of Georgia Press, 1978.

Singer, Peter. *Animal Liberation: A New Ethics for Our Treatment of Animals.* New York: Avon Books, 1977.

———. *Writings on an Ethical Life.* New York: Ecco, 2000.

Slobodchikoff, Con. *Chasing Doctor Dolittle: Learning the Language of Animals.* New York: St. Martin's Press, 2012.

Stap, Don. *Birdsong.* New York: Scribner, 2005.

Suddendorf, Thomas. *The Gap: The Science of What Separates Us from Other Animals.* Philadelphia: Basic Books, 2013.

Tudge, Colin. *The Bird: A Natural History of Who Birds Are, Where They Came From, and How They Live.* New York: Three Rivers Press, 2008.

Weisman, Alan. *The World Without Us.* New York: Harper Perennial, 2007.

Wenner, Adrian M. and Patrick H. Wells. *Anatomy of a Controversy: The Question of a "Language" Among Bees.* New York: Columbia University Press, 1990.